AF263690

REDEMPTION
THE GOD STONE TRILOGY

Joaquin Lopez

DIAMOND
MEDIAPRESS

Content

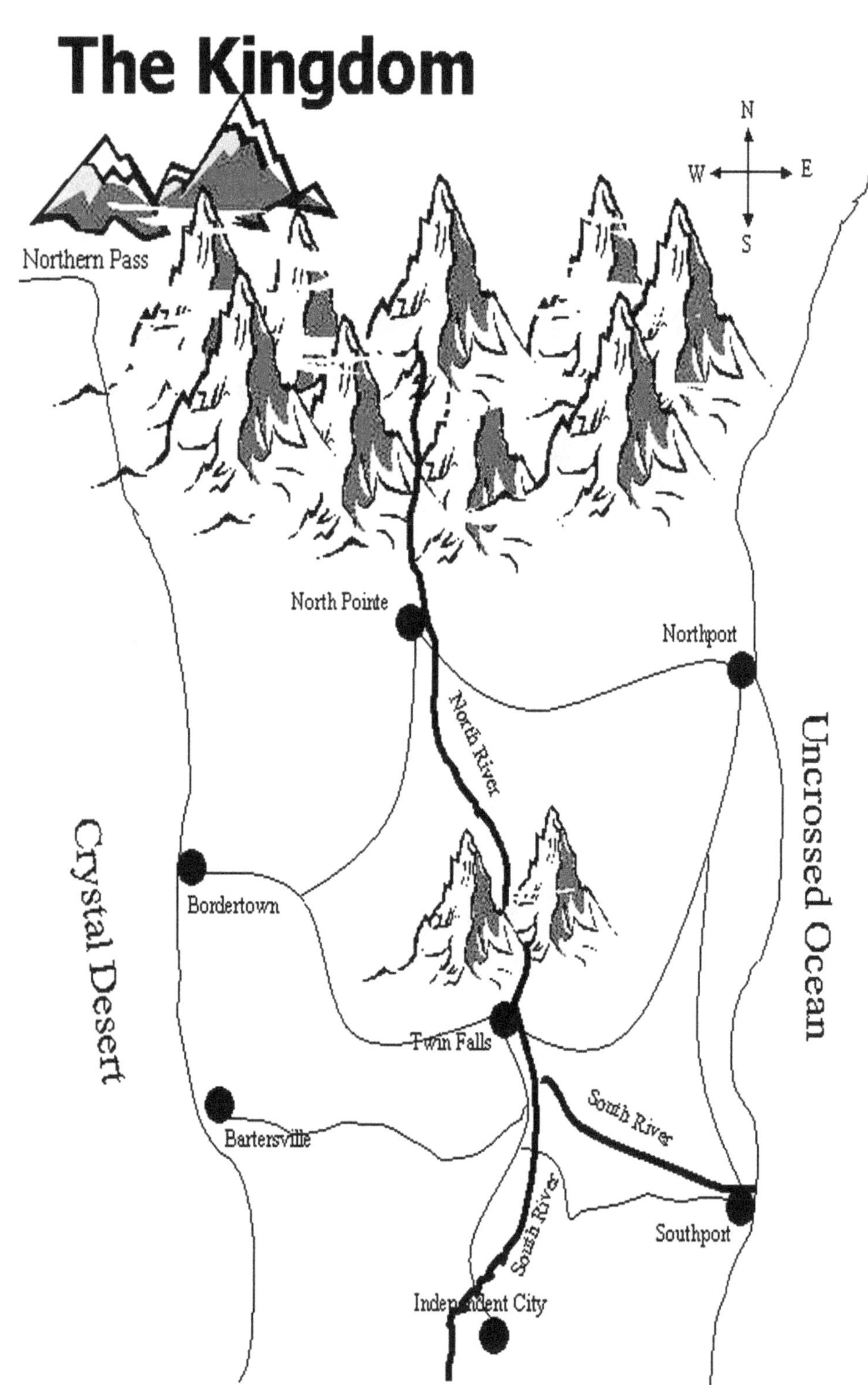

The Kingdom
N
W   E
S
Northern Pass
North Pointe
Northport
North River
Crystal Desert
Uncrossed Ocean
Bordertown
Twin Falls
South River
Bartersville
South River
Southport
Independent City

PROLOGUE

Anna looked outside. It was a beautiful sunny day, yet she was not feeling very cheerful. She knew it would be another long hard day. Anna spent her days resolving minor disagreements amongst the staff, taking care of minor emergencies, or organizing yet another royal function. She didn't mind because all the work kept her mind off what was really bringing her spirits down. Most of the time, working could overcome her melancholy mood; however, not during this time of year. First, it was spring, and it was during the spring when Jack had been taken away from her. Second, it was also Jack's birthday.

This time of year always made Anna sad. Her resentment or hatred of Ariel and Boris would rise during this time of the year. She missed Jack so much even though she realized it had been seventeen years; to her, it seemed like just yesterday. She knew it had been enough time that she should not feel the pain so much. No matter how hard she tried, she just could not get over losing her son. Anna had never told anyone, not even her best friend Betty, that she felt that Jack was alive. She could not explain why she felt this way, but she just knew. It was this feeling that kept the wounds open over time. Anna shook herself in order to snap out of her daze and left her quarters and went to face the problems of the day.

Today had been no different than any other day. As soon as Anna left her quarters, she was confronted with one problem after another. Before she realized it, it was lunchtime already. She went to eat and found Betty waiting for her.+

Betty asked, "What is wrong with you today? You are all business and no fun."

Anna smiled and said, "I have lots of things on my mind, that's all."

Betty knew better than to believe that and said, "Anna, you really need to accept the fact that he is gone. Holding on to any kind of hope is just plain crazy, after all this time." Betty knew that Anna had been thinking about her son because she was like this every time she thought about him Anna sat there and listened to her friend go on about her being smarter than that and how she should instead find herself a good man. Anna had heard all of this before from Betty and a few others. She would listen politely and then keep thinking and hoping that Jack was alive.

After lunch, time flew just as fast as the morning. There was always something that required her immediate attention. Today she had had to stop Kain from throttling a young squire for what he felt was disrespect to Prince Willard. Anna, and everyone else on the palace staff, disliked the prince. He was arrogant and full of himself. When she had first met the prince, she thought he reminded her of Jack. However, she quickly realized that the prince was nothing like Jack. Everyone had liked Jack, and no one liked the Prince.

Needless to say, by the time Anna quit for the day, she was exhausted. But that did not stop her from thinking about Jack. Jack would be twenty- five years old now. She tried to imagine what he would look like. She pictured him as being tall and handsome; what mother wouldn't? She wondered why after all these years she still felt that he was alive.

With that thought, Anna lay down on her bed and closed her eyes. She was about to start a prayer when she felt a sudden heat like that from a bright light. She opened her eyes and saw a bright light in the middle of the room. Suddenly the light was replaced by a figure. At first Anna panicked. As she looked at the figure, she realized that a woman had come out of the light. Anna was frozen with fear; she tried to move or speak but couldn't. The woman came to the bed and sat next to Anna. The woman appeared to have an old yet ageless face.

Anna began crying when she recognized the face of the goddess Athena. She said, "Athena, mother of the gods, you honor me with your presence. I am not worthy of such a visit."

Athena smiled and said, "Anna, you have always been faithful to the gods and especially to me. Your loyalty means a lot to us. I have noticed over the years that you think about and hope beyond reason that your son is alive. I have come here to you tonight to let you know that your son indeed is alive. He survived for over three months in the desert and made it across to Rumalia. Rumalia is a country on the other side of the desert that the people of the Kingdom do not know exists. Jack was rescued by the Rumalians and has been living there ever since. He has grown to be a fine young man and an exceptional warrior."

Anna was shocked; she could not believe what she was hearing. Not only was Jack alive but he had also become a great warrior. She had never imagined he could have survived the desert. All this time, she thought she was a mother that refused to accept reality.

Athena continued. "It was I that kept your hopes alive about your son. You do not have to worry about him anymore. You will see your son again, Anna, but you must be patient. He is fine, and we have many plans for him." Having said that, Athena rose from the bed and walked to the middle of the room. As she walked away, the light reappeared, and she walked into the light.

Anna was in shock; she could not believe what had just happened to her. First, the mother of the gods had visited her. Second, the mother of the gods had told her that Jack was still alive. Third, she was told that she would see her son again but she had to be patient. This was mind-boggling. I must be totally crazy. The grief has driven me totally insane. As she was thinking that, the face of Athena appeared in the middle of the room and assured her that she was not crazy.

That night, Anna dreamt about Jack. She dreamt about him as a fierce warrior. She saw him fighting and winning battle after battle. When she awoke the next morning, she felt like a burden had been lifted from her. She knew that she could not tell anyone about her visit from Athena because they would definitely think she was completely insane. She decided that she would keep the visit to herself. She decided that when anyone noticed her new, happier self, such as Betty, she would say she had finally accepted what had happened to her son and was starting to move on.

CHAPTER 1 - BREAKING THE NEWS

Jack just sat there staring at the map. He was completely shocked; he never thought he would find his way home by chasing after some Horde raiders. He closed his eyes and prayed to the gods. He thanked them for letting him survive long enough to find a way home. He thanked them for giving him a chance to fulfill his promise to Linnie. When he finished praying he continued to sit and stare at the map. After a while, he noticed the map began to get blurry. He wiped his eyes and realized that he was crying.

Jack hadn't noticed the time. He had been staring at the map all afternoon and into the night. He had not eaten all day and just now began to feel hungry. At that moment, Anjie walked into the tent. She was carrying a plate of food for Jack. As she walked over to Jack and he looked up at her, she saw that Jack was crying. Immediately she placed the plate down and went to him. "What's wrong?" she asked. Jack didn't say a word; he simply handed her the map.

Anjie took the map and looked at it. She was confused. She didn't understand why this map would make Jack cry. "It's apparently an old map. Why should this make you cry?" she asked.

Jack said, "It is not just an old map. Look at it more carefully. You will see that it shows Rumalia, the Crystal Desert, and the Kingdom. Following the map north you can see that the desert ends up north somewhere. At the end of the desert, you can read the words 'Northern Pass.'"

Anjie still did not understand what Jack was trying to say. She said. "I'm sorry, Jack. I just don't get what you are trying to tell me." "This is what I have been looking for ever since you found me all those years ago. That pass is my way home. I can go north till the desert ends then go east to the Northern Mountains and head south for home" said Jack.

Finally Anjie understood why Jack was crying. Her face went pale, and she hugged Jack. She was happy that Jack had found his way home. At the same time, she was afraid that she was about to lose him. Suddenly she felt afraid. She did not know what to do, so she simply held onto Jack. The two held each other for a long time. Finally Anjie began to kiss Jack on the neck and cheek. Jack responded to her affection, and they made love. When they finished, Jack picked up the plate of food that Anjie had brought and began to eat.

Anjie asked, "What happens now?"

Jack finished eating before answering her question. He said, "Remember how I told you that for several months now I had been feeling a strange sensation pulling me north? That feeling has been growing ever since I found the map. I feel as if someone has cast a magic spell to compel me to go north. The feeling is so strong and getting stronger. I do not know how long I can fight this. I think that since I have been praying to the gods all these years to help me find a way home, and now I have found one, they are telling me I must go home."

Anjie felt her stomach tangling into a great big knot. This was the moment she had always feared would come. She had to decide if she would go with Jack or stay with her family. She understood there was more to Jack's desire to go home than to simply fulfill his promise. She had noticed a look of admiration on Jack's face whenever he spoke of Princess Linnie. That look always made her feel a little jealous. She realized that the princess had been Jack's first true love. She also understood that deep inside Jack was still in love with her.

Anjie felt that knot getting tighter. She cared for Jack a lot. She definitely felt desire for him, but could she be mistaking her physical desire as love? She remembered a conversation she had with her mother just before Jack asked her to marry him. Her mother had asked her if she really loved Jack or if she simply enjoyed the attention that seemed to always be drawn toward Jack. Anjie had replied that she loved Jack. Thinking about it now, she realized that her mother had been right. She did care for Jack, but she really enjoyed being the center of attention. Being with Jack automatically put her in the middle of all the attention. She knew now that she could not leave her family behind and go with Jack. She began to cry.

Hearing her tears Jack immediately took her in his arms and said, "What's wrong? Why are you crying?"

She hugged him. After composing herself, she looked him in the eyes and said, "Jack, I care about you very much. Remember when you asked me to go with you to your home and I avoided the question? The reason I avoided the question is not that I thought it foolish, like I said back then, but instead it was because I did not want to make that decision. However, lately I have been thinking about it a lot, and I have realized that I have to make that decision. Now the time has come, and I must make a choice. I think my decision was made when you first asked me to go with you. I just didn't realize I had made my choice. As a result, I have always tried to change the subject. Jack, I cannot go with you. I have thought about this, knowing that you would expect me to give you an answer soon. I understand your need to go home, and I fully agree with your decision. I just cannot go with you. I'm sorry."

Now they were both crying. They held each other tight and cried. After about half an hour, Anjie asked, "Have you decided when you will be leaving?"

"No, I have not. I think that it would be best if we just got it over with. What do you think?"

"The sooner we tell my parents and Jerris and Myra the better. After that, it would probably be best on everyone if you left right away," said Anjie as she began crying again. Neither one of them wanted to talk about it anymore, so they just went to bed.

Neither of them could sleep that night. Jack felt excitement because he was finally going home. At the same time, he felt guilty for leaving Anjie. As he lay there, he thought about his feelings for Anjie. Jack knew that he did have feelings for her, but he wasn't sure that he loved her. He couldn't explain why. All he knew was that when he thought of Linnie, he would get butterflies in his stomach and sometimes when he was with Anjie he would pretend that it was Linnie. Jack enjoyed being with Anjie; she was a lot of fun, but not once had he considered not going home and staying with her. For this, he prayed to the gods for forgiveness.

Anjie was having trouble sleeping also. As she thought about what had been agreed by them, she began to get angry. She was angry with herself for being so understanding. She was angry about Jack's promise and his commitment to keep it. Most of all, she was angry with Jack. The more she thought about it, the angrier she became. She decided that she would end her marriage to Jack. In the morning when they told her parents, she would also announce that the marriage was ended. That will be my revenge.

The next morning when they arose, they both looked tired and not rested. They had a quiet breakfast and headed to Tanner and Merna's tent. When they arrived at the tent, Tanner and Merna had just finished eating breakfast. Tanner and Merna immediately noticed the distraught look on both their faces.

"All right, you two, what's wrong?" asked Tanner.

Jack handed Tanner the map and said, "I found this in one of the trunks we brought back from the Horde." Tanner opened the map and looked at it for a few moments without saying anything. Finally he said, "This is an old map. It appears that the people of long ago knew of both your Kingdom and Rumalia. But I do not understand why this map should make you two look so distraught."

Jack said, "If you look at the top or northern part of the map you will see the words NORTHERN PASS. The Crystal Desert ends, and this pass allows travel to the east and to the Kingdom. This map is the answer I have been looking for since the day Anjie found me all those years ago."

Tanner looked at the map again and realized that Jack was right. According to this map, it would be quite easy to cross over to the Kingdom using the Northern Pass. Now he understood that Jack was trying to tell them that he was leaving. He looked at Merna and could tell by the look on her face that she was not quite sure what was happening. Tanner turned to Jack and asked, "When will you and Anjie be leaving?"

It was Anjie who responded, "Jack will be going alone tomorrow. I will not go with him. As a result, we have decided it would be better to formally end our marriage." Anjie could tell, by the look on Jack's face, that she had struck a heavy blow straight to Jack's heart.

Jack was shocked by what Anjie had said because they had not discussed formally ending the marriage. He looked at her face, and the anger he saw in her eyes struck him even deeper. Jack thought that she had understood to make it easier on him. Jack was too shocked to say anything. Tanner broke the silence and said, "Well, Jack, I don't suppose we can change your mind."

Jack could not talk so he just shook his head no.

Tanner continued, "That being the case then the formal termination of your marriage is the right thing to do. Let's go talk to Jerris."

The four of them left the chief 's tent and walked, without saying a word, to look for Jerris. Jerris was still in his tent with his wife. When the four of them walked in, Jerris immediately asked, "What's wrong? Has someone died?"

He had said it as a joke, but when no one even smiled, he knew that whatever was going on was dire. Tanner handed Jerris the map and said, "This old map was in the trunks that were brought back from the Horde. It clearly shows a way to cross to the Kingdom without crossing the desert. Jack has decided that he will be leaving to go home tomorrow. He and Anjie have decided to formally end their marriage. Anjie will not be going with Jack and as a result have come to this decision." Jerris and Myra both had to sit down.

Jerris's face was pale. He asked, "Jack, is there no way we can change your mind?"

Again Jack could not speak, so he simply shook his head no.

For several moments, no one said anything. When the silence was finally broken, it was Myra who spoke. "Jack, as much as it hurts us to see you go, we are very happy for you. Tanner, I think we should have a feast in honor of Jack tonight." Jerris said, "Jack, we love you like our own son, but we understand your need to go home. Honestly I am surprised we were able to hold you here as long as we have." Jack decided he needed to explain to them about the pulling sensation he had been having. Jack said, "First of all, I want to let all of you know that I love you very much. I have come to see all of you as my family. However, for some time now, I have been feeling a strange sensation pulling me north. I mentioned it to Anjie before we headed north, but we decided that it was probably anxiety because of the Horde situation. The farther north we came, the stronger the feeling was. Ever since I found the map, the feeling has become even stronger. It is so strong now that I have to fight the need to start running north. I feel like a spell has been cast on me to compel me to go north. It is this need along with the desire to go home and attempt to keep my promise that I have decided to leave. I will always be grateful for the kindness and love the tribes and especially the Claws have given me. I will never forget you."

Jack was crying when he finished, and so was everyone else. They all came to Jack and hugged him.

Tanner pulled himself away and said, "Myra, I think that your idea of a feast is an excellent idea. I will go make the arrangements." Tanner and Merna left.

Jerris looked at Jack and said, "Are you sure you want to end the marriage?"

Jack looked at Anjie and said, "We feel that it is the best thing to do since we probably will never see each other again."

"Very well then I will talk to Tanner about making the formal announcement at the feast tonight."

CHAPTER 2 -THE CHOOSING

Jack went back to their tent to begin the process of packing and getting ready to go. Unfortunately for him, he was not left alone for very along. Word spread throughout the entire tribe that a feast was being held that night because Jack was leaving. At first it was only a few friends that came by to see him. Later came the warriors; all of them came by to visit him. Most of the warriors simply came in to say that it had been an honor to fight with him. The last warrior that came to visit was Dar and his wife, Claudia.

Dar stared at Jack before speaking. "Jack, my friend, I truly am happy for you. However, I am sad for the Claws. You have been an inspiration not only to the people but also to me." Jack knew how proud Dar was and that for him to say these words must be very difficult. Dar continued. "When the tribal elders came to me and asked me to train you I accepted only because I wanted to be the one who would break you. I resented you because I thought the attention that you were receiving was unwarranted. That is why I was so hard on you when we started your training. After I realized I was not going to break you, it was too late. I had to keep up the training as I had started. Your unswerving desire to learn made an impression on me. Never had I seen anyone take the punishment you took from me, but you kept coming back for more. Your attitude made me realize that I should not only lighten up on you, but on life in general. I had had my eye on Claudia for some time. However, I had always seen it as a privilege for any woman to be with me. After all, I was the leader of the warriors. As a result, I was unapproachable. You changed all of that. Because of you, I did lighten up on life and I approached Claudia and, well, the rest you already know."

Jack was surprised; he had never heard Dar speak so much before. Now it was Claudia's turn to speak. "Before Dar began training you, I also had noticed him. But I was afraid of him. He was always so solemn, serious and downright mean. Then one day out of the blue, he approached me, and I discovered he actually had a personality. I told him I had always been afraid of him. He told me about you and how training you had affected him. I could see the admiration and respect he had for you when he spoke of you. I thought to myself that anyone who can impress this mighty warrior so deeply is truly special. Once I met you, I saw the same admiration and respect on your face for Dar. I knew then that you two would become good friends. It was your friendship that brought Dar and I together, and for that, I will always be grateful. We want you to know that you will always be very special to us. We wish you the best."

Jack had tears in his eyes and had to compose himself before he spoke. "Dar, when I first learned you were going to train me, I was afraid. But I also knew that if I ever wanted to become a great warrior and someday be in a position to keep my promise to the princess, there was no one better to learn from. At first I was angry with you for what I considered brutal treatment. The anger then led to hatred. However, after just a few short weeks, when I realized that my stamina and skill level was so much higher than my fellow trainees I knew that it was because of your method. I changed my attitude from 'I will show him' to 'I can learn a lot from him.' So I can honestly say that the warrior I am today is because of you. For your training and advice, I will always be thankful. It is your friendship since then that I will cherish for the rest of my life. I will never forget you." With that, they all hugged each other. It was getting late, and the feast was already starting. Jack asked Dar and Claudia to excuse him for a few minutes so that he could finish packing. When he finished, he went out and joined the festivities.

The entire tribe had turned out for the feast. Jack saw children, women, and elders he had never seen before. Everyone knew him, and they came to tell him they were sad to see him go. Many shed tears, including Jack, when Tanner, Jerris, Merna, and Myra were finally able to get to him. Jack saw Anjie only briefly during the feast. When he did see her, she would always turn and head the other way. He could tell that she had been crying because her eyes were swollen and bloodshot. The festivities just kept going and going. Just before midnight Jack excused himself and thanked everyone for their support and affection. However, he had a long trip ahead and needed to rest. Finally, he was allowed to retire for the evening.

As Jack was leaving, he looked around for Anjie, but he did not see her. He had not expected to see her since Tanner had made the announcement that their marriage was terminated. Therefore, when he went inside his tent and Anjie was there, he was shocked. He stood there not knowing what to do. Anjie did not say a word. She simply took off her clothes and with her arms begged him to come to her. For the next several hours, they made love. Neither of them said a word. They just enjoyed each other's bodies.

Finally, Jack could not stand it anymore; he had to know why she had said that they had agreed to terminate the marriage. He asked, "Anjie, why did you tell everyone that we had agreed to terminate our marriage?"

Anjie replied, with tears in her eyes, "I became angry overnight, and I wanted to hurt you for leaving me. I know that it was very selfish and childish, but you know me."

"You did hurt me, very much," said Jack.

"I know, and I am truly sorry," she said. Even as she apologized to Jack, a seed of anger took root inside of her without even realizing it. That seed would lead to some dire circumstances. For the rest of the night, they slept a little and then made love over and over.

As a result of their escapades the night before, it was midmorning before they got up and prepared to go outside. The members of the tribe heard the rustling inside the tent and started to gather outside. When Jack and Anjie came out, the people of the tribe were all lined up outside. Jerris and Tanner had prepared Jack's horse. Jerris took Jack's pack and secured it to the saddle of the horse. Jack took the reins from Tanner, and the four of them walked between the lines of people. The tribe had lined up heading north. The tribe was so large that the lines stretched for about a mile north from his tent.

The people said good-bye and wished him well. Jack smiled and waved to everyone. Merna and Myra joined the small group walking with Jack and the horse. When they finally reached the end of the line, Dar was the last one. Jack stopped and one by one hugged them all. By the time he got on his horse, he was crying, but then so was everyone else. At first Jack could not turn the horse and leave. He finally looked up at the crowd and said, "Thank you, all. I will never forget you, and I love all of you." With that he turned his horse north, and with a quick kick on the sides, his horse took off. Jack turned back once after being gone only a few moments. Everyone waved and wished him good luck. Jack hardened his heart and headed north.

It took Jack about half an hour to reach the foothills and head east. It did not take long before he was heading due north along the grasslands at the foot of the mountains and about half a mile from the Crystal Desert. Jack was going through every emotion possible. He felt guilty for leaving Anjie. He already missed all his friends. He was also afraid that he might encounter some Horde. Also, he was excited about the possibility of seeing Linnie and his mother. He prayed to the gods for the strength to make this long trip home. He thanked them for letting him find this way. Through all these emotions, the sensation pulling him north kept growing stronger and stronger. Jack was beginning to wonder if maybe the Horde had cast a spell on him to make him leave so they could attack the tribes. However, deep inside something told him he was doing the right thing. He did not know where that feeling came from, but it was there.

For two weeks, Jack headed north. He saw many plants and animals that he had never seen before. He never went without food thanks to his hunting skill. It was midmorning one day when he saw more mountains in front of him heading east. He became very excited because he could finally see that the map was correct and he would soon reach the Northern Pass. At mid afternoon, Jack stopped to eat and rest a little. He had picked up the pace when he saw the mountains heading east, and now he could tell the horse was beginning to get tired. He rested for an hour before he got up and started to get ready to keep going.

He would have liked to rest more, but he couldn't. The sensation pulling him north was unbearable now. He could no longer fight it. His will was no longer his own; it belonged to the pulling sensation. This made him uneasy and afraid. Jack reached the Northern Pass shortly after having started out. The desert ended, and the mountains jumped out in front of him to the west, north, and east. From the edge of the desert, the sand gave way to grassland then to rocky foothills with a few scattered trees. Jack knew he had made the right decision. However, he was terrified because the sensation he had been feeling was not pulling him east now; instead, he was already heading northwest up the mountains.

No matter how hard he tried Jack could not make the horse stop and go back. He could not make himself instruct the horse to turn around. Jack was beginning to get worried. For several hours now, he had been going up the mountains. It was starting to get dark, and the higher he climbed, the colder it got. He knew he had to find shelter for the night. The trees were too small and too few to help. The mountains did not appear to have any caves or outcroppings. When the sunlight was gone and it was fully dark, Jack stopped and looked around. Ahead of him, about a half a mile, he saw what looked like a small red glow. To him, it looked like it could be a small campfire. Quickly, Jack started climbing again. He did not care who it was as long as he found shelter for the night.

As Jack got close to the spot where the red glow was coming from, Jack realized that the glow appeared to be coming from inside the mountain. At last, when he reached the spot where the glow was coming from, he realized it was coming from within the mountain. Jack was confused. He looked around but saw no cave entrance or smoke. The only thing he saw was the red glow coming from inside the mountain directly in front of him. Jack drew his sword and poked at what he thought was the solid side of the mountain. He discovered that what he had thought was rock was instead just a growth of weeds covered by dirt over time.

Jack saw that the growth was covering an entrance to a cave and that the red glow was coming from inside. The sensation he had been feeling was now pushing him inside the cave. Whatever it was, he knew now that he had to go inside this cave in order for it to stop. With his sword drawn and at the ready, Jack slowly walked into the cave. The cave was only about ten feet deep, and the ceiling was about ten feet high as well. At the back of the cave was an old skeleton. Next to the skeleton leaning against the back of the cave was the most beautiful sword Jack had ever seen. It was from this sword that the strange red glow was coming from.

Jack started moving forward toward the sword. It was the sword that was pulling him toward it. He recognized that it was this sword that had been pulling him north all this time. As he reached the sword, Jack was sweating and very nervous. He reached for the sword and slowly grabbed it. As soon as he had the sword fully within his grasp, he felt a sudden stream of pain. The pain started in his hand shot up his arm and into his chest. Jack tried to release the sword. The pain intensified until he could no longer stand it, and he passed out.

As soon as he passed out, the cave lit up as all the gods entered the cave. They waited for Jack to awaken. Jack was confused. He could not understand what had happened to him he thought he was dying. Then he noticed that the pain was gone and he was lying face down on the floor of the cave. He opened his eyes and turned around. The light inside the cave immediately blinded Jack. He covered his eyes and turned his face.

Ator said, "I am Ator, father of the gods, you may open your eyes and look upon us." Jack could not believe what he had just heard. He thought, if this is Ator, then I am dead. "You are not dead, Jack," said Ator. Jack looked up and saw five people standing before him. There was an older man and woman, two young ladies, and a young man. Jack thought they were old and young, respectively, because he could not really tell their ages; they all seemed to have an ageless look about them.

"This is Athena, mother of the gods. This is our son Atlas, god of wisdom and honor; our daughter Zephra, the warrior goddess; and Pearl, the goddess of love and Life," said Ator.

Zephra spoke next. "You have been judged by the God Stone Sword and found worthy."

Jack was numb; he was in a cave with all the gods and the God Stone Sword. He had been judged by the Sword and been found worthy. With this understanding came shock.

"Now that you understand what is happening, Jack, I will explain," said Zephra. "Thousands of years ago, we tested a young mercenary with this sword. The sword found him acceptable. We gave him our blessing and the Sword. For a short period, he was worthy of the blessing. But alas, he forgot about the gods, and his vanity overtook him. Therefore, we forgot about him and we removed our blessing and he was defeated. That is his skeleton you see on the ground there. After that I fought with my fellow gods and convinced them that the human race deserved another chance. We then let it be known throughout the land that a chosen one would come and that he would have the blessing of the gods. For over three thousand years, we have searched and found no one worthy of even testing. Until now. We have found you, Jack. You have been tested and found your heart worthy of our blessing. Before we name you as our chosen one, we must know if you will accept this honour."

Jack was completely stunned. All this time he had been feeling the strange sensation to come north, it had been the gods pulling him so that he could come here, to this cave, and be tested. He could not talk; he kneeled at the feet of Zephra and Ator. With his head bowed, he said, "I am just a queen's maid's son who grew up on the plains. I am not worthy of this honor. However, who am I to question the wisdom of the gods? If you will bestow me with this great honor, I will do everything humanly possible to fulfill your expectations of me." Zephra beamed with pride as she heard Jack's response. She looked at her fellow gods, and they all nodded approval.

Ator said, "Rise, Jack, and take possession of the God Stone Sword."

Jack stood and picked up the sword.

Ator placed his hands on Jack's head and said, "Jack of the Kingdom, we choose you to be our promised chosen one."

Jack looked up at the gods fell to his knees and kissed each of their hands and feet.

Ator continued. "The God Stone Sword is yours now. However, before we give you the full use of its power, you must pass one more test. We do this because we must be sure of you before bestowing you with the full power of the sword. My daughter Pearl will instruct you on the final test."

Ator stepped back, and Pearl came forward. She said, "There is an abomination on this land put there by human wizards trying to play gods. A long time ago, these wizards created the man beasts. It was we, the gods, who never allowed them to succeed. However, once created, we could not just eradicate them. The final test for you, Jack, is this. For the next three years, you will go to the Northern Mountains of the Kingdom. There you will fight and kill these man beasts. If your heart remains as true to us as it is today, then at the end of the three years, the God Stone will once again shine. When it shines again as you it does now, then you will have the full blessing of the gods and will be free to leave the mountains and pursue your promise to the princess. Will you accept these terms?"

Again Jack was stunned. Not only had the gods heard his prayers, they were giving him the ability to try to keep his promise to Linnie. Once again Jack fell to his knees looking up and said, "Yes, I will gladly accept your test."

Pearl stepped back, and Ator said, "Very well then. For the next few days, Zephra will instruct you in the powers of the sword." As soon as Ator finished speaking he, Athena, Atlas, and Pearl disappeared. Jack was now alone in the cave with Zephra.

Zephra had loved Jack for many years. She decided instead of verbally instructing him on the powers of the sword she would implant the knowledge in his brain as she touched him. She walked over to Jack and took him by the hand. They walked to the back of the cave and sat down, and then she kissed him. For the next week, they made love day and night. Zephra had been craving Jack's attention for a long time. Jack made love to every inch of her. The more he touched her, the clearer his understanding of the powers of the sword became.

Zephra did not want Jack to learn so fast. But she knew that she had to let him go so that he could perform his test. She told Jack that this night would be their last together. "In the morning when you wake, I will be gone. You will be on your own with the God Stone Sword, and your test will begin." They made love again, and Zephra put Jack into a deep sleep so that when he woke in the morning he would be completely rested. Then she left.

CHAPTER 3 - THE NORTHERN PASS

The next morning when Jack awoke, he was alone in the cave. He sat up and recalled what had happened. At first, he thought maybe it was a dream. Then he realized that he no longer felt the pulling sensation. He looked around, and there it was, just a few feet away, the God Stone Sword. Jack reached for the sword. As he touched it, he remembered what had happened to him the last time he had touched the sword. This time, however, there was no pain.

As he sat there, he became aware of the knowledge that Zephra had given him while they were together. The sword would enhance Jack's natural fighting ability when he needed the help. The sword would protect him from any magic or sorcery that was directed at him. The sword also had the power to allow its wielder the ability to use magic. However, Jack would not be able to use that power until the stone was shining. No one could touch the sword other than Jack. If anyone did, the sword would strike him or her down. If Jack gave someone permission to touch the sword, then that person could touch it or admire it. The sword would also allow Jack to sense magic being used around him. All these abilities and many more were or would be at Jack's fingertips with the sword.

He gathered his things and prepared to go. He took one last look around and walked out of the cave. Jack was surprised to find his horse just a short distance away. He packed everything on his horse and started the long climb down the mountain. It took Jack all morning long to get back down the mountain. Once he was down, he stopped to eat and rest. The rest was not very long; he was too excited to just sit and rest. Jack was ready to start his final test. Jack broke camp and headed east through the Northern Pass.

Jack was amazed at the natural beauty of the mountains. The snow- covered peaks rose high into the sky. Some of the peaks rose out of sight hidden by clouds. These mountains were a lot higher than the mountains behind Twin Falls that Jack had explored with the old wizard Morten. The memory of Morten made him remember the gruesome murder of the royal court. This memory made him sad and also gave him the determination he would need to fulfill his promise to Linnie.

As he headed east, he looked south at the desert. He still got shivers just thinking about his three-month ordeal crossing the desert. Occasionally he would have a nightmare about the desert. He remembered how he had constantly prayed to the gods not, knowing if his prayers were being heard and never dreaming that they not only were they being heard but were also being answered.

For the first time since he had left the tribes, he thought about them and Anjie. Zephra had explained to Jack that even though Anjie had cared for him, she was more interested in being the center of attention. It was all the attention that Jack got that made Anjie stay with him. She explained to Jack that there were many people like Anjie who were drawn to whomever or whatever was attracting attention.

After a week of travel east, Jack was still amazed with the mountains and their beauty. He would take short trips up the mountains, on foot, to hunt for food. His skill with the bow and arrow were as sharp as ever, and he never lacked for food. One day when he returned from one of his hunting trips, he noticed that his horse was acting a little fidgety. He thought this to be unusual because the horse appeared frightened. Jack had never come across anything that would frighten the horse. He looked around and found no tracks. He also looked around to see if he could spot anything that would explain the horse's behavior. Jack could see nothing that should frighten the horse.

Not finding a visible explanation, Jack mounted up and headed east. The horse was headed east, but Jack could tell that it was still a bit uneasy. He kept a sharp eye out just in case; he knew something or someone had spooked his horse. It took only moments for Jack to discover the cause of the discomfort to the horse. As they rounded a large boulder that had fallen from the mountains, Jack saw the problem. About thirty yards away was a large bear, and it was charging directly at them. The horse froze and would not move. Jack tried to get the horse to run away from the bear, but it was no use. The horse had smelled the bear for some time now and was completely frightened.

When the bear was about ten feet away, it stood up on its hind legs. Standing like that, the bear, it seemed to Jack, was ten feet tall. Jack had never seen a bear before, but he recognized this creature from drawings he had seen in the palace. In the drawings, the bears always looked ferocious and mean. As he sat there watching this enormous animal attack him, Jack thought the drawings were wrong. The drawings could not capture the look of anger and hatred on the bear's face. The bear roared as it walked toward Jack.

The roar of the bear shook Jack out of the fear-induced trance he was under.

Without thinking twice, Jack grabbed his new sword and jumped off the horse. His horse began backing away slowly. The bear became even angrier when it realized that Jack intended to challenge it. The bear went straight for Jack. As the bear came within reach of his sword, Jack swung with all his might. The sword hit the bear on one of his paws, and then the tip cut a gash across its belly. Jack quickly moved out of the way under the swinging arms of the bear.

The bear was now furious and hurt. Jack knew he could not outrun the infuriated animal. He had to stand and fight. As the bear attacked him again, he said a quick prayer to the gods. Jack swung his sword again. His swing caught the bear off guard, and it cut a deep gash in the right shoulder, arm, and across the chest of the bear. Jack ducked and rolled under the swinging arms of the bear. This time Jack stopped and began another swing at the bear. Much to Jack's surprise, the bear swung itself away from the sword, and he completely missed. The might with which he had swung caused Jack to momentarily lose his balance. The bear attacked immediately, and with its uninjured left hand, the bear swung at Jack. It hit Jack's left shoulder, and the bear's claws left deep gashes.

The surprise of the hit caught Jack unexpectedly, and he scampered back a few feet to try and regain his balance. When Jack looked back at the bear, it was charging full speed at him. There was a small clump of rocks that stood about four feet high. Jack jumped up onto the rocks just as the bear reached for him. The bear missed but recovered quickly. As the bear was standing up, Jack jumped up and over the head of the bear. As Jack started his descent, he brought the sword down on the bear. The sword struck the bear on the side of the head and tore off half its face. The sword then struck the bear's left shoulder. The force of Jack's swing was so strong that the hit broke the bear's shoulder, rendering his left arm useless.

Jack saw the bear hesitate, and he wasted no time. He struck the bear across the back with the sword. The sword cut deep into the back of the bear, breaking the backbone and causing it to drop to the ground. Jack wasted no time and stabbed the bear through the chest right into the heart. The bear growled one last time and died. Jack pulled out his sword and fell to his knees. He was exhausted, and his shoulder was bleeding and hurt.

Before looking after his shoulder, he said a prayer of thanks to the gods. After praying, he got up and went to find his horse. The horse had gone back around the huge rock that had hidden the bear from his sight. When Jack first approached his horse, the smell of the bear's blood was fresh on him, and the horse backed away. Jack had to talk softly and reassuringly to the horse in order to approach it. Once he calmed the horse, he reached into his pack and took out some sort of salve that

Jerris had given him. Jerris had told him that it would stop deep cuts from bleeding and help them heal.

Jack quickly finished taking care of his shoulder and immediately mounted up and headed east. He did not want the smell of the dead bear to scare his horse anymore. He also did not want to be around when other animals came to eat the corpse of the bear. Jack kicked his horse into a trot and headed off east. As he rode, Jack understood that just because he now carried the God Stone Sword did not mean he could let his guard down. Having the sword and the gods' blessing had made Jack overconfident, and as a result, he had almost lost his opportunity to keep his promise. Jack prayed and asked for forgiveness. He had not fully understood what it meant to accept the sword and the blessing. Now he understood the magnitude of his responsibility and told the gods that he would not let them down.

A few days after his encounter with the bear, Jack spotted the Northern Mountains of the Kingdom. He could see the mountains heading south. Jack took a deep breath and prepared himself for what he knew would be a long, hard-fought three years.

One week after the encounter with the bear, Jack had reached the Kingdom. Just like in Rumalia, the desert gave way to grass, which turned into the rocks of the foothills and then eventually the Northern Mountains. It would be a quick trip south to get out of the mountains and reach the farmlands of the Kingdom. Jack led his horse east into the mountains. He was ready to begin his final test.

CHAPTER 4 - THE MAN BEASTS

Jack had never seen a man beast. He had heard that they were half- man and half-animal. According to the stories around the palace, the beasts were mean ferocious fighters. Jack was not prepared for the grotesque sight of a man beast. It did not take long before he found his first group of man beasts. Jack was riding through the Northern Mountains enjoying the majestic beauty of them when suddenly he heard a woman screaming.

Immediately Jack kicked his horse into a trot in the direction of the scream. As they crested a small hill, he spotted ten man beasts. They were gathered in a small circle with a woman in the middle. The beasts appeared to be arguing about who would get the woman first. Jack watched for a brief moment. The beasts were truly atrocious. Now he understood why the gods had called them an abomination. Jack drew the God Stone Sword and charged down the hill. The beasts were too busy arguing that they did not see Jack charging until he was on them.

Jack reached the circle of beasts and swung the sword. The swing cut the head off one of the beasts. Jack jumped off the horse and attacked the beasts. He had killed four beasts before the rest understood that they were being attacked. Jack took on the remaining six beasts using speed, agility, and brains. He would not be caught overconfident again. Jack swung at one beast, taking off an arm. Immediately Jack turned away from the beast and swung in the opposite direction and cut another beast in half. Now there were only four left and one badly injured.

Two of the beasts came at him together. Jack watched them. As they got close, he jumped into the air and kicked the beasts, one with each foot. He landed and struck so quickly the beasts had no time to react. The last two beasts were already coming after him. Jack ducked to dodge a swing by one of the beasts. As he did, he swung around with his legs and tripped the beast. Before the beast hit the ground, Jack had already plunged his sword through its chest. The last beast was in the air jumping at Jack when he looked up. Jack had just enough time to pull the knife from his knife belt he wore at his waist and stabbed the beast. The knife went deep into the chest of the beast. The weight of the flying beast smashed both of them to the ground. Jack rolled the beast off of him and pulled out his knife.

Jack looked around and saw the beast with one arm crawling toward the scream ing woman. Jack quickly pulled his sword out from the other dead beast and ran to the crawling one. With one swing, he cut off the head of the beast. Jack stood and looked around. There were body parts and dead bodies all around. He himself was covered in blood.

The woman said, "Warrior, thank you" as she ran to him crying. She held on to him and sobbed. After several minutes, she asked, "Who are you? How did you find me?"

Jack said, "I am a warrior, and I found you by your screams."

Jack cleaned himself off and his weapons. His horse came back to Jack, and he offered the woman some water. He said, "We should get moving. Undoubtedly there are others around."

"The beasts attacked our farm," the woman said. "They took me, another woman, and the farmer's son then headed back to the mountains."

"How many of them were there?" asked Jack. "I think it was about twenty-five or thirty," she said.

"Did you see where the others went?" he asked. The woman pointed east. Jack mounted his horse and then lifted the woman up behind him and headed in the direction she had pointed.

After several hours of riding east, they heard screaming and crying. Jack kicked the horse into a trot. They came around a bend, and there were the remaining beasts with the boy and woman. The boy was crying and was standing up against the rock of the mountain. The woman was naked standing next to him. Jack stopped the horse and got off. Jack told the woman to get off and hold the horse. He told her that if anything should happen to him to get on the horse and ride home as fast as she could.

The beasts were all facing the boy and woman so they did not know that Jack was behind them. Jack took his bow and went about twenty- five yards away. He got down on one knee and began to fire arrows at the beasts. Because he was so close, the arrows struck hard and were deadly. Seven beasts were down before they noticed that something was wrong. When one of the beasts turned and started growling to sound the alarm an arrow in his mouth cut off the scream. This alerted the other animals, and they all turned to see what was happening. While they were turning and trying to figure out what was happening, Jack kept firing arrows.

He had killed a dozen of the beasts when they charged him. Jack fired three more shots and three more beasts went down. Jack climbed up the rocks and turned to face the beasts. He was too high for the beasts to reach him. He steadied himself and began to shoot more arrows at the man beasts. When he finally ran out of arrows, there were only five beasts left. Jack carried two knives in the knife belt at his waist. One had a fifteen-inch double-edged blade; the other was a ten-inch serrated blade. With the double-edged knife in one hand and his sword in the other, he jumped down among the remaining beasts.

He came down stabbing with the knife and swinging the sword. He stuck the knife into the skull of one of the monsters, and it dropped to the ground dead. The swing of the sword cut off the arm of another. Jack never stopped swinging the sword and quickly killed the rest of the man beasts. Jack pulled his knife out of the skull and then went to retrieve the arrows. He did not have a way to replace his arrows, so he had to get as many as he could back. When he had gathered all the arrows, he then turned his attention to the survivors.

The woman with Jack's horse had gone over to the naked lady and the boy. She had opened the packs on the horse and found a shirt and gave it to the woman. She was a small woman, and the shirt hung to her knees. As Jack approached them, the boy ran to him and hugged him. The woman thanked him and asked him to please stay with them until they were safely home. Jack said, "I cannot take you all the way home, but I will see you to safety."

That night they came across a large group of beasts. Jack estimated that there was about fifty of them. It was already dark, and Jack knew this was his only chance of killing the beasts. He left the women and boy with the horse and instructed them to stay hidden and very quiet. He went into the camp and with his long double-edged knife started slicing the throats of the sleeping monsters. Jack moved quickly but quietly and was able to kill all the beasts without them discovering what was happening. He returned to the survivors, and they slept there hidden for the night.

The next morning when they started out, they were shocked at what they saw. In addition to the dead bodies of the beasts, there were remains of five humans. Each human had missing parts that had been bitten off. One woman had obviously been raped and then killed. Jack was grief-stricken and sickened by the gruesome sight. However, he mustered up his emotional strength and dug a large grave. He then buried the bodies and all the body parts he could find. The women thanked him for his kind gesture but were very nervous that more man beasts might catch them.

For the next week, Jack and his survivors came across several small groups of man beasts. Most of them did not have any captives. Sometimes they found the beasts in the process of eating or raping the humans. Jack killed every beast he found. He rescued as many people as he could. He was torn apart inside when he was too late to save the life of the humans or too late to prevent the raping of a woman. The brutal treatment he witnessed from the man beasts made him hate the animals, making him all the more determined to kill them all.

It took Jack eight days to reach the southern edge of the Northern Mountains with the survivors. He had rescued three little boys, two teenage girls, and eight women from the beasts. He led them out of the mountains for a couple of miles and then stopped. "You are safe now. I will let you return to your homes on your own. I must go back to the mountains and continue the fight with the man beasts." All the women tried to convince him to go with them. They promised him anything he wanted as payment for saving them. Jack simply thanked them and headed back to the mountains.

The survivors chased after him for a little bit, but when Jack kicked his horse into a trot, they stopped giving chase and turned to head home. All the survivors could talk about was the handsome young warrior that had saved them from the man beasts. When they finally made it home to their families, they told the story of how this great warrior had rescued them. They told of his skill with the sword, bow, and knife. Soon others were rescued and returned to tell about the young warrior that had saved them. In a matter of a few months, the legend of the warrior in the mountains had spread throughout the North Pointe area and Northport.

CHAPTER 5 - A CALL FOR HELP

Emily and Silas had just finished having lunch when Linda and Vanessa returned home from town. The girls came running in the house, looking for Emily and Silas. They were so excited that they both started talking at the same time. Silas and Emily just laughed, and the girls realized what they were doing.

Silas said, "If you two will control yourselves, maybe one of you can tell us what has excited you so much."

The girls looked at each other and laughed. Vanessa nodded for Linda to go ahead. Linda said, "In town everyone is talking about a great warrior that is fighting the man beasts. He has rescued several people from the beasts. They say that he rescues the captives, brings them to a safe point out of the mountains, and then goes back to look for more captives. They say he is the greatest warrior alive. He fights with a sword, knives, and even a bow."

Linda stopped to catch her breath, and Emily said, "Yes, yes, and I am sure he is ten feet tall and the most handsome man you ever saw."

Vanessa said, "Seriously, Mother. Everyone is talking about him. They say that he hates the man beasts and wants to kill them all." Emily looked over to Silas, and he said, "I heard something about some young farm boy being rescued from the man beasts last week when I was in town. The young boy supposedly tells of a great warrior that saved him and his nanny."

Emily said, "Well, Commander Wallace should be coming any day now to give us his quarterly report. I will ask him about these rumors when he arrives."

The next morning, Commander Wallace arrived to give his report. For several hours, they discussed the business of the garrison and the financial costs and reimbursement the queen would make. The commander informed them that he now had twenty thousand men under his command. After he told them this, the Commander stopped talking and looked at Emily then Silas. He was curious to see if either of them recognized the significance of this number. Silas looked at Emily and found she was looking at him.

They both turned to the commander, and Silas said, "That is a significant number. It has taken a long time. Are you saying that we are ready?"

The commander sat silently for a moment before he continued. "I am not sure that all twenty thousand men would join our cause. The recruitment standards are still the same. However, implementation of the requirements may have been relaxed, or so I am told by Sergeant Miller."

Emily asked, "How many men can we count on?"

"Sergeant Miller tells me that he is confident that fifteen thousand of the men will join our cause," answered the commander.

No one said anything for a few moments. The silence was interrupted by Sara coming in and saying, "Excuse me, but a rider is coming, and he is in a big hurry."

A few minutes later, Sara led a young courier into the parlor where they were waiting for him. The courier handed a sealed message to the commander and said, "I apologize for barging in like this, but the Duchess Sheila instructed me to ride day and night as fast as I could and to deliver this message to Commander Wallace. When I arrived at the garrison, I was told that you were here, so I came as fast as possible."

The commander had been reading the message while the courier spoke. "It appears as if the man beasts are on the loose again. A force of about two hundred has just left the mountains and is heading for Northport. The duchess asks that we send at least one thousand men. She asked that these men be temporarily assigned to the garrison at Northport. It seems that the beasts have been attacking around the city for several months now. She is formally requesting the reopening of the garrison at Northport. She has even volunteered to pay for half the cost of sustaining the garrison" said the commander.

Silas asked, "Will one thousand men be enough to handle this uprising?"

The commander answered, "One thousand should be enough to handle this bunch now if we can get them there fast enough."

Silas added, "Well, Commander, I see no other option than to send them the troops they need. However,

I think we should send a message to the duchess asking if we should not increase that number to twenty- five hundred just in case the beasts attack in larger numbers and if she would still be willing to help with half the costs."

Emily turned to the commander and asked, "Whom will you send to Northport as the commanding officer?"

The Commander thought about it for a brief moment and answered, "Sergeant Miller has earned the opportunity for a command of his own. I will send him as the military leader to the garrison." Silas and Emily both shook their heads in approval. The commander said, "Since we are in agreement then I must hurry back to the garrison and make arrangements for the sergeant to leave.

As they were walking the commander out, Emily remembered the rumor the girls had mentioned. She asked, "Oh, Commander, I was wondering if you have heard any of the rumors going around about this great warrior who rescues people from the man beasts?"

The commander stopped and turned around and said, "It is not a rumor, my lady. I have personally spoken with over a dozen rescued captives. They all have described this warrior exactly the same. I do not know who he is, but for months now, he has definitely been killing the man beasts and rescuing our fellow citizens. According to these survivors, when they asked him his name, he answers simply 'warrior.' When they ask him where he came from he says, he is from the Kingdom. I had intended to speak to you about him, but with the arrival of the courier, I forgot to mention it."

Silas said, "I believe this mysterious warrior deserves some investigating. But we can talk about it some other time. For now you have some very important business to take care of at the garrison."

Silas and Emily walked back to the house hand in hand, talking about the rumors. "I think that this warrior is someone who has been deeply hurt by the man beasts. They probably took his wife or children. He went after them and has been lucky, so far, that he has not been killed," said Silas.

Emily said, "I don't know about that because according to all the survivors this warrior is very skilled with many sorts of weapons." As she finished saying this, Linda and Vanessa came out of the house and immediately asked if the commander had confirmed the rumors. Emily told the girls that indeed the commander had said that the rumors were true.

Vanessa asked, "Why did the commander leave so quickly?"

"A courier came from Northport. They are being attacked by the man beasts and have requested help. The commander is returning to the garrison to send help to them," said Emily.

The Commander rode as fast as his horse could carry him back to the garrison. When the watchtower spotted him in such a hurry, they immediately sounded the alarm. Sergeant Miller met the commander in the middle of the yard. The commander leaped off his horse and handed the message to the sergeant. He issued orders for all command staff to meet in his office immediately.

It took less than five minutes for everyone to gather in the commander's office. He had Sergeant Miller read the message to everyone. The message gave everyone a long face. The commander said, "Sergeant Miller, you will lead a force of one thousand men and go to Northport. Let's hope you arrive in time. Your orders are to handle the immediate emergency, then go to the garrison and fortify it. You will then report to the Duchess Wells and let her know that the situation has been handled and that you will be staying there until further notice. In addition you will deliver a message from me to the duchess. You need to leave immediately." With that everyone left his office and started making preparations for the men to leave.

It took Sergeant Miller three hours to prepare his troops to leave. The commander was impressed that such a large force could be mobilized so quickly. The trip to Northport normally would take an army of that size twelve days to make. The sergeant set a steady pace and maintained it all day long. He gave orders that breakfast would be cold and lunch would be in the saddle. Dinners would be the only hot meals they had. They rose before dawn and started moving before daybreak and rode until well after dark. On the morning of the seventh day, they rode into the garrison at Northport.

Sergeant Miller immediately took command and ordered for reports of the situation. He was told that the man beasts were close by, but no one could say exactly where they were. The sergeant sent out scouts to find the beasts. The scouts returned about mid afternoon and reported that the beasts were ten miles out to the northwest. They were heading straight to the city and were running very fast. The sergeant ordered his men to mount up. He gave orders to ride in full battle gear. He wanted to get to the beasts before they reached the city. The scouts reported that they estimated about two hundred beasts were charging.

Within half an hour, the soldiers had left the garrison and were riding out to meet the beasts. One hour later, they were face to face with the man beasts. The sergeant ordered a full charge. The beasts heard the rumble of the charge but did not realize that they were being attacked until the charging army was on them and one third of them were already dead. With the surprise attack, the sergeant had not only stopped the beasts from charging forward but also spooked them into complete disarray. The soldiers killed all the beasts quickly and efficiently. The soldiers returned to the garrison shortly after dark. They had killed all the beasts and only suffered one hundred casualties. This was a great victory for the sergeant. Normally the beasts killed more than twice their own number before they were defeated. This time the quickness of the attack had completely surprised them and created havoc amongst them. The sergeant gave orders that everyone should have a hot meal and bath that night before retiring for the evening. He himself did not participate in the meal and bath until several hours later.

The sergeant headed to the duchess's palace. When he arrived, the head mistress was upset that he would come calling at such an hour. However, he insisted, and the mistress had no choice but to announce him to the duchess. The headmistress led the sergeant to a small waiting room in the back of the palace. A few minutes later, the duchess arrived.

The sergeant stood, took a bow, and said, "My lady, I am Sergeant Miller, and I have come to report to you that the group of man beasts that were charging on the city have been eliminated."

The duchess said, "That is good news, sergeant. How many men did you bring with you?"

"I brought one thousand men. We have orders to move into the garrison and stay until I receive orders from Commander Wallace to return. I apologize for the late hour, but my orders were to notify you immediately after we had taken care of the man beasts. I also have this written message for you from the commander."

The duchess took the message from the sergeant and read it. She said, "Thank you, sergeant. That will be all. I will send my reply directly to the commander by courier. Thank you for your prompt response to my request for help. You have my never-ending gratitude." The sergeant bowed and left the palace.

The next morning, the duchess dispatched a courier to the commander. In her response, she told the commander that she would accept the additional troops and help pay for the costs of maintaining the garrison if the Duchess Winston and the commander agreed to leave the troops for a minimum of two years. She would like to keep the troops there indefinitely, but she would settle for two years. Three weeks later, she received a reply from the commander. In the reply, the commander stated that the troops would stay, under the leadership of Sergeant Miller, for a minimum of two years. He stated that the additional troops should arrive within a month.

CHAPTER 6 - A NEW SORCERER

Things in Twin Falls and the palace had been running smoothly for some time now. Ariel was finally beginning to feel relaxed and totally in control of the world. The only bad news to come to them lately had been the small uprising of the man beasts in Northport. As usual though, Commander Wallace had rapidly dispatched troops and taken care of the situation. As a result, the two duchesses, Sheila and Emily, had agreed to reopen the garrison at Northport. They had agreed to keep 2,500 troops there and split the cost between each other. This arrangement was fine with Ariel because it provided the extra protection needed for the citizens and did not cost the royal treasury anything.

As Ariel looked at the map in front of her, she studied each Kingdom city individually. Southport had accepted her from the beginning without any problems. Southport had been the first city she conquered in the Kingdom, and she had stayed there longer than any other city. It was also the nearest Kingdom city to her home and stronghold Independent City. She had left a full garrison of five thousand troops there, and they never had any problems.

Looking further along the map, she came to Bartersville. Bartersville had always been the most rebellious of all the Kingdom cities. However, since Boris had taken care of the Longs and left Kain with 2,500 troops there, the resistance had slowly withered away. Over the years, the number of troops there had slowly diminished. Now they had about five hundred soldiers in the rebuilt garrison.

Heading north on the map along the desert was Bordertown. She never understood the name of this city because it was not on the border. She thought if anything it should have been called Edgetown because it was on the edge of the Crystal Desert. Bordertown fascinated her.

It was a strange city. The people were rugged and tough. The wall that protected it from the desert sandstorms had in the last five years been increased to thirty feet high. Ariel thought that the citizens of Bordertown were paranoid and obsessed with the desert. However, she liked them because they had a unique way of controlling their criminals. Criminals were aware that if caught they would be exiled. The practice of exiling criminals had been restarted after Ariel had exiled that stubborn little boy. The people of the city had quickly turned the city into a law-abiding and prosperous and rapidly growing city.

As she followed the map north to North Pointe, Boris walked in. Neither of them spoke; Boris went to his desk and started working. North Pointe was the fastest growing city in the Kingdom despite the always-present threat of the man beasts. She knew that this was because of the excellent job that Commander Wallace had done over the years in protecting the city. In addition, the Duchess Emily along with her husband, Silas Jones, was very astute in business. They had created an economy in the city that was conducive to business and personal growth. She liked Emily very much; Ariel considered her a close friend and thought of her like a sister.

Ariel could not help herself; whenever she looked at the map of the north, she always looked at the Northern Mountains. These mountains were ominous but beautiful, and yet they contained the single greatest threat to her empire, the man beasts. However, lately she had heard about a warrior that seemed to live in these mountains and was determined to wipe out the beasts. She and Boris had discussed these rumors and investigated them last year when they had made their trip to the cities. Commander Wallace had confirmed that the rumors were true. This warrior had rescued hundreds of people. Everyone described him as the greatest fighter they had ever seen. When Boris used his sorcery to make the survivors tell the truth, their story was still the same. When Boris used the memory spell he had first used on Commander Wallace, what they saw was always from the perspective of the warrior. Boris could not explain why his spell would work like that. As a result, they had not been able to see what the warrior looked like. They had only been able to prove that he indeed existed. Boris had finally rationalized that as long as this mysterious warrior stayed in the mountains and fought these beasts there was nothing that he or anyone could do.

Finally, she followed the map to Northport. She always thought of Northport with fondness because of Duchess Sheila. Sheila had married and had two children of her own now. However, Sheila had somehow managed to keep herself slim and fit. Sheila was still as beautiful as the first time Ariel had seen her. Her marriage had not stopped the two women from keeping the annual tradition they had started long ago. Every year when they met, the two women would seduce each other and spend one night together.

Sheila had been young when Ariel appointed her as Duchess of Northport. As a result, it had taken a few years for her to learn the ropes of politics. Eventually,

Sheila had grown into a smart and brave leader. She had stopped being influenced by the political groups and started running the city according to her own beliefs and ideas. Shortly after she began implementing her own ideas, the city began to respond to the duchess, and now Northport was booming.

As Ariel was following the map to Twin Falls, Boris startled her. Boris had been working at his desk when suddenly, without apparent cause, he fell over backward on to the floor. Ariel ran over to Boris. He was pale and looked like he had been struck by a sudden illness. She asked, "What happened? You look sick. Are you all right?"

Boris blinked and then slowly stood up. After composing himself, he said, "Someone in the palace has just used sorcery. The blow was so strong and unfocused that it not only affected the intended target but also anyone with the ability in the vicinity of the wielder. Whoever it was is untrained and therefore very dangerous. I must find this person."

Boris and Ariel left their private quarters and began to look for the source of the sorcery. It did not take long for word to reach them that a young girl had just been killed over in the servants' quarters. When they arrived, there was a large group of people standing around just staring at the bloody scene. As Boris and Ariel worked their way to the front of the crowd, they came to a sudden stop when they stepped out from the crowd.

There before them was a horrible scene of blood and body parts scattered around. Up against the opposite wall of the room in the middle of the blood and body parts was the prince. Prince Willard was in an apparent state of shock. Apparently, so was everyone else. No one said anything they just stared, even Ariel and Boris. Finally it was Anna that came to her senses first. She started shouting orders. "Don't just stand there gawking," she said to the servants. She picked three men and ordered them to pick up the prince and take him to the royal suite. She then told several other servants to start cleaning up the mess. She ordered everyone else to go back to their chores.

Ariel finally snapped out of her shock and looked over to Boris. Boris nodded, confirming that it had apparently been the prince who had used the sorcery. Ariel turned to Anna and said, "Thank you, for your quick thinking in taking care of this mess." Then she turned to Boris and said, "We must go talk to our son and find out what happened here." With that being said, they both took off after their son. Anna turned to inspect the cleanup process and decided to ask a few questions about what had happened.

When Ariel and Boris got back to the royal suite, the staff had already started cleaning the prince up. When the staff finished the cleanup and had laid the prince in bed, Boris ordered everyone out of the royal apartments. He wanted complete privacy for the discussion he was about to have with his son. The prince was still in shock but was starting to come around.

Boris and Ariel sat on the bed with the prince. Boris looked at him and said, "Son, I want you to tell me exactly what happened. I want every detail. Do not leave anything out." The prince knew by the look of intensity on his parents' faces that if he was not careful he could be in a lot of trouble. He decided that he would not tell all the facts but would instead embellish the truth for his own protection.

He began. "I had been hearing rumors that this girl liked me and that she had been having dreams about me. She was very pretty, and lately I noticed that she had been flirting with me and literally teasing me. I went to her room and began flirting with her. At first she was very cooperative, but when I made a pass at her, she rejected me. At first I thought she was just playing hard to get. I kept trying, and she began to scream and call me a rapist and slapped me. Then she raised her knee and kicked me in the privates. I was in great pain and furious. I am not sure about what happened next. All I remember is looking at her with complete hatred and wishing she were dead. I was thinking that I would cut her to pieces as soon as I was able to move again. The next thing I knew she blew up into pieces. Her body just burst into pieces, and blood and guts were everywhere. I screamed."

The prince had lied about the rumors about the girl in order to save himself. Boris and Ariel just stared at each other knowing that based on what their son had just said he was a sorcerer.

Boris asked, "Willard, has anything like this ever happened before?"

"Yes," the prince replied.

"Tell me about it, son" said Boris.

"Well, I thought it was just my mind playing tricks on me because it has always been little things. Like once last winter when it was real cold and we were having liquids freeze in our cups. Some of the guys and I were sitting around one night, just talking nonsense. One of the guys was bragging about how he was the best swordsman in our class and how he could beat us all. I remember thinking how I wished his drink would freeze in his mouth. The next thing I know he takes a drink and he starts gagging and he cannot talk. His drink had frozen in his mouth. Another time I was having a cup of coffee one morning. The coffee was not fresh or hot. I remember thinking how I wished my coffee were fresh and hot. The next drink I took from my cup, the coffee was very fresh and very hot. I thought it was just my mind playing tricks on me."

Boris looked at Ariel and then turned back to his son. Looking him straight in the eye, Boris said, "Son, you know that I am a wizard and a sorcerer. As a result, the possibility exists that some of my ability could have been passed on to you. Until now I thought that you had not received any of my abilities. However, now based on what you have been telling me, I can see that my abilities have indeed been passed on to you. Willard, sorcery is very dangerous. Without the proper training, you could not only hurt people around you but you may also hurt yourself. We must get you trained in order to teach you to control your power before you kill someone else or yourself. I can only think of one way to train you properly. That way, however, means that you will have to return to Independent City and study under the same teacher that I learned from. Are you willing to do this?"

Willard, lay there in his bed in complete shock. He was a sorcerer. His mind was racing with the possibilities. He became overwhelmed by the possibilities. He was so excited that he could not even speak; his response to his father was simply to shake his head yes.

Ariel said, "Very well, you will leave tomorrow. I will make the travel arrangements."

Boris said, "I will make the necessary paper work for you to take with you. In the meantime, you need to rest."

Willard was ecstatic about going to learn to be a sorcerer. His mind raced with all the things he would do to all the people who had never shown him the proper respect.

Anna had been careful not to be obvious about her investigation. She had uncovered a very different story from what the queen had made public. She however was glad to hear that the prince was leaving for a while. The prince was going home to learn how to be a sorcerer. Anna had discovered that the prince had been, as usual, trying to force himself on a young servant girl. As was normal with all the girls in the palace, they wanted nothing to do with the prince. As was also normal, the prince did not care if the young servants would not cooperate; he would force himself on them. This time when he tried to force himself on this young girl, she had managed to get away from him by kicking him hard in the privates. As the young servant girl walked away, she burst into pieces. Anna now knew that the prince had, not realizing, used sorcery on the girl and killed her.

The thought of the prince as a sorcerer scared Anna very much. She feared for the lives of those that would not please him. However, the fact that he would be leaving the palace for an extended period of time pleased her very much. The news that the prince was leaving the palace spread throughout the palace and the city like wildfire. The next day when Boris and Ariel were escorting the prince to the ship he would be taking downriver, they were surprised to find a large group of people waiting at the docks.

As the royal family entered the docks, the crowd began cheering. Boris and Ariel were touched by the show of emotion. They took it as a heartfelt sadness to see the prince go. However, the truth was that the cheers were of joy and not sorrow. The citizens of Twin Falls had also come to dislike the prince. The prince would visit various establishments around the city. If he was not pleased with the reception or services he received, the prince would create a scene. At first the citizens went to the palace to complain about the prince and his behavior. The merchants complained about the prince's temper, his taste for the unusual, and his bad manners. Unfortunately for the merchants, the complaints went to Kain. Kain was in charge of the grievance committee the queen had established. Every complaint that Kain received about the prince was seen as an act of treason or conspiracy. The merchant would be tortured and killed, and his business would be closed. Word got out quickly that merchants who complained about the prince were tortured and condemned as traitors. Soon the merchants quit complaining about the prince because they feared for their lives. As a result, the prince was free to do as he pleased throughout the city.

Ariel almost began to cry at the show of support for the prince. However, she would not allow herself to show emotion in front of these people. Even after eighteen years, she still could not call them her people. Today, the citizens of Twin Falls earned a little trust and respect from both Boris and Ariel. The crowd stayed until Boris and Ariel left the docks.

As the word spread around the town that the prince was gone, a spirit of cheer came over the entire city. Ariel had no idea what had caused the change in the atmosphere around town. All she knew was that lately everyone seemed to be happier.

CHAPTER 7 - A NEW PLAN

It had been a year since the devastating and demoralizing defeat to the desert warrior, and the wounds had not totally healed yet. Karn's physical wounds had healed very well, and he was now in the process of rebuilding his strength. Gar's wounds had healed sooner than Karn's. Emotionally, neither one had recovered yet. Both men were depressed and felt ashamed. Not only had they lost a battle with overwhelming odds in their favor but they had been spared their lives only out of the mercy of their most hated enemy.

When the survivors had returned to the mountains and told about how the desert warrior had defeated them by setting traps and surprise attacks, the entire Horde nation was devastated. Sam and the elders were in shock when they heard the news. Then when Gar and Karn had finally made it back, both were badly wounded physically and emotionally. They told the elders how the forest had been filled with traps. They explained that no matter where they turned the traps were there. Then when the traps were sprung, they told the elders of the hit- and-run tactics used against them. They told how the desert warrior himself had participated in the hit-and-run tactics. They told of his superior ability and how easily he had defeated all who stood against him, including both Gar and Karn.

When word got out that the desert warrior had easily defeated both Gar and Karn, the spirits of the Horde sank into depression. Gar was a big man, in his mid thirties, and a very good fighter. He was considered one of the best fighters in the entire Horde. Yet even so, the desert warrior had easily defeated him. The elders were in shock and for the first time afraid for their people. If everything they had experienced up to now was mercy, what would the desert warrior do to them if he attacked?

After the devastating loss, when Gar and Karn delivered the message the desert warrior had given them the elders were crushed. The warrior had warned them that his people wanted peace. He warned that if the attacks continued, he would not show mercy again. This word got out to the people of the Horde, and they all feared for their lives. When anyone hinted about striking at the tribesmen, they were rebuked by the people, sent before the elders, and made to swear that they would never consider an attack against the tribesmen again.

Sam's daughter Faithe was the one who first broke out of the slump. She wanted to get married, and she would not take no for an answer. Faithe would hear no more about waiting and healing. When she threatened to cancel the entire engagement, Sam finally realized that his daughter was right. The Horde nation was indeed in a state of depression, and if they did not snap out of it, the entire Horde nation would die. Sam went to Karn and asked him to go through with the wedding plans. At first Karn was reluctant to go through with the wedding, but not because he was no longer in love with Faithe; he still loved her very much. He felt ashamed that he had been so easily defeated. With this shame, how could he possibly marry the daughter of the leader of his people? Faithe's answer to that was quick and simple: "Because you love me."

When Faithe told Karn that if he did not marry her right away, she would call the whole thing off, he reluctantly agreed to go through with the wedding. Faithe and Lana, her mother, went wild with plans for the ceremony. Every day they came up with something new that they wanted to add to the ceremony or the decorations. With all the planning and preparations for the ceremony, the Horde nation slowly came back to life.

Most Horde wedding ceremonies were simple and usually only attended by the clan members of the couple. However, when the daughter of the leader of the entire Horde got married, that was a different story. The ceremony was held at the valley of meetings. The actual ceremony would happen on the ledge where Sam or the elders spoke. By holding the ceremony here, the entire Horde nation could witness the event. When the daughter of the leader married, the chosen mate was usually someone of importance among the clans.

On the day of the wedding ceremony, the entire Horde nation attended. There were over two hundred thousand in attendance in the valley that day. The ceremony was conducted by one of the elders. Faithe and Karn had asked Nicolas to perform the ceremony. The ceremony was more of a ritual than ceremony. The Elder would first introduce the bride. The introduction was a description of her family lineage. Then the Elder would introduce the groom. The groom traditionally gave the Elder a recap of his family's lineage and a list of his personal accomplishments. Karn came from a good family line, and he personally was well liked. His accomplishments were, in his opinion, not sufficient to claim the hand of the daughter of his leader.

Nicolas met with Karn at length about his accomplishments. It was during this meeting that Nicolas realized that not only Karn but the entire Horde nation was depressed. Something had to be done immediately. Nicolas told Karn to relax and work on building his strength up for his wedding night and not to worry about the ceremony; he would take care of everything.

The ceremony began at midmorning as was customary. First the mother of the groom spoke to the mother of the bride and assured her that her son would love her daughter. Then it was the groom's father who spoke to the bride's father about how his son would care for his daughter. This went on for about an hour. Then it was Nicolas's turn to speak. First he introduced Faithe; and after he finished, accompanied by music and surrounded by her wedding court, Faithe came forward and joined Nicolas on the ledge.

Nicolas paused for a few moments and let the crowd enjoy Faithe and her party. Faithe was a very pretty young lady, and dressed in white, she truly looked like an angel. After several moments, Nicolas asked for silence and began his introduction of Karn. He discussed his family lineage with little fanfare. Then he started by talking about Karn as a young and courageous warrior. He explained how when no one else even attempted to devise a method to defeat the evil desert warrior, Karn had had the courage and foresight to invent the shield. Then he had the courage to test this new weapon himself. He was the youngest Horde warrior to ever lead them into battle. His invention of the shield would forever change the way of fighting for the Horde nation. He went on to state that despite setbacks he kept trying and never gave up. Nicolas was laying the foundation for a plan he was going to present to the elders that night after the first day of celebration.

Karn could not believe what he was hearing. This old man had taken his failures and made him sound like a hero. His respect for Nicolas grew tremendously and knew that he would be forever in his debt. After the introductions, Sam and Lana came forward and announced that they would accept Karn as a husband for their daughter. The entire council of elders came out next and blessed the couple. Finally, Nicolas took them by the hand and pronounced them as man and wife witnessed by the entire Horde nation and the gods.

The celebrations usually lasted three or four days after the pronouncement. It was out of the ordinary for one of the elders to call a meeting of the elders. Sam was concerned that this could be bad news for him. When Sam arrived, he was the last one to get to the meeting. Nicolas had refused to start without Sam being present.

Nicolas said, "I am sure you are all wondering why I have asked you here tonight. Sam, you can thank your new son-in-law for this meeting. It was while I was visiting with Karn that I first accepted that our entire nation is in a state of depression." Everyone began speaking at once and nothing could be understood by anyone. Nicolas signaled with his hands for silence. When everyone stopped talking, he continued. "I know you all think that statement is foolish. But consider this: What have we done in the last year, since the battle with the desert warrior? Nothing! We have hidden out up here in the safety of our mountains. We have chastised anyone who tried to do anything. We let this warrior dictate to us how to live our lives. You all know I am saying the truth. Sam, your daughter's wedding has been a good start to help bring life back to normal among the clans. Now it is up to the council to insure the continued resurgence of our people."

For a moment, no one spoke. Finally, Sam said, "Nicolas, as much as I hate to admit that our nation is in a state of depression, I must agree with you. If not for my daughter insisting on this wedding, I think we would all be in worse shape than we are now. When Faithe approached me about the wedding, my first reaction was to try to talk her out of it. I told her the time was not right. What I was really saying to her was that I was in shock and did not want to do anything that might be considered aggressive by the desert warrior. I was afraid. Once I realized what was happening to me, I was able to deal with it. I too feel that we are at risk of losing our unity and agree that we need to save our nation. However, I have thought about this, and I can think of nothing that we can do to build up our spirits."

No one said anything. Everybody just shook his or her heads in agreement with Sam. Something needed to be done, but no one had a clue as to what.

Finally Dora spoke up. "All right, Nicolas. You must have an idea or you would not have called this meeting."

Nicolas smiled and said, "I have an idea. Since it was a battle that we lost that got us this way, we need a battle that we will win to snap us out of it." Everyone erupted; they were all yelling and screaming at each other.

Finally Sam stood up and shouted, "Shut up!" The group was caught by surprise, and they all stopped talking. Sam continued. "Nicolas, with all due respect, I think the desert warrior has proven to us time and time again that we cannot defeat him. He has repeatedly bested even our best warriors and strategies. What you are suggesting would be a useless loss of life."

Everybody agreed with Sam, and they all looked at Nicolas.

Nicolas was still smiling, "What you just said is part of the problem, Sam. Who said anything about attacking the desert warrior and the Claws? I didn't. You made an assumption when I mentioned fighting. There are six other tribes that we can attack. For the last several years, we have only sent small raids against the other tribes. These raids have been somewhat successful. Because of our pride, we have continued to send our main forces against the desert warrior." Sam was dumbfounded. How could he have been so blind, so focused on one warrior? "Nicolas, are you suggesting that we attack another tribe? I think I see where you are going with this. If we attack another tribe, we should be able to defeat them and therefore restore our pride."

Nicolas said, "Now you are thinking like the Sam we selected to be our leader. However, it must be more than just a victory. We must make a strong showing, and the victory must be decisive."

Sam was already thinking along those lines and was forming a plan.

One of the other elders, Martha, said, "I agree with Nicolas, but, Sam, it will be up to you to make the call to arms. Based on our recent failures, I am not sure that we will get the response we need to make this plan work." Sam replied, "I will make the call tomorrow at about midday. That will give the revelers time to recover somewhat. I have a plan that is not finished yet, but I think will work. If we are in agreement, then I suggest we adjourn so that I can finalize my plan and you can spread the word about the meeting tomorrow."

Word spread throughout the Horde that the council was calling a meeting at midday. Everyone was surprised; this sort of thing was not done specially on the day after the chiefs' daughter was married. Karn heard about the meeting, and he and Faithe went to find Gar. They found Gar talking to Lana.

Karn immediately asked, "What is going on?"

Faithe said, "Mother, why is the council doing this to my wedding celebration?"

Lana replied, "Your father was called to a council meeting last night. When he left, he was convinced that the council was going to ask him to step down from his role as leader of the Horde. However, when he came back, he was very excited. All he said was that the Horde nation was going to return to the days of victory and glory." Lana was interrupted by the excitement of the crowd. Looking up, they saw Sam standing on the ledge, ready to make his speech.

Sam stood at the edge of the ledge for a few moments; he wanted to make sure everyone knew he was ready to begin. Finally he spoke, "Clans of the Horde, I realize that this meeting is unusual. However, given the importance of what I am about to say you will understand. As many of you know, the Council has for the last year been very hard on anyone who was considering any actions against the tribes of the plains. There was a very good reason for this. I have heard all the rumors that have been spread around the clans. I am here today to lay all the rumors to rest. They are not true. The council has not accepted defeat." When he said this, a roar of cheers from the crowd made Sam wait a few minutes before he could continue. Waiving for the crowd to be silent, Sam continued. "The council was hard on these individuals for many reasons. First we wanted the tribes to think that they had won. We wanted them to think that we had accepted their peace offering. We have not!" Again Sam was forced to wait before continuing. "Second and most importantly, the council were formulating a new plan that will rid us of the tribes forever." The crowd became ecstatic, horns started blowing, old war songs were sung, and dancing broke out.

Sam turned back to the council members, and they all nodded with approval. After a long time, Sam was able to bring the crowd back under control. He continued. "The new plan is the same as the old plan but with a twist. We will attack, and to that means, I make a call to all warriors who want to be part of this plan. We will attack from the west. We will attack the Arians. This is the westernmost tribe. We will attack them just before they head to their annual gathering. The Arians will not be attending this year's gathering. Instead, the survivors will be begging us for mercy and become our slaves. After the Arians are dealt with, we will pull back for the winter. Next spring when the tribes return, we will attack again from the west. We will attack one tribe at a time until we reach the Claws. The Claws will have no choice but to surrender to us without a fight. This is how we will defeat the desert warrior and eliminate the tribes. I call all warriors who want to help rid us of the tribes to arms." The crowd erupted again. Sam turned around and walked back to the council. The council members all came to him and congratulated him on a great speech and an even better plan.

Karn turned to his new bride and said, "I know this is our wedding, but I must go."

Faithe kissed him and said, "I know."

Karn turned to Gar, and they headed up the trail to go and sign up. By the time Gar and Karn reached the elders' cave there was a line already. Sam spotted them and called them forward.

Sam told them, "I took the liberty of putting your names at the top of the list."

Both warriors were bursting with pride. By the end of the day, 7,500 warriors had volunteered. Sam took Gar and Karn into the council chambers. The council members were there and anxious to hear the rest of Sam's plan.

Sam said, "We have 7,500 warriors ready for battle." Everyone was pleased and surprised, including Sam, by the large number of volunteers. Sam continued. "In order to ensure complete victory, we will split the warriors into two forces. The main force will consist of five thousand warriors and will attack straight ahead from the north. The smaller force will circle around from the east and cut off any escape routes." Turning to Gar and Karn, he said, "It is up to you two to decide who leads the main force and who leads the smaller force. You will need to coordinate so that both forces attack at the same time from both sides."

It was Gar who spoke immediately, "Since it is Karn's wedding that we have interrupted, I believe he should lead the main force, and I will take the smaller one."

Sam turned to the council members; each nodded their head in approval. Turning back to Gar and Karn, he said, "Very well, you will need to act fast to make sure the Arians have not left for the gathering yet."

Gar and Karn thanked the council, and Sam then immediately started making plans.

The Arians were packed and ready to go the gathering. The sun was just beginning to set, and Jerum, Chief of the Arians, decided to wait until morning before they left. Jerome, leader of the warriors and husband to Jessica, Jerum's daughter, posted a scattered few warriors to the north to act as watchmen. The Arians had indeed been lulled into a false since of safety. All the tribes had heard about Jack's defeat of the Horde last year and the peace offering he had made them. All the tribes had been grief stricken when they heard that Jack had found a way home and had left. However, the Horde had not attacked since Jack had defeated them in the forest.

At around midnight, Karn sent his scouts out to eliminate the posted watchmen. Three hours later, the Horde attacked. They charged without the customary screaming and hollering. All the Arians heard was a rumbling. They were caught completely by surprise. When the alarm finally sounded, it was too late; the Arians were already defeated. Chief Jerum tried to organize a retreat, but they were cut off by another Horde force attacking from the east. By the time the sun rose, the Horde had gathered up all the Arians and were ready to head back up the mountains. It was Horde custom to kill the leaders of their opponents. Gar took it upon himself to kill chief Jerum, his wife Jade, and Jacob their son and next in line to be chief. He had not killed Jerome, the leader of the warriors, because Gar had mistakenly thought that Jacob was the warrior leader. Jessica, Jerome's wife and daughter to, the chief, was spared because she was very pretty and considered good breeding stock.

The Horde army returned to the mountains. The clans had all agreed to stay at the valley of meeting until the warriors returned. Gar sent a courier ahead to notify the clans that they had had a complete victory. When the warriors arrived, there was already a celebration going on. The prisoners were locked up in caves while the celebration was on. The council honored Karn and Gar for a great victory. The plan had worked out exactly as Sam had hoped. His people's pride was restored, and they were full of life and ready to take on the rest of the tribes. Volunteers were already starting to sign up for next year's attack on the tribes.

At the gathering of the tribes that year, the Arians never arrived. The chiefs' meeting was very heated with discussion about the missing tribe. Some of the chiefs wanted to send a scout team to the Arians to ask why they had not attended. It was Kail, chief of the Wolf tribe, who finally brought order to the meeting. Kail said, "If you remember at last year's gathering Jerum and his family took the news of Jack the hardest. If you remember, he even stated that the tribes would live to regret the day that Tanner and Jerris allowed Jack to leave. He would not be appeased. I think this is his way of letting us know that he is still upset. The Arians will be back next year." The chiefs reluctantly accepted Kail's explanation, and the tribes ended the gathering and headed south.

On their way south, Tanner and Jerris talked about Kail's reasoning. Jerris explained that Jerum and his family had become very close with Jack ever since Jack had gone after that mountain lion that had attacked Jerome. Jessica had gone with Jack and witnessed Jack's courage against the lion and then the Horde. The family had been very grateful to Jack, and as a result, they had become very close. Tanner knew that all the reasoning made by Kail and Jerris were correct and probably were right. However, something about this just did not sit right with him. He knew he could not prove anything. He had no evidence. All he had was a gut feeling, but he knew something was wrong. He explained his fear as a sense of loss. The Claws, especially his family, had not completely recovered from Jack's departure. It had been almost two years now, and they still missed him like it was yesterday.

CHAPTER 8 – LEARNING

The large crowd that had shown up to see him off did not touch Prince Willard. He noticed the surprise on his parents' face and the small show of emotion that the people of Twin Falls were showing for the prince. Prince Willard knew that the people were probably glad to be rid of him for a while. He knew that inside of him, hidden away from his parents, was the real prince—the prince the citizens of Twin Falls had come to know and despise. As he looked at the crowd, the prince thought, once I learn how to use my newfound powers, I will make this city quiver at the mere mention of my name. Turning back to his parents, they hugged one more time and left the ship.

Prince Willard was fifteen years old, and for the first time in his life, his parents were sending him on a mission. The prince was feeling a little odd and nervous, but most of all, he was very excited and anxious. The prince was positive that he was going to be a very powerful sorcerer, so powerful that he would rival his father. His father awed Prince Willard. His father was not only the biggest man Willard had ever seen but he was also the most powerful wizard and sorcerer the world had ever seen. His father's size and powers made the prince afraid of his father, and at the same time, he envied all the strength and power. The prince wanted all that strength and power and could not wait to inherit the world.

It took the ship carrying the prince two weeks to make the trip downriver to Independent City. The city did not seem to have changed much to the prince. This was his first trip back since he had been taken to Twin Falls to live with his parents. There was no fanfare, no crowds, and no royal reception waiting to meet the prince. This was because no one knew he was coming. His parents told him that he was to go straight to the palace and ask for Governor Bran. Boris had prepared a letter of introduction and instructions for the governor. The governor was to introduce the prince to Master Tam, and the prince was to deliver a letter to the master.

Willard rode his horse slowly through the streets. He watched and noticed that the city appeared to be booming. There were many new businesses and houses that he did not remember from before. He noted the location of several inns that he would return to visit, enjoy the cuisine, and other things. The ship had arrived at mid afternoon, and it took the prince until nightfall to get to the palace. When he arrived at the palace gates, the guards did not recognize him and as a result would not let him in. The prince demanded that he be allowed to see the commander of the watch. The guards ignored his request. The prince made such a commotion that the commander of the watch decided to come and see what the problem was. The commander of the watch recognized the prince right away and reprimanded the guards and allowed the prince to enter.

The commander apologized for the incompetence of the guards and asked the prince to have mercy on them. The prince told the guards that this one time he would show them mercy but never again. The prince was hungry and had the commander escort him to the kitchens. While the prince ate, the commander ordered the staff to go prepare the royal suite for the prince. By the time the prince had finished eating, the word had spread that the prince was in the palace. As Willard left the kitchen, all the palace staff was waiting for him, ready to obey his every command. Willard said, "I am tired, and it's late. I will retire for the night. Tell Governor Bran that I have a message for him from my parents, and I will present it to him in the morning."

Much to the surprise of everyone on the palace staff, the prince was up early the next morning. The prince was anxious to get the preliminary introductions over with so that he could start his training. Governor Bran had always been an early riser and therefore was already in his office when the prince arrived.

"Good morning, your highness," said the governor. "I must say that I am surprised to see you up and about so early."

The prince replied, "I am to start training in sorcery and wizardry. My father has discovered my ability and wants me trained by his teacher. This letter will explain everything. I am very anxious to get started and at the same time a little nervous and as a result I could not sleep anymore. So here I am."

The governor took the letter handed to him by the prince and read it. The letter contained some instructions from the queen on the ruling of the city and some instructions from Boris on military matters. Finally, the letter introduced the prince and spoke of his newfound ability. The prince was to be trained by Master Tam beginning immediately. The governor was instructed to take the prince to the master instructor to begin his learning. After he finished reading the letter, the governor said, "It seems that your parents are as anxious as you are about your training. I have been ordered to take you directly to Master Tam. If you would like, we can go there right now." The prince signaled for the governor to lead the way.

Master Tam had his quarters toward the back wall of the palace. They were also underground. It took them about half an hour to reach the quarters of the master instructor. Master Tam was a tall slender man with a long white beard and long shoulder-length white hair. When the knock at the door interrupted one of his experiments, he immediately started yelling at the intruder, "This had better be a matter of life or death. You are interrupting my work." When Master Tam opened the door he was surprised to see the governor and a handsome young man standing there. He said, "Governor, good morning. I am surprised to see you here." Looking at the prince, he said, "You, young man, I have never met but based on the fact that you look exactly like Boris, I assume you are his son or related to him."

The governor said, "Your eyes and your logic are quite astute, Master Tam. This young man is Prince Willard, the son of Boris and Queen Ariel."

Master Tam said, "Your Highness, I am pleased to meet you. Won't you gentlemen come in please?" The master instructor led them through a long narrow hallway. At the end, it opened up into a rather large sitting room. The prince was surprised at the few furnishings in the room and hallway. He was also appalled at the smell in the entire place. Master Tam noticed the wrinkling of the prince's nose and said, "I must apologize for the smell, but I have many different experiments going on. Each one contains various herbs and or minerals that unfortunately do not always agree with folks."

The governor explained to the master the reason for their disturbance this morning. He said, "Boris has asked that you take the prince in and begin training him immediately. He hopes that he has not discovered the prince's talents too late and that he can still reach his full potential. I believe that the prince has a letter for you from Boris."

The prince reached inside his tunic and pulled out the letter and handed it to Master Tam. The master took the letter and read it. The letter told the story of the instantaneous combustion of the young woman and the force with which Boris had felt it. He asked his old teacher and friend to please do the best he could with his son." Reading the letter brought back some memories to the master that made him smile. He said, "Normally training is started when the gifted are no more than seven or eight years old. You are twice that age. This means that you will have to work twice as hard. In cases like this when the gift is discovered so late, the best we can hope for is to teach the gifted how not to kill himself or anyone else. However, if what your father says in this letter is true, then you have tremendous potential. That being the case, you and I will both have to work very hard and very long hours."

The governor left the master's apartments as quickly as he could. He was glad to leave the prince in someone else's care. He remembered the spoiled little brat that ran around the palace all those years ago and did not want to have to deal with him if he did not have to. He could still detect an air of stubbornness and arrogance in the prince. He thought the master instructor would have his hands full.

Master Tam informed the prince that he would have to move into the guest room that was down the hall from this sitting room. The prince immediately objected and refused. Master Tam explained that the prince had no choice and could no longer leave the master's apartments. The prince's anger was raging. He got up and headed for the door. As soon as he reached the front door and tried to open it, he was shocked by the door. The shock was so strong that it knocked him off his feet, and he landed rather roughly on his ass several feet back. The prince rose and headed straight to the master instructor. As he got to about ten feet from the master, he pulled out his knife. The master just stood there with a smile on his face, and watched the prince. This made the prince even angrier. When the prince tried to stab the master, he found that he could not reach the master. The master was protected by some sort of shield. The prince struck the shield over and over, and each time, he struck harder. The harder he tried, the less effect he had on the shield that protected the master. When the prince was finally exhausted, he went to his knees and panted.

Master Tam said, "If you will give that type of effort to your learning, your late start will not be a problem." This infuriated the prince even more. He remembered how he had just thought and the young girl had exploded. He tried to think of several different things to punish the old man. The master just smiled and said, "I see that we will have to teach you humility and respect before we can do any kind of real training."

"Are you ready to start your training now?" asked Master Tam. The prince just looked at him. Master Tam said, "Your belongings are already being moved here, so do not worry about anything."

The prince was exhausted and realized that he had no choice and said, "Let's get started."

Master Tam got up and led him to another hallway that shot off the main hall. After about fifteen feet, it opened into another room. "This room will be your training room," he said. "But before we start, there are a few things you need to understand. First you will do as I say when I say. You will devote yourself completely to your studies. You will have limited access to the outside world. I will control your every move and thought. Do you understand?"

The prince was furious again. "Who the hell do you think you are, you old bastard? Wait till I tell my father about this. You will be made to pay for your insolence."

"Your father instructed me to do whatever it takes to train you. Because of your late start, we must take drastic measures. If we do not take these precautionary measures, you will kill yourself and others within a short time. The first lesson is to teach you how to reach and hold your gift as if it is a natural extension of you." The master placed the prince in the middle of the room. He had him sit down and cross his legs with his hands holding on to his knees. "You must concentrate on nothing but your gift. Close your eyes and think about the gift. Look for a light in your mind's eye. That light is your gift. Keep looking for the light until you find it. Once you have found it open your eyes."

The prince closed his eyes and concentrated but could not see a light. He said, "There is no light. Even if there was, how could I see it with my eyes closed"

"You must concentrate completely on finding the light. If you cannot find it, you are not concentrating solely on finding the light. Once you find it, open your eyes then close your eyes again and find the light. Keep doing this until you can find the light instantly without thinking about it. Then leaving your eyes open, find the light. Keep doing this until you can find the light instantly with your eyes open. Once you can do this, you have learned to reach your gift naturally. You will not be allowed to leave this room until you can accomplish this. Do not think that you can fool me about being able to find your light. I will know when you find your light. I will know this because when someone uses his gift even in such a minute way it can be felt by others who are gifted. I will leave you now so that you may practice," said Master Tam.

The prince figured that he would not be able to walk out of the room because the old man had told him he would not be allowed to leave this room. He closed his eyes and concentrated and searched for his light. Willard could not see the point to this exercise and resisted it. As a result, he was not fully concentrating on his light, and he could not find it. After about an hour, he finally was able to see his light. He became very excited. He opened his eyes. He was tired of sitting, so he rose and walked around the room. As he walked by the door, he reached for it with his hand. He could not reach the door handle because it was protected by a magical shield. After resting for a few minutes, he went back to the center of the room and sat down. Once again, he closed his eyes and searched for his light.

True to his word, the master would not allow the prince to leave his training room. He had food and drink brought to him. He even brought a bedroll in the evening for him to sleep on. This entrapment made the prince very angry; as a result, he could not fully concentrate on finding his light. The prince's lack of full commitment angered the master. The master told the prince that if he wanted to have a battle of wills, he would be glad to oblige him. However, you will lose he had told the prince. At first the prince's arrogance made him resist and swear that he would show this old man. After several days, the prince finally broke. He was exhausted both mentally and physically.

It had been two weeks since the prince had arrived, and he still refused to cooperate. Master Tam thought that this could not be the son of Boris. Boris had been a model student. This prince was a spoiled, stubborn, and arrogant brat. As a result, he was in shock when he went into the training room to find the prince practicing. When the master entered the room, the prince had just found his light. The look on the prince's face was one of defeat; his eyes were aglow because he had found his light. By the end of that day, the prince was able to find his light with his eyes open and closed.

Master Tam said, "Very well. Now it is time to use your gift to do something with it. Now that you can find your light, you need to concentrate on making the light grow. I want you to make the light grow until it illuminates this room. First you will do it with your eyes closed. Once you have accomplished this with your eyes closed, you will do it with your eyes open. I will make the room go dark so that you will have no doubt of your success. Once you have accomplished this, you will be allowed one day of rest and be allowed to go out of the apartments." While the prince was listening to the new instructions, he was once again feeling defeated. How could he make the light grow? When he heard that he could get a day of rest, he became determined to succeed.

Willard thought to himself, how can I make the light grow? He concentrated as hard as he could without any success. He was starting to feel the effects of not having slept the night before. He had wanted to be successful and had not stopped to rest. He was sweating and felt weak. While he was

concentrating, he was about to give up and rest when suddenly the light grew. It had not been much, but it was noticeable. With his momentary success, the prince became energized again. He figured out that it was his thought processes that controlled his ability to make the light grow, and it also controlled his ability to reach his gift. After that realization, it did not take him long to light up the entire room. He was so excited he wanted to continue with his eyes open, but he was too tired and his fatigue overcame him and he fell asleep.

The next morning, when the master came to check in on his student, the prince was standing with his eyes open, and the entire room was lit up. The look on the prince was one of total ecstasy.

"Congratulations," said the Master. "You have earned your first day of rest. You may clean up and go outside of the apartments. However, you may not leave the palace grounds. If you do attempt to leave the grounds, well, I think you know what will happen. In addition you must be back here as soon as the sun sets. If you are not back by then, you will suffer great pain until you re-enter the apartments." The prince once again was furious. How dare this old bastard place such restrictions upon him, the future king of the world? He kept his anger to himself and said to himself, I will make you pay old man. One day you will pay.

The prince ran to his room, grabbed some clean clothes, and ran out of the apartments. He went to the bath chambers of the palace. There he found some young ladies who were more than willing to please their prince. All day long the prince wandered around the palace grounds. Every time he came to a gate he would concentrate on the gate. Each time he felt the same thing, a strong magical sensation. He knew he could not walk out through any gate. Finally as the sun set he realized that he was on the opposite side of the palace grounds and he could not make it back to the apartments in time. He started walking back to the apartments. He would not run; he would not let the palace staff sees him run. Just as he entered the clearing in the back of the grounds, with the front door of the apartment only fifty yards away, he thought he was going to make it. Then suddenly he froze, he could not move. He felt the pain start at his feet and run up his legs, abdomen, chest, and arms. His head began to pound. He had never felt such excruciating pain before. He panicked. He could not move. He knew the pain would not stop until he was inside the apartments. Using all his physical strength, he managed to take a step forward. He thought he was going to pass out from the pain. Concentrating completely on making the pain go away, he was able to make the pain subside enough to allow him to walk a little better.

When the prince opened the door to the apartment and stepped inside, the pain was instantly gone. He was panting, out of breath, and extremely tired. He went straight to his room and fell asleep. The master watched the prince as he felt the first pain. The master thought this will make him or break him. The master was surprised at the sheer physical determination of the prince as he forced himself to take that first step. However, the master knew that if the prince did not change his approach, he would not make it across the yard. More surprising was the strength with which the prince reached for his gift, forced himself to calm down, and made the pain subside enough to allow him to walk. The master thought, good, he is learning, then went inside and went to bed.

CHAPTER 9 - REALITY

The prince had been gone for over a month now, and Ariel was still not used to not having him around. She missed him. One day she was walking down the hallways of the palace when she heard voices giggling. As she got closer, she heard the prince's name. This made her freeze instantly. She listened to the conversation for several minutes before she continued on. The conversation bothered her and had touched her deeply. Ariel went straight to her quarters and sent staff members in search of Boris, Kain, and Anna. Boris was the first to arrive, and Ariel relayed the story she had heard to him. He also became bothered.

Anna was already in her chambers when the queen's maid found her. The maid told Anna that the queen wished to see her right away. Anna told the maid she would be right there as soon as she got dressed again. The maid left, and Anna's first reaction was to panic. Then she quickly got dressed and nervously headed to the queen's quarters.

When Anna arrived at the queen's quarters, she found that Kain had also been summoned. Ariel said, "Anna, I am sorry to bother you so late in the day, but I have something I need to have answered right away. Please sit down." This kindness from the queen and the queen's obvious nervousness made Anna scared. Ariel continued. "Earlier today I was walking along the corridors of the palace, and I overheard a conversation by two of the staff maids. They were talking about the prince. They said that they were glad that brute was gone." The queen went on for several minutes, relaying the story she had heard. As the queen continued, Anna became more nervous because she knew the queen was going to ask her if the stories were true. The queen said, "I have already asked Kain if these stories are true. He denies them of course, but he is loyal with every inch of his soul.

Therefore, I ask you, Anna, what you know about this. I know that this is putting you on the spot, but I ask you to please be honest and know that whatever you say you will not be punished so long as it is the truth." Anna looked at the queen, then Boris, and finally at Kain. Kain was giving her a look of warning. It was the look on his face that made her decide to tell the truth.

Anna said, "Your Highness, if I answer truthfully, I fear that I may suffer retribution from Kain." The queen looked at her and said, "I assure you that no one will seek to harm you in any way." Then looking at Kain, she said, "Is that understood?" Kain just nodded. Turning back to Anna, she said, "Please continue." Anna took a deep breath and began to talk "Honestly, the prince was not very well-liked. He was not liked because he took advantage of his position. He bullied the men and women. At first when he would go into town and mistreat a lady of the night, the innkeepers came to the palace and filed a complaint. However, those complaints were given to Kain. As you said he is loyal with every inch of his soul. Kain would go to the establishment in question and question all those involved. In the end, he would kill the young lady, beat the proprietor, and/or imprison him. After a while the proprietors quit filing complaints for fear of losing everything they had worked so hard for. The same thing happened with the palace staff. Eventually they also quit complaining for fear of losing their jobs or more importantly their lives. This sort of thing has been going on ever since the prince came to live here. What made matters worse was the way the prince would hide his true nature from the both of you. I am sorry that I had to tell you this, but you asked me to say the truth."

Ariel looked over at Boris when Anna finished speaking, and Boris looked to her and said, "She is telling the truth." Ariel looked at Kain and asked, "What do you have to say about this?" Before Kain could say a word, the queen said, "Remember Boris will know if you are not telling the truth."

Kain swallowed hard and finally spoke. He said, "My queen, I only did what I thought was best in the protection of the prince and the Kingdom. At first, I thought these Northerners were just trying to make trouble for us. So I did the only thing I know how to do."

The queen said, "Now I understand why the locals call you Kain the Butcher. No one blames you for what you did, Kain. I am, however, disappointed that you kept the truth about our son from us. What is done is done. You may both go and remember that no one is to seek retribution of any kind."

Kain and Anna left the royal chambers together. As soon as they were out of the chambers, Kain stopped Anna and said, "That was very smart in there. The way you were able to manipulate the queen. I must say I am impressed."

Anna said, "I did not manipulate anyone in there. I simply told the truth. You know damn well that if I had not made you commit to the queen, you would be in the process of having me flogged right now."

Kain said, "Now I understand why the queen likes you so much and has kept you around all these years."

Boris had come up with the idea that he and Ariel should do things with the local nobles and more prominent merchants. He thought that this would help to endear the people more with them. In an effort to promote good will among the nobility, Boris had planned and scheduled a hunting trip. He would be taking Kain and several of the local nobles with him. They would go into the Twin Mountains north of the city and hunt for deer. Boris had heard that the deer hunting in the woods of the mountains could be lots of fun.

The hunting trip was scheduled for the next morning after the meeting with Kain and Anna. When the small hunting party left the palace grounds, there were a dozen soldiers, Boris, Kain, two bankers, and the owners of the text tile mill, the sawmill, the largest ship-making yard, and the largest hotel and inn. Altogether there were twenty men that went out on the hunt.

The hunting party left early in the morning. It took them several hours to reach the mountains. They stopped to eat before going into the woods and beginning the hunt. Boris offered a reward of one hundred gold crowns for the first hunter to make a kill. Soon after heading into the woods, they picked up a trail. It appeared to be several deer heading toward the river. When they finally came upon the deer, it was a small herd of about eight does and two bucks. One of the bankers got off the first shot, and it was deadly. The innkeeper also killed a doe. With that, the deer were off and running up river. The hunters kicked their horses and went after them. The deer were running through the rocks on the bank of the river. The deer were faster and more sure footed than the horses.

Boris spurred his horse, and the horse took off. The horse was not as sure-footed as the deer. His horse began to slip on the rocks. Boris knew he was in trouble, but everything happened so fast that he did not have time to react. His horse slipped and broke its leg. The horse fell down and pinned Boris beneath him. The soldiers immediately lifted the horse off of Boris. As soon as the weight of the horse was lifted off his leg, the pain shot through his leg and his entire body. Boris was barely able to remain conscious. It was his ability with sorcery that allowed him to mask the pain. When he was able to move again, he asked for help to sit up. He looked at his leg and knew it was broken. His leg bone was sticking out of the skin about eight inches above the knee. Below the knee he had suffered some deep abrasions.

Boris said, "I can control the bleeding with my skills, but that hampers the healing. I will do that until you gentlemen get me back to the palace medical staff. You will need to build a litter that can be carried between two horses." The soldiers went to work right away on the litter. Boris also ordered some men to stay with the kills and bring them back to the palace. His leg was hurting more and more as he rode between the two horses. The pain was so intense that he would pass out for short moments from time to time.

When they finally reached the palace it was dark already. Boris was sweating from the strain of using sorcery to stop the bleeding. He looked like he had a fever. When they arrived in the palace, Ariel happened to be in the courtyard. She ran over to the litter and immediately started issuing orders for Boris to be taken to the infirmary. Boris was able to tell the palace doctor what he had done with sorcery and that he would have to lift the spell in order for the doctor to heal him. As soon as he let go of the spell, the pain overcame him, and he passed out.

The doctor said that it was good that he had passed out because what needed to be done would be very painful. It took the doctor half an hour to clean the wounds and stop the bleeding. Then he asked for all nonessential visitors to leave the infirmary. He was about to set the leg and needed the room. He asked four soldiers to stay. He had each soldier take hold of a limb and hold Boris. Ariel had refused to leave. The doctor had the soldiers pull on the legs, and he pushed the broken bone back in place. Boris screamed and then passed out again. The doctor quickly took two wooden boards and placed the injured leg between them. Then he had the soldiers wrap the leg and boards together tight. He forced some medication into Boris and thanked everyone for their help and asked them all to leave. He explained that Boris would sleep well into the next day and that nothing would be gained by them staying there.

The queen asked if Boris could be moved. She wanted him moved to their quarters. The doctors agreed to allow him to be moved to the royal chambers because it would be easier to stop visitors from coming to see him. They determined that this would allow Boris to rest and heal quicker. The nobles and merchants in the hunting party were afraid that Ariel would blame them for what had happened. When Boris had been moved into the royal chambers, she came out and asked the hunters for an explanation of what had happened. It was Kain who spoke up immediately. He said, "My queen, it was an accident. We came upon a small herd of deer by the river. We starting shooting, and the deer took off running. They ran upriver along the river bed. There were lots of rocks, and the horses were not able to maneuver very well among the rocks. Boris's horse slipped on the rocks. The horse broke its leg and fell. It all happened so quickly that Boris had no time to react. The horse fell and pinned him between it and the rocks. We lifted the horse, and he screamed in pain."

Ariel looked at each of the nobles, and they all agreed that Kain's account of the events of that day were accurate. Ariel thanked the men and asked them to go home. She told them she would keep them posted on his progress. Lastly, she thanked them for bringing Boris back so quickly. The nobles were rather surprised by her reaction. However, they were not swayed and still did not totally trust her.

It was two days before Boris became fully awake and able to talk with his caretakers and Ariel. Ariel asked him what had happened. She was pleased to hear that Kain had told her the truth. The doctors told Boris his leg had been set and would heal over time. He would have to stay off the leg for at least two weeks and then could start walking around using crutches. With Ariel's insistence Boris agreed to stay off the leg for two weeks. After that he made no promises.

It took a week for Ariel to accept the fact that Boris was okay. Then she went to him and told him her plan. She said, "This year is our turn to visit the Kingdom. Given what we have learned about Willard, I thought we would start by going to Independent City. As a result of your accident, I will have to go alone. I will visit with Willard, and on the way back, I will go to Southport and Bartersville. When I get back, if your leg is healed sufficiently, you can join me on the trip north. What do you think?"

Boris said, "I was thinking along those same lines, except I was planning to go with you. I think we do not have a choice in the matter."

"Very well, it will take a couple of days to get ready. I will leave in three days," said Ariel.

Boris added, "Be sure to let Willard know how disappointed I personally am with him." Ariel just shook her head in acknowledgement.

Three days later, Ariel was ready to leave. She would be taking the usual three hundred soldiers on the trip. As she was saying good-bye to Boris, he said, "I am casting a spell of protection around you."

She said, "That is not necessary."

He added, "It is too late for you to disagree the spell is already cast." She smiled, thanked him, kissed him, and was gone.

Ariel had told the captain of the ship there was no hurry and she wanted to enjoy the countryside. As a result, the trip down the river had taken eight days; normally the trip was made in five. When the queen arrived, word spread throughout the city quickly. By the time she reached the palace, the courtyard in front of the palace entrance was full of people. As she entered, the crowd roared. Governor Bran was waiting at the gates of the palace. Ariel stopped to thank the crowd for the warm welcome. She immediately went to the meeting rooms and began holding her usual meetings with the governor and his various support staff. The meetings went on for two days. When they finished, she asked the governor about her son.

The governor explained that the prince had been under the strict care and teaching of Master Tam. Ariel said, "Thank you, Governor. Now I would like to see my son. Does the master still live in his apartments behind the palace?"

"Yes and very seldom does he come out. I must warn you he does not like to be disturbed." Ariel just smiled as she remembered the master getting very upset every time she would come to visit Boris.

It had been so long since she had walked the corridors of the palace that Ariel took her time. She found herself comparing the two palaces. Each palace had its own style, but both were beautiful. She could not determine which she liked best. As she stepped outside, she saw the entrance to the apartments where Master Tam lived. She walked slowly across the courtyard, taking in the smell, sounds, and sunlight.

She walked up to the door. She checked the door, but it was locked as usual. She knocked on the door. After a few moments, she knocked again. A voice from inside said, "This had better be important. You are interrupting my work. I am very busy. I do not have time for you. Go away." Ariel knocked again.

The door opened, and there he was, Master Tam. Ariel thought that he looked the same as the last time she had seen him. She made a comment about it, and he reminded her that he looked exactly the same as the last time she saw him because of the long-life spell he had on him. Ariel smiled, thinking the old man has not changed. The master asked her to come in and apologized for his rudeness.

"I assume you are here to see your son. Let me tell you that we had a rough time in the beginning, but he has come a long way since."

At that time, the prince was heard coming down the hallway, saying, "Did I hear someone knocking at the door?"

Ariel stood up at the sound of his voice.

The prince entered the room. His eyes went wide, and he ran to hug his mother. "Mother, I am so glad to see you. Where is Father?" Ariel told them about the hunting accident and that she had come alone as a result of the injury.

Willard thought this was perfect; now he would get even with the old man. They all sat down, and the prince immediately started in on the master. "Mother, you should know how this old man has been treating me." For the next twenty minutes, the Prince went on and on about the horrible treatment he had received from the master. Ariel just listened and watched her son's eyes. She noticed the intensity in his eyes. As he was winding down, his eyes lost the intensity.

Ariel said, "I know all the methods that Master Tam uses. He used those same methods on your father. It is because of his methods that we sent you to him. Did you know that it was on one of those rare free days that I met your father? It is your behaviour that has brought me here. Your father and I have learned all about your abusive behaviour back in Twin Falls. It is no use you trying to deny anything. Your father used his truth spell on everyone who told us about you. We even got a full confession from Kain. What do you have to say for yourself?"

The prince was stunned. He had not expected this turn of events. It was his pride and arrogance that got the best of him, and he said, "Yes, it is true. I did all those things, and why shouldn't I? I am the son of the queen of the world. That gives me the right to do whatever I want."

Ariel said, "No, Willard, it is because you are my son that you have to be better than everyone else. Respect is not something that is given to you because of who you are. Instead, respect is something you must earn. It saddens my heart to hear you say these things. Your father and I have obviously been too busy conquering the world that we failed to teach you how to be a decent human being. We are both very disappointed in you. I am heartbroken." Her eyes were filled with tears as she stopped speaking.

For the first time in his life, the prince felt ashamed. He knew that he had hurt his parents and lost their trust. He could see it his mother's eyes. He had to do something to regain their trust. He could see the hurt and disappointment in her eyes. He went to his knees in front of her and placed his head in her lap. He began to cry. Also, for the first time in his life, the prince was genuinely crying because he understood that he had done wrong.

His mother said, "Power comes with respect. Power can be taken, but in order to keep it, you must earn the respect of your subjects. When I took power here in Independent City, I poured everything I had into improving living conditions and righting the wrongs of the previous rulers. By doing so, I earned the respect of the citizens of the city. Today these same citizens would give their lives for me. I never once took advantage of them. Your behavior has brought shame to me, your father, and the citizens of our home."

Her words hit home with the prince. They were both crying. Master Tam just sat there and watched and listened. He was impressed by the queen's honesty. He remembered her when she was determined to succeed. It seemed that her success had also made her wise. He felt pride to be allowed to witness this moment. He could also see that the prince was genuinely distraught.

After they had both cried for several minutes, the prince said, "Mother, I am truly sorry that I have disappointed you and Father. I know that I have lost your trust. I can see it in your face and eyes. I promise, Mother, that I will regain your trust."

Ariel took his face in her hands and said, "Son, I love you very much, and so does your father." With that, they hugged and she asked him about the training. The prince then spent the next several hours showing his mother all he had learned.

Master Tam gave the prince the next few days off so that he could spend it with his mother. Before the prince left the apartments with his mother, he asked the master, "Master Tam, I think that I have detected some sort of spell around Mother. Am I right, or is it a figment of my imagination?"

It was Ariel who responded. "It is not your imagination. Your father cast a protection spell around me before I left Twin Falls."

Master Tam said, "It is a sign of how much you have learned about sorcery and magic that you can detect the spell. Very good, young man."

The prince smiled with pride.

The queen and the prince spent the next week together. Over that week, the prince watched his mother. He watched the way she dealt with people, talked to them, gave orders, and never talked down to them. He noticed how people looked at her. They had respect and admiration in their eyes. He could see the love for her in their eyes. He also noticed that when they looked at him, he saw fear and dislike. Willard wanted the love and respect from the people that his mother had. He decided that he had to change his ways. He had to change the way he dealt with people. He would have to keep his true feelings hidden and only show them to a selected and trusted few. By the time his mother left, the prince had decided that the first step he had to take was to learn as much as possible about magic.

When the queen left and the prince returned to his studies, he applied himself completely to learning. Master Tam immediately noticed the new dedication and was pleased. The prince learned quickly and began advancing his learning.

Ariel left Independent City, feeling good about the visit she had with her son. She was heading to Southport.

Ariel had decided to go overland instead of taking the river. She wanted to see the countryside. Unfortunately, what she saw was not to her liking. The farmhouses were in poor condition, and the livestock was limited. Many fields were left unplanted and unworked. Ariel was concerned about this. The closer they came to the city, the worse the conditions became.

When they arrived at Southport, Ariel was shocked at what she saw. Outside the city wall were hundreds of tents. The smell that filled the air was that of human waste. When she rode through the tents, the people just stared at her. As she came closer to the gates, the people realized that she was someone of importance and rich. The people started to beg for money and food. Ariel was shocked and became afraid of what the people would do. As her party approached the gates, her soldiers had to force the people away. The city guard recognized the queen's party and opened the gates and helped clear the way for her party.

Once inside the city, Ariel thought that things would improve. She was disappointed. There were no more tents. Instead, the people were just sitting around on the ground. They were in every alley that she could see. When she arrived at the garrison, she went straight to the commander in charge and demanded an explanation. In Southport, she had left the military in charge. Until now she had been pleased with the way the military had governed the city. The commander's name was Dellbert.

Commander Dellbert explained that the alleys and tents were filled with the poor and homeless. He explained that the farmers slowly stopped farming because they could no longer afford to buy the seed and supplies needed to keep up the farms. As they gave up farming the people started heading to the city. At first everything was okay until the people ran out of money and goods to trade for food and services. That is when the alleys started to get filled up. Once we realized the alleys were getting overcrowded, we ran hundreds, no, thousands of people out of the city. These people erected the tents. The steady flow of people kept coming, and the number of tents grew into the city that exists today.

Ariel was shocked by what she was hearing. Southport was struggling economically. She knew she had to do something before the people rebelled. Ariel had always been a very decisive person, and she was not going to change now. Ariel immediately called a meeting of all the merchants. The meeting was to be held in the yard of the garrison. The yard was the only place large enough to hold the meeting and keep it private.

The merchants were a bit timid about attending the meeting. They were afraid that Ariel would blame them for the current state of the economy in Southport. What the merchants did not know was that the current situation was a result of Ariel's greed and had nothing to do with them. Ariel had for almost twenty years been taking money and sending it to Independent City to her private treasury. Southport was the first Kingdom city that she had conquered and was therefore the first city to start suffering from her policies. Ariel heard about the merchant's reluctance and let it be known that she was planning to make changes to the governance of the city and that no one had anything to fear.

The meeting was scheduled to begin at midmorning. The merchants started to arrive in small groups. By midmorning, the yard was full. Asmall stage had been set up at one end of the yard. Ariel was standing in the center of the stage. Ariel raised her hands to get everyone's attention. She said, "It has become obvious to me that changes need to be made in the governance of the city. The military has served well, but they are not qualified to deal with this type of situation. Therefore, effective right now, the military will no longer be in charge of city government. I have called this meeting to name a city council. The council will consist of five of you. The council will be in charge of the city government. The military will continue to serve as the policing authority. The military will enforce all laws and regulations passed by the council."

The merchants were pleased with what they heard, and they started cheering. Ariel gave the merchants a few moments to cheer. "I have asked you here today to elect the five council members that will lead the city. At this time, I would like you to nominate your leaders." For several minutes, the merchants discussed and shouted out names. After an hour, they had selected five candidates. When the five had been selected, Ariel said, "Now you must choose one of them to be the head of the city council." It was clear that the merchants trusted their banker the most, and he was named the head of the council.

Ariel continued. "The first order of business for the council is to have a city wide election for mayor. The council will lead the city along with the mayor. The next step will be for the council to select a spot to build a city hall. Since the military will no longer be running the city, the city headquarters can no longer be inside the garrison. The royal treasury will pay for the construction of the new headquarters and will also pay for the property. The treasury will then donate ten thousand gold crowns to the city." The merchants erupted with cheers. It took several minutes to calm down the crowd. Finally, Ariel was allowed to continue. "The poor people living in the alley and outside the city in the tents will be the labor force used to build the city headquarters. When they finish the new building, they will clean up the streets. Once the streets are cleaned, they will be used to build houses outside the city wall for all the people living in the tents. By the time all these projects are completed I am sure the city will have another project for them to work on. Projects like a sewer system to clean up the air. The point is to keep them busy working. If they are working, they do not have time to create problems." Again the merchants cheered.

It took Ariel one week to organize the city government into something she was comfortable with. She did not know if this type of city organization would work in the long term. All she knew was that she had to try. It was the least she could do; after all, she knew it was her fault for the current condition of the city. A week later when she left, she was confident that the city would never know that she was responsible for their current condition.

Jenna was about to turn twenty-three years old in a few months. It had been almost twenty years since her father had been taken away from her—twenty years of hatred building up and promising herself she would avenge her father. Jenna was the illegitimate daughter of George Long. The Freedom Fighters thought they had wiped out the entire Long family. However, no one knew of George Long's affair with her mother. Jenna could remember a man that would come to visit her all the time. She remembered her mother telling her that the man was her father. Her father had been kind to her. He would always bring her presents and give money to her mother. One day he stopped coming to visit. Jenna asked her mother why her father had stopped coming to visit her. To this day she could remember her mother's words, "Jenna, your father has been murdered by the Freedom Fighters." Since that day Jenna was a different person. She became determined and hard. She learned how to fight with her bare hands. She learned how to use a bow and arrow. She learned how to use a sword. She had become quite an accomplished archer and knife fighter.

After twenty years of promising, Jenna told herself, my day has come. Ariel, the bitch queen, as she was referred to, was coming to Bartersville for her official state visit. This time she was coming alone. Boris the sorcerer was not coming with her. Jenna knew this was her chance for revenge. The queen always followed the same route to the council building in the center of town. All Jenna had to do was find the right place for her revenge. It had not taken her long to decide from where to take her revenge. There was a small butcher shop that had a storage room in the back. The shop was about six blocks from the council building. Jenna had broken into the shop many times in her younger years to steal food. The shop had an attic from where she would take her revenge. On the street side, there was a small hole about three inches in diameter. The butcher had covered the hole, but Jenna had used that hole many times to spy on people. It was through this hole that she would take her revenge on Ariel.

According to reports, Ariel would arrive tomorrow around midmorning. Ariel's caravan could have made it to the city that night, but the queen liked to make a grand appearance, so she would always make sure she arrived at midmorning. Ariel was anxious to get to Bartersville. She wanted to return to Twin Falls and see Boris. She was worried about his leg. She hoped he would be able to accompany her on the trip north to Northport and North Pointe. Ariel noticed some of the same signs of an economic slowdown around the city as she had seen at Southport. However, here she had an excuse. When that fool, George Long, had rebelled, the city had been almost wiped out and destroyed. Only in the last few years had the city finally recovered from that destruction. The homeless were still around, but it was not as bad as Southport.

Ariel arrived as usual to the city gates at about midmorning. The normal daily traffic going to the city stopped to allow the Queen's caravan to enter the city. The citizens of Bartersville had learned the hard way to show admiration and love for the Queen. As a result, the citizens were lined up along the streets. The citizens cheered and threw flowers on the street. The caravan took a steady but slow pace through the streets. Usually it took her about two hours to get to the council building. Today would be no exception.

Ariel was riding her white thoroughbred stallion. It was a beautiful horse. When Ariel rode the horse in complete ceremonial armor, she made a regal appearance. Ariel was beginning to wish she could just kick her horse into a trot. She was tired of the fake smile on her face, and her arm was tired of waving. Suddenly Ariel felt a sudden jolt of pain. It felt like she had been hit with a rock on her ribs. The hit was so fast and hard that she rocked on her horse and almost fell off. Before she had recovered from the shot, she was rocked again by another blow. This time she saw that it was an arrow that had been shot at her. Her soldiers also saw the arrow this time. Immediately they surrounded the queen. They made sure that Ariel was all right first. Then they started to try and figure out where the shots had come from. No one had any idea. The queen ordered fifty of her men to stay there and secure the area. She wanted every one of the citizens there arrested and all the surrounding buildings searched. Ariel made sure everyone saw that she was not injured then kicked her horse into a trot and stormed off to the council building.

Jenna was anxious and nervous. The queen's trip from the city gates to her spot seemed to be taking longer than usual. When she finally saw the queen's entourage, her heart started to beat faster, and she started breathing heavily. Jenna closed her eyes and took deep breaths. This helped her calm down. When she opened her eyes and saw the queen, she could not believe her luck. The queen was too sure of herself that she took little precaution to guard herself from an attack. Jenna notched her first arrow and took aim. She had gone over this moment over and over, in her mind. Now the time had come. Jenna pulled back on the bow and fired. The shot was a direct hit. Jenna saw Ariel rock and almost fall off her horse. Quickly she notched a second arrow and took aim. Again she released, and the shot was as true as the first; it was a direct hit. However, Jenna noticed something was wrong. The arrow had hit Ariel but had not penetrated. They fell down as if she was being protected by some sort of magic.

Jenna was stunned as she watched the chaos on the streets. Boris was not with Ariel, but apparently, he had cast some sort of spell on her to protect her. Jenna knew that there would be a search and questioning of all the people. She had brought some food and was prepared to stay in the attic until nightfall. She knew that the cover of night would be her only chance to get away. After the queen rode off, Jenna covered the hole and sat down with her back against the wall.

As she sat there she could not believe what had just happened. All these years of planning and brooding had come down to this. All her hopes and dreams had just come crashing down before her eyes. Tears began to run down her cheeks, and she cried for hours. As she sat there in the attic crying, she lost her resolve and thought that life was meaningless. If she could not avenge her father's murder, then what was there to live for?

Jenna began to sink into a state of depression and lost all hope. Then suddenly there was a bright light. Jenna closed her eyes the light was too bright. Then she heard a voice, "Open your eyes and look upon me." Jenna opened her eyes and looked up. There in front of her was a beautiful young woman. Jenna thought she was the most beautiful woman she had ever seen. Jenna thought that she was either dead or dreaming. The woman then spoke again. "I am the goddess Pearl, and you are not dead or dreaming. Your state of mind worries me. I understand why you think that all hope is lost because your long- awaited moment has failed. However, I assure you that all hope is not lost. There will be another who will come, one who has waited longer than you, suffered more than you, and has kept his faith in the gods. So do not fear. All hope is not lost."

Jenna sat there staring at this beautiful woman and listening to what she was saying. She did not know what to say or what to do. Jenna said, "Why are you telling me this? Who am I to deserve the visit of a goddess?"

Pearl smiled and said, "My sister, Zephra, has shown all the gods that you humans are worthy and deserve the affection of the gods. So fear not, my child, and keep your head up. There is hope. Now I am going to help you get out of the predicament you are in right now. I will place you several blocks away from here, away from the soldiers so you can return home safely.

In the blink of an eye, Jenna found herself standing in an alley several blocks away from where she had been. She took a moment to reflect on what had happened. Her plan to avenge the death of her father had failed. She had lost all hope, and then in the midst of her self- pity she had been visited by a goddess. The goddess had told her not to worry that someone else would come—someone who had waited longer, suffered more, and been blessed by the gods. The goddess had not exactly said that the gods had blessed this person, but what else could she have meant? Jenna decided that indeed there was hope, and things were looking up. She decided that there was something to live for. With her mind at ease, she headed home. As she walked home, she thought, "How long will I have to wait this time?" Then from the air, she heard the goddess's voice say, "Not long at all."

Ariel was in shock as she rode her horse down the street as fast as she could. Her side and chest were throbbing. When she reached the council building, she jumped off the horse and ran inside. Once inside she went to the suite upstairs, where she would be staying. Once upstairs she locked herself in her bedroom and sat down on the bed. She quickly took off her clothes and saw two large bruises. One bruise was on the right side of her rib cage, and the other right in the middle of her chest. She had been waving at the crowd with her right arm when the first shot hit her. Then as she was regaining her balance the second shot hit her. If the second shot had not been aimed directly at her chest, she may not have realized that it had been an assassination attempt. Then she remembered that Boris had placed the protection spell on her just before she left Twin Falls. She smiled and thanked the gods for Boris.

Ariel called her maids in and had them tend to her bruises. Once they finished she went back down stairs. Ariel did not want the rulers of Bartersville to think that she was weak or vulnerable. She immediately started giving orders. She wanted the person responsible for this attempt on her life found and punished. She ordered round the clock searches of the entire city. She wanted this criminal found. The members of the city council were as shocked as Ariel. Ariel could see the look of fear in their eyes. They were completely clueless as to who could have done this. They were falling all over themselves trying to apologize and assure the queen that this had to be the act of a single person and that this individual was an exception and that the city stood behind her.

When nightfall made it difficult for the searches to continue, Ariel ordered the city gates locked, and no one was allowed to leave the city until she was gone. It was close to midnight when she finally went back upstairs to go to bed. As she lay there in bed, she thought about the day's events. She thought Bartersville had always been the only city that had given her real opposition. During the war, they had been the most difficult to defeat then they had actually rebelled and declared themselves a free city. With the economic situation in Southport and the rebellious attitude of the citizens of Bartersville, she realized how fragile her hold on the Kingdom was, even after almost twenty years.

With the help of the local garrison, it had taken the soldiers one week to search the entire city. Nothing had been found that would indicate a connection between the assassination attempt and any of the citizens of the city. Ariel decided she would leave but made it clear that if the guilty party was not found soon the entire city would suffer. The city council understood what that meant. It meant that she would turn Boris and Kain loose on the city again. Nobody wanted that so they promised her they would find the guilty party.

Ariel ordered a quick pace on the trip back to Twin Falls. She wanted out of Bartersville; she did not feel safe, and she was starting to get irritable. Ariel told the soldiers that they would not stop for meals except for supper; breakfast and lunch would be cold. It took the queen's caravan ten days to make the trip back to Twin Falls. As fast as the trip was, the word of the assassination attempt got to the city before the queen arrived. Word of the attempt spread like wildfire throughout the Kingdom.

Word came to the palace that the queen had entered the city. Boris was relieved and excited to have Ariel home. He took his cane and started walking toward the front entrance. Boris's leg had been healing quite well until two weeks ago. He was taking a bath and tried to get out of the tub too quickly and without help. His foot slipped, and he fell on the stone floor. Pain shot up his leg immediately. Boris lay on the floor for several moments before he was able to call for help. Boris was taken to his bed, and the doctor called. The doctor examined his leg and said that Boris had apparently broken his leg again. The doctor had just yesterday taken off the splint. The doctor warned Boris that he had to be very careful or risk permanent damage to his leg.

So now here was Boris limping along the hallways very slowly. He knew it would take Ariel some time to get to the palace grounds, so his speed, or lack of, did not bother him. He just wanted to see Ariel so he could confirm that she was all right after the attempt on her life.

As usual Anna put out the word that the queen was returning and asked the citizens of Twin Falls to turn out and welcome the queen home. As soon as the queen's party entered, the city the crowd started cheering. Ariel was surprised at the level of intensity with which the crowd greeted her. In all reality, the crowd was glad that she had returned safely. Ariel was not liked in Twin Falls, but no one wished her ill will nor did they want to see her killed and her army left in place. So the crowd welcomed her home. When the queen finally reached the palace grounds, she kicked her horse into a fast trot and headed for the palace.

Boris was standing at the top of the steps waiting for Ariel to arrive. Ariel took one look at Boris as she jumped off her horse and knew that his leg was not fully healed. She ran up the stairs and jumped into his open arms. Boris's eyes filled with tears as he wrapped his arms around Ariel. She immediately asked him about his leg. Boris started walking back inside the palace and told her the story of how he had broken his leg again.

When they finally made it back to the royal suite, Anna was waiting for them. Anna took a risk and hugged Ariel when she entered the suite. She told her how glad she was to see her return home safely and unharmed. Ariel once again noticed that Anna was the first one to state what was really on her mind. She was grateful for Anna. As was expected, Ariel called a meeting of all the heads of state in two hours.

It took Ariel two weeks to feel comfortable that the Kingdom was okay, and she decided to continue her trip around the country. In reality she was hoping Boris's leg would heal enough that he could accompany her north. Much to her dismay, the doctors were adamantly against such a trip for Boris. Boris cast another spell of protection on her. He said this one was stronger than the last. He had made this one stronger in case she encountered the man beasts.

Ariel set out with her usual retinue of three hundred soldiers plus her personal staff. Ariel was curious as she rode north to see if the downturn of the economy was also afflicting the cities of the north. She set a steady pace. Breakfast and dinner were both hot meals, but lunch was cold and eaten usually in the saddle. The landscape did not show the deterioration that the landscape in the south had shown. In the villages, there did not appear to be any homeless people in the streets. This made Ariel feel a little relieved.

When the party reached Northport, Ariel was feeling good about the economic condition of the north. In the city itself, she did see some homeless people and beggars. However the numbers were not more than what would be expected in a large city.

The Duchess Sheila had prepared a feast for the queen. Ariel was pleased with the reception. For the first time in twenty years, Ariel was not filled with desire for Sheila as soon as she laid her eyes on her. This year would be the first year since they had met that they would not seduce each other.

The evening was going well. The music and food were excellent. Ariel made it a point to complement the staff and musicians. It was only a matter of time before the conversation turned to the man beasts. Sheila made a point of introducing Sergeant Miller to Ariel.

Ariel asked him, "Have the beasts slowed down any in the last years?"

He replied, "Unfortunately, they have not. In fact, I believe the attacks are becoming more frequent and in larger numbers."

This news gave Ariel concern for her safety as she travelled to North Pointe. She asked, "Do they attack the roads or are travellers fairly safe?"

Sheila smiled and said, "Don't worry. You will be safe on your trip to North Pointe."

Sergeant Miller added, "The beasts seem to be giving all their attention to the larger settlements and towns. They have not attacked any travellers."

"What about that warrior who was fighting them in the mountains?" asked Ariel?

Sergeant. Miller said, "The warrior is still up there and by all accounts is killing the beasts by the hundreds. It is truly amazing that for almost three years now he has been up there and survived."

Sheila called a young recruit over to join them. "Your Highness, this young recruit is Mark. He was saved from the man beasts by this mysterious warrior." Young Mark was speechless. He did not know what to say or do; all he could do was blush.

Ariel said, "Relax, Mark. I want to hear about the warrior that saved you."

Mark said, "The beasts attacked our village. They took me, three other boys, and about five women. They took us and headed north at a very fast pace. For two days, we travelled into the mountains.

On the morning of the third day, they stopped. They tied all the males up in a circle. Next they took the women and started some sort of auction to see who would get the women. There were five women and about twenty five beasts. The beasts had been arguing and fighting amongst each other for about an hour. Then suddenly out of nowhere came the warrior. He had decapitated four of the beasts before they even realized that they were being attacked. He had a sword in each hand. For the next half hour, they fought. There were body parts and blood flying all over the place. The warrior was relentless and deadly with both swords. When the fighting stopped, all the beasts were dead. The warrior had only a few minor wounds. He accompanied us to the edge of the mountains and turned around and went back up the mountains. We asked him to come with us, but he said his job was not done yet. I turned sixteen a month later and as soon as I did I enlisted."

"That's quite a story. What does he look like?" asked Ariel.

Mark replied, "He is definitely from the Kingdom. If I had to guess I would say that he is probably from somewhere around Twin Falls."

"What makes you think that?" asked Ariel.

"His size, facial features, and overall appearance match that of someone from that area. Of course he is a seasoned warrior used to living under harsh conditions. I would say that he is twenty-five to thirty years old."

Ariel said, "Well, maybe someday I will get to meet this mysterious warrior. That day will not be tonight for I am exhausted, and I think I will turn in for the day."

Ariel, having said that, caused the other guests to take their leave, and the feast ended.

Over the next few days, Ariel met with the city leaders and Sheila. It seemed that everyone was pleased with the current economic conditions and with the Duchess's leadership. In fact most of the city leaders credited her leadership for the continued success of the economy in the Northport area. They even supported the reopening of the fort and had no problem with the city contributing to maintain the fort, satisfied that everything was under control in Northport Ariel headed west.

The trip to North Pointe was at a slower pace. There were several villages along the way, and Ariel made it a point to stop at each village and talk to the people. These visits extended her trip by three days. When they finally reached North Pointe, the mayor was beside himself with worry. Word had come to him that the queen was on her way. When she did not arrive at the expected time, the mayor became worried. Ariel thanked him for his concern and explained about the stops in the villages.

Ariel spent one day with the mayor then headed to the garrison to meet with Commander Wallace. Commander Wallace gave Ariel the report that he normally gave to Boris. Ariel was surprised to learn that between the fort at North Port and the garrison at North Pointe, there were almost twenty thousand soldiers. In her discussion with the Commander she realized that all the soldiers were needed to protect the North and the Kingdom from the man beasts. When she left the garrison, she felt safe from the man beasts. At first the number of troops had given her cause for apprehension, but now she realized that she reacted that way because of what had happened at Bartersville.

Ariel was anxious to see her friend Emily. She set a fast pace from the garrison to the Winston estate. As she had expected, Emily's first concern was to make sure she was all right after the attempt on her life. The two women talked all day long. If Sara had not interrupted with dinner, the two would have continued talking long into the night. They had discussed the cost of the soldiers, the economy of the North Point area, the warrior fighting the man beasts and many other topics. Silas was exhausted from just listening to the two women carry on. The ladies talked so much that Ariel decided to stay the night and leave the next morning.

The next morning, everyone said their good-byes, and Ariel headed south. Ariel once again set a fast pace. She wanted to get back to Twin Falls and Boris. Her stop in Bordertown never lasted more than a few hours. Bordertown was a prison. The city had sprung up around it as the prison grew. The more the prison grew, the bigger the city became. The military ran the city. The city was about to outgrow the ability of the military to run, but no one seemed concerned about the matter. Thus, Ariel saw no reason to do something about it. She decided to leave the city alone and headed back to Twin Falls.

CHAPTER 10 -THE HORDE

For Jessica, it had been a long, cold, and hard winter. It started with the devastating capture and imprisonment of the Arian tribe. Then the Horde had killed Jerum, Jade, Jacob, and Jon. They had not killed Jerome, her husband; because they did not realize that he was the leader of the warriors. The Horde had thought that Jacob was the leader of the warriors. However, shortly after their capture Jerome had been killed.

As leader of the warriors, Jerome felt he had to do something. He could not just stay in the cave and not try to escape. Jessica pleaded with him to forget about escaping, but he would not listen. Jerome had felt that as leader of the warriors he was expected to be brave and he had to try to escape. He told Jessica that he felt as if everyone was looking at him for guidance and leadership. Jerome had noticed that when their evening meal was brought to them, the guards were not as many as with the other meals. He thought he could sneak out at that time. He would then hide until night and make his escape to the plains and warn the other tribes. That night when the evening meal was brought, Jerome stood alone up against the wall of the cave. When the food was brought in, he slowly moved with his back to the cave wall. After about half an hour, he had made it to the entrance. The sun had started to set, and it was already getting dark outside. Jerome looked around chose his moment and walked out of the cave. He quickly ran around the edge of the mountain and disappeared.

The next day at about noon, a loud commotion was heard heading toward the cave. There were several Horde warriors laughing and hollering; they were celebrating. When they arrived at the caves, they called all the Arian tribe out on the ledge. About fifty feet from the cave entrance stood four warriors. In the middle of them was Jerome. He was tied up with his hands behind his back and with a pole stuck between his back and arms. His face was bruised; his lips were swollen, and he was limping. Another warrior, the one in charge, stepped forward to address the tribe. Jessica would always remember him; Karn was his name.

Karn said, "This tribesman has made a fatal mistake. He tried to escape. His actions while brave were foolish. He was caught this morning at daybreak about a mile from this camp. I had hoped it would not come to this, but I must show you what happens when you try to escape." As soon as he finished speaking, he turned his head back and nodded. Upon his signal, the two warriors standing next to Jerome reacted. The one on his right took his knife and sliced his throat. The one on his left took his knife and stabbed him in the gut twice. Jerome fell over dead before he hit the ground. Jessica screamed. For weeks after that, she didn't care if she lived or died.

At first Jessica became mad at Jack. This was all his fault; the only reason the Arians had been attacked was because the Horde could not defeat the Claws. The Claws had Jack, the desert warrior as he was called by the Horde, the great and feared warrior. After a week or two of being mad at Jack, she realized that even though the Arians had been attacked because of Jack, it was not Jack that had made Jerome try to escape. Therefore, she became mad at both of them. After a while, being mad at Jack and Jerome became boring, and she realized that her anger was misdirected. The Horde was the ones who were responsible for all the deaths. The Horde, whatever their reason, had killed Jerum, Jade, Jacob, Jon, and finally Jerome. Her anger was now totally focused on the Horde. She swore that she would see them pay for what they had done.

As the weeks become months, Jessica slowly started to return to a normal state of mind. All the women of the tribe had tried to get her to snap out of her grief and depression. All attempts had failed until one day Jessica was approached by a little girl. The girl had asked her what was wrong with her. The girl told her that all the tribal women were saying that she had gone crazy. It was the words of this little girl that had reached deep within her soul. Jessica made another promise that day. She prayed to the gods and asked for the strength to survive this ordeal and to live long enough to see the Horde pay for the evil they had done.

Through the course of the winter, more and more Arians were slowly integrated into the Horde. The women were taken as lovers; children were taken in by Horde families to be raised as their own. Those that did not voluntarily submit became slaves. By the time spring came around, the Arians had surrendered both physically and emotionally. The Arians had been totally assimilated into the Horde.

At the first signs of spring, Sam called another gathering. At the gathering, he said, "Clans of Rumalia, hear me. Last fall we won a great victory over the tribes. Now it is time to strike another blow to the plainsmen. We will attack the next tribe from the west. We will attack the Crete. I make a call to all warriors who wish to join in this battle to do away with the Crete."

The crowd cheered and celebrated.

Two days later the warriors were still coming to volunteer for the attack on the Crete. When the warriors had finally stopped coming, Sam asked, "How many did we get?"

Elders Nicolas and Dora had been handling the sign up. Nicolas looked at Dora and said, "Thirty-five thousand."

Sam could not believe what he had just heard. He was dumbfounded. Sam called an emergency meeting of the elders. Sam also asked that Gar and Karn join the meeting.

As soon as all the elders arrived, Sam said, "First I apologize for calling this meeting so abruptly. However, when you hear what I have to say, you will understand. Nicolas, would you tell the entire council of elders how many warriors have responded to my call to arms?

Nicolas looked at Dora then at Sam as he said, "Thirty-five thousand."

Total silence followed the announcement as the number sunk in.

After several moments of silence, Sam said, "Now you know why I called this meeting. I have a new plan. Since we have so many warriors ready to do battle, I say we take advantage of it. I propose that we not only attack the Crete but that we also attack all the tribes except the Claws. That would give us seven thousand warriors for each of the other five tribes. We divide the seven thousand into four groups. The main force consisting of four thousand warriors will attack from the north. The other three forces will each be made up of one thousand warriors, and they will attack from the south, east, and west. By doing this, there will be no way that any plainsmen can escape."

Everyone was silent as they considered the magnitude of Sam's plan. Finally Garish spoke. "Sam, this is truly a full-blown offensive that you have devised. Something like this has never been tried before."

With that all the elders began talking at the same time, and for several moments, they argued and shouted at each other.

Finally it was Karn that brought order back to the meeting. He said, "It can work."

Everyone stopped talking and looked at Karn.

He continued. "The plan can work. The plainsmen will start to arrive at their summer camps in about three weeks. That gives us three weeks to prepare. If we prepare, we can launch a coordinated attack on the five tribes at the same time. That way, if anyone manages to get through our lines, it will be of no use. The other tribes will not be able to help because they will be under attack also."

Gar then added, "Karn is right. If we coordinate the attack on the five tribes to be simultaneous, then we can strike a death blow to the plainsmen all at once.

It was Wanda who finally asked the question that everyone was thinking. She said, "What about the Claws?"

Sam replied, "After we have defeated the other tribes we will rest for a few days, and then we take all thirty-five thousand warriors against the Claws. We can surround their camp at night and attack at first light."

With that everyone agreed; Sam's new plan would be put into action. Gar and Karn were charged with putting together the details of the plan and carrying them out.

The Crete tribe had been at their summer camp for about a week. Jarod, the chief, and his wife, Trisha, were lying in bed early in the morning.

Jarod said, "I hope that Jerum gets over his hurt feelings and returns to the gathering this year. I miss Jessica, and I want to see her." Jessica and Jarod had always been very close.

Trisha replied, "I'm sure that even if he isn't, Jessica will convince him to come to the gathering. After all it is our turn to host it this year. I think she misses us too."

As they lay there, they heard a rumble in a distance. They both thought it was thunder. The rumble kept getting closer and closer. Finally Jarod got out of bed and got dressed. Trisha did the same, and by the time they were ready to go outside, the rumble was no longer a rumble. Instead, there was no mistake that it was shouting.

They looked at each other, and Jarod said, "Oh my god, it's the Horde. They are attacking us, and by the sound of it, there are a lot of them."

They both stepped out of the tent just as the sun was starting to rise. The shouting of the Horde sounded like it was coming from all around. By now the alarm had been raised throughout the camp, and the warriors had started to scramble about trying to prepare some kind of defense. Jarod went to the northern edge of camp where most of the warriors were gathering. When he arrived and saw the sea of Horde coming at them, he froze. He could not believe the number of warriors that were attacking them. This was the greatest number of Hordes he had ever seen in his life. "Quickly sound the alarm! We must escape. We cannot stand up to a force that large. We must try to outrun them to the south and over toward the Rumans."

As word was passed around the camp to retreat, several runners came up to the chief and informed him that they were also being attacked from the east, west, and south.

Jarod said, "We have no choice then but to make a stand here. Prepare the camp for a siege." The word to prepare for a siege did not make it around the camp before the Horde arrived. The Crete was so outnumbered that they never had a chance to prepare a defense. The Crete warriors tried to fight back the Horde but were overrun by superior numbers.

The Hordes were ruthless. If anyone looked at the attackers wrong, they struck them down. The fighting was over as quickly as it started. All the warriors were killed. Chief Jarod, Trisha, and Jon were gathered in the middle of the camp. The leader of the attack, a warrior named Shaun, began to speak. "It has always been the custom of the Horde to kill the leaders of our defeated enemies. Today will be no exception." As soon as he said that, three other warriors took their swords and killed Jarod, Trisha, and Jon. Shaun spoke again, "As for the rest of you. You will be taken to our mountains and made slaves. You will join the Arian slaves that we conquered last year. If you try to escape, you will be killed."

After he finished speaking, the Horde warriors started rounding up the remaining members of the Crete tribe and headed back up the mountains. For the first time, the plainsmen knew why the Arians had not been to the gathering the previous year.

Ral had always been an early riser; usually he just stayed in his tent until his wife, Becca, was ready to get up. Lately he had gotten into the habit of getting up early and going outside for a walk. He found the walking helped him physically. Ral was a proud man, but the truth was that he was getting old. He was sixty-three years old. Rollie, the tribal healer for the Rumans, had told him he needed to stay active physically. Rollie himself was in his sixties also, and together they had started walking around the camp.

Since arriving at their summer campgrounds, Ral and Rollie had started walking together every morning. Ral would usually come out first. Rollie would join him shortly, and they would head to the northern edge of the campgrounds. Once they reached the northern edge, they would head east until they reached the eastern edge of the camp. From there they would head south until they reached the southern edge of the camp. Then they turned west and headed west to the edge of camp. From there they headed north then east until they had made a complete circle of the entire camp. By the time they completed the circle, the sun was up, and Becca would have breakfast ready for them.

Ral and Rollie used the time to talk about various problems that needed solving. When they weren't solving problems, they just carried on casual conversations or else they just walked along without saying a word. This morning the walk had started out the same as every other morning. They were heading south when Rollie stopped and asked Ral if he was hearing a roaring sound. Ral could not so they just kept going.

A few moments later, Ral stopped and said, "Now I can hear it."

The sun was just starting to rise. Rollie said, "It sounds like a stampede."

Ral added, "I can also hear what sounds like yelling."

Both men started looking around. It was Rollie, looking due east, that saw them first. He said, "Ral look at this." When Ral turned to look, they both recognized the Horde and realized that they were under attack.

Both men immediately turned toward camp and started running and yelling. It only took a few moments before the entire camp was able to hear the rumble and shouting. By the time the two old men made it to camp, the warriors had figured out that they were under attack. Raif, the son of Ral and leader of the warriors, was already organizing a defense.

As the two old men arrived to where Raif was, he said, "Father, we are under attack. There is a large force of Horde attacking from the north."

Ral and Rollie looked at each other, and Ral said, "There is another force attacking from the east." As he said that, runners came up to them to inform them that they were being attacked from the south and west also.

Ral realized that they were surrounded and that they did not have an escape route open to them. Raif gave orders for warriors to go to the nearest attack site and fight as best as they could. After giving his orders, he ran north where the largest army was reported. When Raif arrived at the northern edge of the camp, the Horde army was clearly visible and only fifty yards away. Raif was stunned by the number of warriors that were attacking. For a few seconds, he just stood there frozen, not sure what to do. Then suddenly he started running forward, yelling.

Using Raif 's charge as motivation, the warriors of the Rumans tribe charged. Most of the Ruman warriors lived in the northern section of the camp, and therefore, that was where the fighting was the fiercest. The Ruman warriors were gallant and fought bravely; however, the turnout of the battle was decided long before the fighting started. The Horde army was just too large. The fighting lasted about an hour. When the fighting stopped, Raif had been killed in the fighting along with most of the other warriors fighting in the northern front.

Bran was the Horde warrior in charge of the attack. He tortured women until he discovered who the tribal leaders were. He gathered Ral, Becca, and Rollie at the center of camp. He said, "In order to demonstrate that your lives as you know them are over, I will kill your leaders." As if that had been a signal when he finished speaking, three other warriors stepped forward and killed Ral, Becca, and Rollie. Bran continued. "If you cooperate, your lives will be spared. If you resist us, you will be killed. You will be taken into our mountains where you will become our slaves. You will join your fellow tribesmen in our servitude." As soon as he stopped talking, he gave orders to round up everyone and headed north to the mountains.

Elan was a young Horde warrior who found himself in charge of his first real command. Elan did not know how he had been chosen for this responsibility, but he intended to prove his value. Elan had always dreamed of winning great battles. He had even dreamed of fighting and killing the desert warrior. Elan had always known that he wanted to be a warrior. Ever since he could remember, he dreamed about glory in battle. He had learned how to fight with a knife at the age of six. By the time he was ten, he had mastered the bow. He thought for sure that he would be a great leader of his people. Then one day, reality hit him hard. He went to his first warriors training tournament. At the tournament, Elan found out that being better than everyone in his clan did not mean he was the best.

Élan's father had tried to tell him that just because he was able to defeat his clan did not make him the top Horde warrior. Elan had had to swallow his pride when he came home. He had not won any of the events. He had been able to make it to the semifinals but not any farther. He realized that his father had been right all along. Elan had said many awful things to his father for not believing in him. Elan had accused his father of being jealous of him. Yet when he came home with his tail between his legs, it was his father who had come to the rescue.

Elan had come home expecting to hear some sort of "I told you so" speech or worse. Elan had decided he would take his lumps after all his family had put up with all of his boasting. When he got home and told his story to his family, he apologized to them and asked for forgiveness. He told them that he was giving up on being a warrior. His father had not said a word until then.

His father said, "Son, just because you did not win the tournament does not mean that you are a bad warrior and that you should give up your lifelong dream. All it means is that you did not win the tournament. You are still a good warrior, and I would rather have a good warrior as a son than the greatest. As a good warrior, you will stay alive. As the greatest, well, there will always be someone trying to prove that he is better than you. Eventually someone comes along that is just a little faster, stronger, and yes, better that you. I am proud of you."

Elan had run into his father's arms and hugged him and cried.

Elan had been fifteen years old when he had swallowed his pride. Since then he had become a warrior. He was not the biggest, fastest, or strongest, but he was steady and reliable. He had not done anything that should have caught the eyes of anyone. For this reason, he was surprised when he was asked to lead the attack against the Bore. When his father heard of the assignment, he searched out his son and said, "Go make your dreams come true, son."

Now Elan found himself here in the early hours of the day getting ready to fulfill his life's ambition. Snapping out of his trip down memory lane, Elan gave the order: "Begin the attack."

Lar had always been a late riser. However, this morning, he was restless and could not sleep. Letisha, his wife, asked him, "What's wrong?"

He said, "I do not know why, but I have a bad feeling. I cannot explain it, but something is wrong. I just have this eerie feeling. The last time I felt like this was the year that the Claws found Jack. I don't know what is happening or going to happen, but it will be big." No sooner had he said that than they heard a rumbling. They jumped out of bed, dressed quickly, and went outside.

The camp was in chaos; everyone was running around and shouting.

Finally Cole, the tribal healer, ran up to them and told them, "We are under attack!

Lar just stared at him, and after several moments, he said, "It's the Horde with an army so large that we cannot defeat them, right?"

Cole looked at him and said, "How did you know?"

Rita, Lar's daughter, came running up to them and gave them even more dire news. "Father, the Horde is attacking from everywhere. From the North with several thousand, from the east, west, and south are large armies also."

As soon as she said that, an arrow flew by and struck Cole in the chest. He was dead before he hit the ground. A few minutes later, the fighting stopped, and the Horde warriors were gathering all the people together.

It took about an hour before everything settled down, and all the people were gathered. The Horde had managed to torture enough people to find out who the chief and his family were. The warrior who had been giving the orders finally spoke. "My name is Elan, and today your tribe stops to exist." He turned to the men that were holding Lar, Letisha, and Rita and nodded.

Upon his signal the three were killed. As soon as they fell to the ground, Elan spoke again. "The rest of you will go with us to our mountains and become slaves. You will join the other tribes as slaves. Today the tribes cease to exist."

When he finished, he signalled his men, and they started to move the captured tribe north to the mountains.

The Horde had always considered the Wolf tribe to have the fiercest warriors. In the past, every time they attacked the Wolf, the Horde casualties were very high. Only since the coming of the desert warrior had the Claws' tribe becomes the fiercest. Since the Horde were not attacking the Claws today, that made the Wolf the fiercest tribe they had to contend with. As a result, Karn was put in charge of the attack on the Wolf. This was Karn's first command in which he was on his own. All the other battles that Karn had led Gar had been with him. The two together had planned every encounter that Karn had been a part of.

This time Gar would not be with Karn. Gar, as the military leader of the Horde, had to stay behind and coordinate the entire attack on all the tribes. Gar had given instructions to all the leaders of the various attacks. Karn he had taken aside and said, "Today you take your first step toward defeating the desert warrior. Today will be the beginning of the end for the desert warrior. But before we start worrying about the desert warrior, you must first take care of the Wolf. Over the centuries, the Wolf has been the tribe that has caused the Horde the most grief. The Wolf warriors are very determined, skilled, and strong. They will not be easy to defeat. For this reason, I have chosen you to lead the attack against them. I am sending my fiercest warrior against the fiercest tribe." The speech had encouraged Karn and helped to settle the butterflies in his stomach.

Sam the leader of the entire Horde had come to Karn and said, "I just want you to know that I and all the council agree with Gar that you are the best warrior to lead the attack against the Wolf." His wife, Faithe, had come to him and told him how proud she was of him. All the other leaders of the attacks congratulated him and wished him luck. Lor, the leader of the attack on the Coho, had told him "I was with the raid on the Coho, as a young warrior, when the Wolf attacked us. They decimated our western flanks. They had no mercy. They were ruthless.

I myself was gravely injured. It took me over a year to completely recover. I would not want your assignment."

Karn was scared, nervous, and excited all at the same time. Now here he found himself about ready to lead the attack on the Wolf. Karn gave the signal, and the attack began. The plan was to overtake the lookouts before they could raise the alarm. Once the lookouts were dealt with, they would cover most of the distance to the camp before they started the customary Horde yelling and screaming. However, the Wolf lookouts proved harder to overcome than expected. One lookout saw some movement and quickly raised the alarm. With the alarm having been sounded, Karn gave the signal for the all-out attack, screaming and all.

Kolton, the leader of the warriors for the Wolf, had been restless all night. He never slept for more than four or five hours a night. This night he had gone to bed early determined to get a full night's rest. He had tossed and turned for about two hours before he fell asleep. Then his sleep was not a restful sleep; he still tossed and turned. When he heard the alarm, he was out of bed and dressed in just a few moments. He ran out of his tent and headed north. Most of the warriors lived in the northern part of camp. The warriors lived here because the north is where the Horde was and the most likely direction an attack would come from.

When he reached the northern tents, the warriors were already starting to line up. When the warriors spotted him, they pointed to the north. Kolton looked to the north and saw the Horde army. His first reaction was shock. He had never seen an army this large before. His shock did not last long, but before he was able to give any orders, runners came from the west, east, and south with news of the attack from all around. Kolton assigned two hundred warriors to fight the Horde from the south, two hundred to the west, and two hundred to the east. He still had another one thousand warriors; these he led north.

The fighting was fierce. Both sides were suffering heavy losses. Karn saw a young Wolf warrior that seemed to be the leader. He was a very good fighter. Karn started heading in his direction. So far Karn had not found any warrior that could match his skill or strength. The Wolf warriors were good fighters, but still they were no match for Karn. Karn had learned his lesson from fighting the desert warrior. He had practiced all winter long. By doing so, not only had he fine-tuned his skills but he also had strengthened his body.

When he finally was face to face with the young warrior, he asked, "Are you the leader of the warriors?"

Kolton answered, "Yes, and are you the Horde leader."

Karn answered, "Yes, I am. I hope you will turn out to be a worthy opponent. I have heard that the Wolf warriors are the best fighters on the plains. Well, so far, I have not found that to be true." Karn had stolen a page from the desert warriors' book. He made his opponent mad, thus giving himself the edge. As soon as Karn finished talking, he saw the flash of anger in Kolton's eyes. Kolton charged. Karn was surprised, at first, with the strength and determination with which the young warrior fought. However, in the end Karn easily defeated the warrior.

As the young warrior lay there dying, he said, "You are not a bad fighter, but you are not anywhere close to the ability of the desert warrior. The desert warrior defeated me many times in a matter of seconds. I stand here today only because he had mercy on me."

Kolton just stared at Karn as he took his last breath.

Kail, the chief of the Wolf, had been watching the fight between the two leaders. When he saw his son fall, he lost all hope. He ran to him. As he was running to Kolton, he gave the order to surrender. He was devastated with the death of his son.

Karn lost no time when the few remaining Wolf warriors stopped fighting. He figured that the old man crying over the young warrior was his father. He went up to him and asked him, "Where is your chief?"

Kail said, "I am Kail, chief of the Wolf, and this is my son." Karn ordered the chief and all surviving warriors rounded up, and the entire tribe was gathered up.

When the fighting was over, the Horde had lost over two thousand warriors, and several hundred were seriously injured. Karn knew that the Wolf had about 1,500 warriors; the damage they had inflicted on his army was impressive. He decided that the Wolf truly had been a worthy opponent. The battle had lasted for over three hours. It was noon before all the tribe was gathered up. Kail, his wife Sarah, and Star the healer were brought before Karn.

Karn raised his hands and asked for silence. When the crowd quieted down, he spoke. "Life as you have known it ends right now—not only for the Wolf but for all the tribes. Today all the plains tribes will suffer the same fate as you. You will be taken to our mountains and be made slaves. If you resist, you will be killed. If you cooperate, you will have a modest degree of freedom. You will never return to the plains, and you will become part of the Horde. To provide you with an incentive to cooperate, we will show you what will happen to you if you cause problems for us." When he finished, he turned to where Kail, Sarah, and Star were being held and nodded his head. Three warriors came forward and killed them. A collective moan went through the crowd. With that, Karn gave orders to gather up the survivors, and they started north.

Lor was the oldest warrior leading an attack on one of the tribes. Lor was leading the attack on the Coho tribe. Lor was pleased that he had been given the opportunity to lead the attack. Gar had seemed to be going with young warriors to lead the attacks. Lor was the only old warrior given the role of leader. Lor, however, was not completely happy with the tribe he had been given to attack. Of all the tribes, he hated the Coho the most. He hated them because as a young warrior, on a raid almost forty years ago, he had almost lost his life. Lor had been part of the raid on the Coho tribe that had almost wiped them out. The battle that day had started a steady decline in the perpetual war against the tribes. Since that day, the tide had turned against the Horde. In the battle, Lor had suffered two severe injuries. He had taken an arrow in the leg and then a knife stab all the way to the bone on the same leg. To this day, he had a limp due to that wound. However, the injury that had almost cost him his life was a sword wound. He had been fighting for hours and was starting to get tired, not to mention the pain in his leg. A young Coho warrior charged him with his sword. Lor had blocked the attack and countered with an attack of his own. The warriors were pretty evenly matched in terms of strength and ability. The fight lasted several minutes, and both warriors were out of breath. Lor managed to knock his opponent off his feet. The warrior was on one knee as Lor came in for the kill. What happened next was so quick that Lor did not realize what was coming until it was too late. To this day, he did not know how the Coho warrior had managed to find the strength. As Lor approached the kneeling warrior, who was apparently finished, out of the corner of his eye he saw a sword coming at him. The young warrior had suckered him in and was now swinging his sword with both hands. Lor tried to jump back out of the reach of the sword. The sword struck him on the left side of his ribs. The swing continued and sliced open his entire stomach. Lor looked down to see his insides seeping out of the wound. Lor fell back and passed out from the pain and shock.

Now Lor found himself leading seven thousand warriors against the Coho. Finally, after a lifetime of suffering privately, he would have his revenge. Lor gave the signal to begin the attack. Lor knew that the Coho had not totally recovered from that battle all those years ago. As a result, he did not even try to sneak up on the tribe. He ordered an all- out attack from the beginning. His warriors responded with pride that he had that much confidence in their abilities. They charged, running at full speed and yelling and screaming.

Chet, chief of the Coho, was having breakfast with his daughter Alicia when they heard the roar. They dropped their food and ran outside. They both recognized the roar as a Horde attack. May, the tribes healer, found them first and told them the Horde were attacking from the north with an army larger than any he had ever seen. Several warriors ran up to him and informed him that the attack was coming from all sides. Chet knew they had no chance to win or to send for help. He gave the order to surrender.

The fighting lasted only a few minutes when the word came that the Coho had surrendered. Lor tortured a few women to find out who the chief and his family were. Once he had them, he ordered the entire tribe to be brought to him. With the entire tribe gathered in a circle around him, he and two warriors walked up to Chet, Alicia, and May and killed them. He turned to the crowd and said, "As you can see, your leaders are dead. So is your life, as you have known it up to now. From now on, you will be our slaves. You will join the rest of the tribes, who today have suffered the same fate as you. If you cooperate, your life will be spared. If you resist, you will die." Lor looked over to his warriors and gave the signal to round them up and head north.

Gar, as military leader of the Horde, had to stay behind and coordinate the entire attack on all the tribes. He had wanted to be involved in the fighting but knew that he could not. As a result, he found himself nervous, anxious, and scared all at the same time. He had runners going back and forth between all the battles. All the attacks had started on time according to the runners. The second runners had come and said that all the tribes were engaged in fighting. Now it was just a matter of time and patience to see the outcome of the fighting.

It was Lor and the Coho tribe that made it back to Gar first. It had taken Lor less than half an hour to subdue the tribe. The attacking force had suffered no losses and only a few minor injuries. Gar congratulated Lor on his victory and revenge on the tribe. Lor had been surprised that Gar was aware of his personal demons. Lor now knew why Gar had chosen him for the task. Lor thanked the gods for answering his prayers. Lor was ordered to take the captured tribe to the gathering valley where the rest of the clans awaited.

It was Bran and the Rumans who showed up next. It had been about three hours since Lor had arrived, and Gar was starting to worry. Gar received his report from Bran. Bran reported the casualties and injuries. Bran also reported that he had seen one of the other tribes coming up behind him. He estimated that they would arrive within the hour. Gar thanked him and ordered him to take the captured Ruman tribe to the gathering valley.

Bran had been correct in his estimate of the arrival of the next tribe. Less than an hour after Bran left, Shaun and the Crete tribe arrived. Shaun gave his report on fatalities and injuries. So far, this group had suffered the most casualties. Every group that reported in had suffered more casualties than the previous group. The fighting was getting more intense; this worried Gar because he knew that the Bore and the Wolf tribe teams had not reported in. The members of the Bore tribe were not known for their abilities as warriors, but they were a large tribe second in size only to the Claws. Shaun was also ordered to take his captives to the gathering valley.

It was shortly after the noon hour when Elan and the Bore arrived. As expected, the casualties were higher for this team than any of the others. Gar had asked Elan if he had seen any sign of Karn or his team. To the dismay of Gar, there was no word or sign of Karn. Elan explained that he had been delayed because of the number of captives he had to round up and bring. The numbers of captives plus the lack of cooperation from them had delayed him. Elan explained that he had had to kill about one hundred captives on the road before the entire tribe gave up and began to fully cooperate with him and his men. Elan was trying to delay his departure because he wanted to wait and see if Karn would return while he was still there. But his wish was not granted, and Gar ordered him to take his captives to the gathering valley.

It had been before lunch when the last runner had arrived from the battle site. The runner had reported very fierce fighting and strong resistance from the Wolf. Gar tried to convince himself that this was normal and had been expected. However, no matter how hard he tried, he could not convince himself that everything was fine. It was now mid afternoon and still no word from Karn. Finally, as the sun began to go down, Karn and his team were spotted. When Karn and the captured Wolf tribe arrived, Gar finally relaxed.

Karn reported that the fighting had been very intense. The casualties were quite high considering the odds. The Wolf tribe had lived up to its reputation. Karn asked about the other battles. Gar told him that everyone else had already returned and was waiting at the valley of the gathering. He inquired about the casualties.

Gar informed him that total dead were 4,200 and another 800 to 900 were serious injuries. They had attacked with thirty-five thousand and now had right at thirty thousand warriors left. It had been a high price to pay, but the results had been worth the cost.

Jessica did not know what was going on, but she knew that something big was happening. Jessica tried talking to various individuals, but no one would answer her questions. Jessica was the only member of the captured Arian tribe that was still in chains. She had chains around her ankles. They said she was free to do as she pleased. However, she was kept in chains so that she would not try to escape. Jessica had become an outcast even amongst the survivors of the Arians. All the tribe had successfully been assimilated into the Horde except Jessica. As a result, she was kept in chains so that everyone would know where she was at all times. If she tried to run, the chains stopped her. The chains only had enough slack to allow her to walk and then only at a very slow pace. Her own people had disassociated themselves from her.

Even though no one spoke to her, she knew something was going on. It was about midmorning when everything became quite clear. A group of warriors arrived with the members of the Coho tribe. The Coho were taken and locked up in the caves where she and the Arians had been locked up after they were captured. Jessica went to the captives and inquired about what had happened. They told her how they had been attacked from all sides. They gave her all the details of the battle and the surrender. Then with tears in their eyes, they told her of how the chief and his family had been murdered. Jessica then told them about what had happened to the Arians the year before. This made the new captives feel a little better and gave them some hope that they might still be allowed to live.

As the day went on, more and more groups of warriors continued to arrive. Each group of warriors brought with them a captured tribe. Jessica understood now why no one would tell her what was going on. Just as she realized this, it also occurred to her that her family was probably dead. This realization made her nervous. Every time a group of warriors arrived, she held her breath until she knew which tribe they were bringing in. The fourth group of warriors that arrived brought with them the survivors of the Crete tribe. The Crete was Jessica's tribe. As soon as the Crete survivors saw her, they ran to her and hugged her. She asked about her parents, and they told her they had been killed.

As the sun was setting, the final group of warriors arrived; with them they had the survivors of the Wolf tribe. The Hordes were having a party. Jessica overheard that their plan had been completely successful. Every tribe they had attacked had been overwhelmed and defeated. Jessica realized the Claws had not been brought in. She wondered why they had not attacked them. She tried asking some of the survivors if they knew why the Claws had not been attacked. No one knew why, so Jessica turned to the Horde. When she asked, the Horde simply laughed. She finally gathered enough nerve to seek out Gar and asked him about the Claws. At first Gar just laughed like everybody else. Finally all he said were "We have a special plan for the Claws."

After a week of celebration, the atmosphere at the valley of the gathering changed from one of celebration to one of preparation. Suddenly the sound of warriors practicing and weapons being made filled the air. Sam and the elders' council began having meetings to discuss the rest of Sam's plan. They included Gar and Karn in the discussions. The plan Sam had come up with called for all the Horde warriors to attack the Claws. The problem was not everyone thought that they needed to fight. Most of the council members were in favor of a plan that would limit the amount of fighting. They favored this because they knew the losses they had suffered with all the other tribes would be doubled or worse against the Claws. They wanted to avoid the loss of life as much as possible. They were not convinced that the desert warrior had left. They felt this was a trick on the part of the plainsmen in an attempt to lure them into another trap.

Gar had been quiet for some time now. Elder Andrew took notice and asked, "Gar, you have been quiet for too long. I, for one, would like to know why you are so quiet."

At this question, everyone stopped talking and turned to Gar.

Gar said, "I have been formulating an idea. This idea might accomplish both our goals. It will give the Claws the opportunity to surrender without fighting or to fight to the end."

Everyone was totally quiet and anxiously awaited for Gar to reveal his idea. Sam nodded to Gar telling him to continue.

Gar said, "We have the Arian girl Jessica. She was the daughter of the chief of the Crete tribe. My idea is to use her and her potential influence. We take all of our warriors and surround the Claws just like we did with the other tribes. Instead of attacking, we send in a messenger. That messenger would be Jessica. I and Karn would go with her. We let her introduce us and tell the Claws what has happened to the other tribes. When she finishes, I will give the Claws a choice. They can surrender without a fight, and no one, not even their leaders, will be killed. Or they can fight and we will kill them all."

Everyone was stunned with the plan. No one said a word for several moments. Sam finally broke the silence. "Do you think Jessica will cooperate?"

It was Karn who answered, "Yes, she loves her people, and I think she will be in favor of anything that will save the lives of any plainsmen regardless of tribe."

Sam said, "There is only one way to find out. Have the girl brought here." Karn left the meeting to go find Jessica and bring her to the council.

It took Karn about two hours to find Jessica. When he did, all he told her was that the council wanted to speak with her. She asked what the council wanted with her, but Karn would not answer. Karn said, "It is not for me to know the council's business. I am only a messenger."

This made Jessica nervous; never had any member of the tribes been called before the council. First Jessica thought this was the end for her. The Horde finally had enough of her stubborn, unrelenting attitude. However, the more she thought about it, the less likely her idea became. The Horde had just won several major battles with the plainsmen. Why would they want to punish her now? Jessica decided to wait before she made herself sick with worry.

All the council members stopped talking when Karn and Jessica arrived. The council had decided that Garish should speak on behalf of the council. Jessica was seated in front, and Garish began to speak.

"My name is Garish. I am a member of the ruling council. We have been watching you ever since you and the Arians were captured. You are the only member of the Arian tribe who has not surrendered and been assimilated into the Horde. You have shown courage and hope for you and your people despite your situation. When the other tribes were brought in, you immediately went to them and offered moral support. You alone have maintained your beliefs and customs. This is very impressive and worthy of a Horde. It is because of your courage and desire to live that we have called you here today. You have been asking about the Claws and why we had not attacked them. We did not attack them because we do not believe that the desert warrior is gone. We believe this is another one of his tricks to lure us into a trap.

As a result, we have a special plan, and you will play a vital role in that plan. We will be attacking the Claws next week. We have thirty thousand warriors that will be involved in the attack. The attack will be just like all the others. We will attack from all sides. We will send 7,500 warriors from each direction. Then you, along with Gar and Karn, will deliver a message to the Claws. You will introduce our warrior leaders and tell the Claws what has happened to the other tribes. Gar will then offer them a choice. The choice will be simple, life or death. Will you help us?"

Jessica was stunned by the enormity of the plan. Thirty thousand warriors against the Claws—they did not stand a chance. She decided that she would try to convince them that Jack was truly gone. "Jack, the desert warrior as you call him, is gone. He has been gone now for about three years. In the last battle that you had with the Claws, he found some old tribal trunks in one of your caves. In one of those trunks was an old map. On this map, it showed all of Rumalia, the Crystal Desert, and on the other side of the desert, it showed a land called the Kingdom. Jack said that was his home. On this map, it also showed that somewhere up north the desert ends, and there is a way to cross over to the Kingdom. Jack left and headed north to this place where the desert ends so that he could cross and go home. He truly is gone."

The council members sat quietly just looking at her. Finally it was Sam who responded, "You sound very convincing, but you expect us to believe there is another land across the desert. Don't be foolish. Everyone knows there is nothing on the other side of the desert. The desert was created as a result of the war of the gods thousands of years ago. Everything on this world was destroyed except for Rumalia. Everyone knows this. Surely even you plainsmen must know this. I ask you again. Will you help save the lives of many of both our peoples?"

Jessica was surprised at how well-informed the Horde seemed to be. She knew the history of the world and everything that Sam had said was the same as what she had been raised to believe. The arrival of Jack all those years ago had changed all those beliefs for the plainsmen. She now knew there was another land across the desert, and that was where Jack had come from and where he had returned to. Jessica was also surprised at how astute the council members were and had figured her out so quickly. They were right; she did not like to see her people killed, or the Horde for that matter. It was apparent to her also that the Horde had a tremendous amount of respect and fear for Jack. They were afraid that an all-out attack would cost them too many lives. They were even afraid they might lose such a battle. She decided to help.

The week passed by quickly for Jessica. She had tried to come up with something to say that would convince the Claws to surrender. She could not think of anything that would make them surrender. Now here she was along with thirty thousand Horde warriors heading to the campsite of the Claws. Jessica was impressed at how organized and efficient the Horde army was. Karn had told her they had learned that from the desert warrior. Two days after the army headed out, they split into the four groups that would attack from all sides. Jessica stayed with the group that would attack from the North. Gar and Karn were also with this group. As soon as the Horde came out of the woods at the base of the mountains, they heard the alarm horns going off. The Claws knew they were under attack.

As soon as the alarm sounded, Dar was up and headed out to meet the messenger that would be coming to give him the news. The messenger met Dar in the middle of the warriors' camp to the north of the Claw campsite. The message shook Dar when he heard that they were being attacked by at least seven thousand Horde warriors. Tanner and Jerris came running up a few minutes later. Dar informed them of the situation, but before they had a chance to decide on a plan of action, three more messengers came running in. The news was even worse than the large numbers coming from the north because they were being attacked by armies of equal size from the east, south, and west. The three leaders stood there just staring at each other, not knowing what to do.

Fortunately for them, a messenger came running in and decided a course of action for them. The messenger informed them that three warriors were coming in from the north by themselves.

Tanner said, "Let's go see what they want." The three leaders marched to meet the incoming party. It was Jerris who first recognized that one of the warriors was a woman, and the woman was Jessica of the Arians. He said, "The one in the middle looks like Jessica from the Arians. But what is she doing with the Horde?"

As they got closer it was Tanner who spoke. "Jessica, is that you? What are you doing with these…" He stopped in the middle of his question as the two groups came face to face.

Jessica said, "Hello, Tanner, Jerris, and Dar. Yes, it is me, and I am very glad to see you. However, I am afraid I bring bad news. I am sure you noticed that the Arians were not at the gathering last year. The reason we were not there is because we were attacked by the Horde. They attacked us from all directions. They did not have as many warriors as you see here today, but they managed to attack from all directions. We fought bravely, but in the end, they overwhelmed us. They killed the tribal leaders and took all the survivors as slaves. Today they live in bondage to the Horde in the mountains. As the tribes arrived at their summer camp grounds this year, the Horde attacked. They attacked all the tribes on the same day. All the tribes have been captured, and all the tribal leaders have been killed. That was about a month ago. Today they have brought all their warriors, about thirty thousand, and have come prepared to wipe out the Claws. They have brought me along to tell you what has happened to the rest of the tribes and to introduce Gar and Karn. They are the leaders of the Horde warriors."

Tanner, Jerris, and Dar all stood quietly as Jessica explained to them the fate of the tribes. Tanner was saddened to the heart by the news of his fellow tribal leaders and friends. Jerris was shocked that the Horde had been able to think up such a plan. Dar could not believe that they were being attacked by thirty thousand warriors. All three of them were stunned and did not know what to say.

It was Karn who broke the silence. "Where is the desert warrior?

Jerris replied, "Jack is gone. He has been gone for three years."

Then Dar added, "You remember the trunks that Jack and I took from the cave the last time we met? In one of the trunks was a map that showed him how to get home across the desert."

Karn looked at Gar and said, "So it is true then. The desert warrior is gone." All three men nodded their head yes.

Gar spoke for the first time and said, "Very well then, you have a choice. You know that you are surrounded by thirty thousand warriors. You can choose to surrender and be taken as slaves. No one will be killed, not even your leaders. Or you may choose to fight, but if you fight everyone will die—young, old, children, women alike. The Claw tribe will end here today. Make your choice—live or die. Either one is the same to us."

Tanner said, "Please give us a moment to decide." He took a few steps back and pulled Jerris and Dar back with him. They backed off about ten feet and spoke softly to each other.

Dar said, "I would rather die than become a slave to the Horde."

Tanner said, "So would I, but our people have the right to choose for themselves."

Jerris said, "You both are thinking with your heart and not your head. We must surrender and live to fight another day. That is the only choice. We cannot let our pride get in the way of the survival of the tribe."

Tanner said, "You are right, but I still think the people should decide."

The three men walked back to the Horde leaders, and Tanner said, "I am chief of the Claws, but this decision is a choice that must be made by the people together and not by one person. Allow us to go the people and let them decide."

Gar and Karn looked at each other. Gar replied, "You are wise. Your request makes sense. We will give you two hours to decide. If you do not return in two hours, we will attack and annihilate you."

Jessica said, "Gar, let me go with them so that I can tell the people the same thing that I have told their leaders."

Karn did not like the idea, but Gar agreed to let her go.

As the Claw leaders returned to the tribe, it was Anjie that ran out to meet them first. She stopped in her tracks at the sight of Jessica. Jessica ran to her, and the two embraced. On the short trip back to the tribe, Jessica told Anjie the short version of the attack today. Tanner had the entire tribe rounded up. They gathered around one of the wagons. Tanner, Jerris, Dar, and Jessica stood on the wagon and told the tribe the story. Jessica went first and told them about the capture of the other tribes. Tanner then told them about their choices. Jerris added that the tribe must survive and the only choice was to surrender. The people wanted to know what Tanner thought. Tanner explained that in his heart he would rather fight and die, but in his head he knew that Jerris was right and the tribe must survive. The warriors wanted to hear from Dar.

Dar said, "I agree with both Tanner and Jerris. The job of the warriors is to protect the people of the tribe. Normally by fighting we keep harm from coming to the innocent women, children, and elderly of the tribe. I do not want to live as a slave to anyone. However, I cannot go into battle knowing that we will fail in our duty and therefore cause the death of innocent lives. I know you will argue that we have defeated superior odds before. However, we have never faced these types of odds before, and finally, we do not have Jack to fight on our side this time."

After Dar spoke, silence took over the crowd. Tanner was impressed by Dar's speech. He said, "There you have it. Our choice is to live to fight another day. However, we need to know that you the people are behind us on this decision.

Merna, Myra, and Claudia, the wives of the three leaders, climbed on the wagon, and together they said, "We stand by the decision of our husbands." They each grabbed the hand of their husbands and raised them in the air. Slowly the people all around the camp raised their hands in support of their leaders. Tanner gave the order to prepare to be taken to the mountains. Jessica took Anjie with her to inform the Horde that the Claws had chosen life and would surrender.

Anjie had not said a word throughout the whole meeting. The entire time the leaders were speaking, all she could think about was this was happening because Jack had left. This was all Jack's fault. She decided one day Jack would pay for leaving them. Jack would pay for leaving her. When Jessica introduced Anjie to Gar and

Karn, Anjie was impressed by Gar. Immediately she thought this man could help her get her revenge on Jack. As the Claw tribe was taken into the mountains, Anjie was already plotting her revenge on Jack.

CHAPTER 11 - AN OFFER

It had been two days since Jack had had his encounter with the new leader of the man beasts. The leader had been very smart and spoke very well. The leader had said, "Our fight is over, warrior. I will no longer waste my time trying to kill you. I have five thousand fighters ready to follow me. I will lead them to the human city, and we shall feast on your brethren."

Jack had been surprised by the man beasts. He had come over a small hill, and on the other side waiting for him was the man beast leader. As he began to talk to Jack, several hundred man beasts came out of hiding, and he was surrounded. The leader of the beasts laughed as he saw the look of surprise on Jack's face. By the time the leader had stopped talking, the beasts had gone back into hiding.

Jack heard a rumble that sounded like a stampede. He raced over the next rise and saw what looked to him like a sea. It was the five thousand man beasts, and they were heading south out of the mountains. Jack was at the foothills of the Northern Mountains; therefore, all he could do was watch the beasts head south toward civilization. They were close to the ocean, so he expected the beasts were headed to Northport. That had been two days ago. Jack was very worried because if he remembered correctly, the garrison at Northport was no longer open. That meant that the beasts would have a free run into Northport.

Jack had not kept exact track of time since coming to the mountains. However, he thought that it was getting very close to three years. For the first time since coming to the mountains, he thought about the time frame. He knew he was thinking along these lines because of the army of beasts that was headed to the city. Jack began to pray to the gods. He asked for guidance in this matter. He told the gods he wanted to go help the cities, but he was willing to abide by their decision. He asked, "May I leave the mountains and help the people? I will come back after the threat is defeated."

The goddess Zephra had come to visit Jack every three months or so since Jack had been in the mountains. They would spend a few days together making love and then she would leave. Zephra always told Jack the gods were pleased with his efforts so far. Jack was hoping Zephra would come to him soon so he could ask her personally if he could go help the people. That night Jack was pleased when Zephra came to him. Jack immediately wanted to ask if he could help the people. However, Zephra stopped him before he could get started. She took her finger and placed it on his lips and said, "Later." She kissed him passionately, and they began to make love.

Jack was surprised at the desire the goddess had for him. Then as the session became more passionate, Jack realized that something about Zephra was different. She looked like Zephra, but it was not her. In the heat of the moment, Jack pushed away from her and said, "You are not Zephra, so why are you here and who are you?"

Immediately the woman under him shimmered a bit and took on her real form. It was the goddess Pearl. She said, "Zephra said I would not be able to fool you. She said you would know it was not her. Very impressive." Pearl pulled Jack toward her and kissed him passionately. Both of them were very excited and let their desires take over. For the next several hours, they explored each other as they made love.

During a break in the action, Pearl said, "I understand now why my sister has made it a habit to visit you on a regular basis. She claimed she wanted to teach you more about the sword, but I now know better. She had other motives."

As Pearl said that, Zephra appeared and said, "Well, sister, what do you think? I told you he would know, and I also told you he was amazing."

No sooner had she stopped talking than she joined Pearl and Jack in bed. The three of them made love for several hours. Of course the goddesses used their power to give Jack the strength he needed in order to keep up with them.

The next morning when Jack woke up, both Pearl and Zephra were still there. With a snap of her finger, Pearl made breakfast, and they ate.

After breakfast, Pearl said, "Now, Jack, it is time for me to tell you why I am here. Your three-year test period is over today. You have passed your test, and we are quite pleased with you. However, before we grant you the full blessing of the gods, we have a proposal for you.

How would you like to spend eternity with the love of not one but two goddesses? We offer you immortality and the chance to become a god."

Jack did not know what to say or do; he was shocked at what he had just heard. After several moments of just staring at them, he finally spoke. "If my history is correct, we all remember what happened the last time two gods were interested in one human. The world was changed forever by the War of the Gods. The Crystal Desert still remains as a haunting reminder to humankind to be wary and respect the gods. The gods almost wiped each other out. Only your father, who eventually won and claimed his prize, your mother the goddess Athena remained. Of course we mortals do not know what your father, Ator, did with his brother Zultar, after he defeated him. There are many theories about that, but we know for certain he did not kill him. Why then would I want to start another cataclysmic battle between the gods?"

Zephra and Pearl looked at each other and smiled. Zephra said, "Jack your memory of history serves you well, but you knew that. That war happened because our father and his brother let their pride get in the way of reason. We will not have that problem now. Pearl and I are happy to share you. We assure you there will not be another war because of us. Our parents have learned from their mistakes and have taught us to share with each other and not let personal pride get in the way. You will not have to worry about us. We will joyfully share you between us."

Again Jack was shocked. It appeared to him that Pearl and Zephra had considered this proposition very well. They had come up with this plan and were apparently willing to share him for eternity. Jack knew that he could easily accept the offer and be reasonably happy for eternity. But even though he was willing to lay his life down for the gods, in his heart he knew he would not be happy, and he would have broken his promise to Linnie. His word would not mean anything if he broke his promise. Of course that would not matter to anyone except himself. He tried to convince himself that he wanted to accept this offer. The harder he tried though, the more apparent it became to him that he could not. For the first time in his life, he admitted that he loved Linnie, and he could not live with himself if he broke his promise to her. After all, it had been that promise that had kept him going all those years. It was his promise that had been his reason for living, the driving force behind his faith and purpose in life. He could not break his promise; he could not give up on his life's goal.

Jack stood up and walked over to Zephra and Pearl. He took them by the hand and sat them down on a large rock. He paced back and forth for a few minutes. Finally he stopped, in front of the two goddesses and went down on one knee. He said, "Ladies, I really do not know what to say or how to respond to your very generous offer. However, I do know my feelings. You both know that I would gladly give my life in support of any or all the gods. What you ask me is more than giving up my life. I do not have to tell you that all my life the single driving force that kept me going was my promise to Linnie. That promise has been the foundation of my life. It has been my reason for living. Even after I was rescued by the Claws and time passed, I remained true to my faith in you, the gods, and my promise. If I accept your offer, I could be reasonably happy. Unfortunately, deep inside I would know that I had intentionally broken my promise to Linnie and that I did it for personal gain.

"I could not live with myself knowing that I had done this. I realize that Linnie probably thinks I am dead and most likely has forgotten me and my promise. I would know that I had the opportunity to keep my promise and did not by my choice. My word would not mean anything. I would stand for nothing, and my whole reason for striving would be gone. You know that I love you, but for the first time in my life, I realize that I am in love with Linnie. For this reason, I cannot accept your offer. I apologize if I have offended you. If you feel I deserve punishment, I will gladly accept it. If this also means you will not let me keep the sword and receive your blessing, then so be it. I must remain true to my beliefs and my heart."

As soon as Jack finished speaking, a loud thunder was heard overhead. The sky was clear yet the thunder came. Zephra and Pearl knew that it was their father, Ator, and he was very upset. Jack never knew what happened to him, but as soon as he stopped talking, he fell to the ground sound asleep. Ator, Athena, and Atlas joined the two sisters around Jack.

Ator spoke up immediately, "How dare you two make such an offer without coming to me first?! Are you crazy? Did you ever stop to think about the implications of taking Jack out of the world today? There are things happening in the world today strictly because of him and for him. The two of you have even had a hand in causing certain events to happen. Jack was right. There would have been cataclysmic results had he accepted your offer."

Ator was furious and could not speak anymore that he began to pace.

Athena added, "I think Jack refusing your offer only proves what you have been saying all along, Zephra. Humankind does deserve a second chance, and there is a basic goodness to most humans. I must admit Jack surprised all of us by refusing your offer. However, if you read his heart, you will see everything he told you is true. His refusal is all the more reason why he should be given our blessing and allowed to fight against the forces of evil in the world. We all know Zultar will take advantage of any opportunity to get revenge on your father.

With Jack in the world, Zultar will not be able to so easily manipulate humankind against us. Your father has every right to be upset."

Zephra and Pearl were shocked at the anger in both their parents. They had never seen them act like this before. Zephra said, "Father and Mother you are right. We did not give consideration to the effect on humanity should Jack be taken from the world before his time. I for one now realize how fragile the balance between good and evil or Father and Zultar is. I do not believe we considered the effect removing Jack would have on that balance. We were being selfish, and I now realize how lucky we are that Jack turned us down."

Pearl, noticing the calming effect that Zephra's apology had on the mood of Ator, quickly added that she too realized the error of their ways.

Ator stared at Zephra directly in the eyes then turned to Pearl and stared into her eyes. He was satisfied with their repentance. Ator said, "Very well, since you both seem to have learned your lesson, I will forget this ever happened. If both of you try something like this again, you will be banished from the heavens and become human."

Both goddesses made personal notes to not do anything to upset Ator again.

Ator continued. "Now Jack has performed remarkably during the last three years. He has convinced even me that he deserves our blessing and to be granted the full power of the God Stone Sword. Unless any of you has any objections, then I grant Jack our blessing and give him access to the full power of the God Stone Sword."

None of the gods had an objection, and they left.

CHAPTER 12 - ATTACK

It was late autumn, and Sergeant Miller had not completed his quarterly report to the Duchess Sheila. As a result, he now had Mark in his office with a message from the Duchess.

Mark said, "Sergeant, the duchess would like to know why you have not come around with your quarterly report." Mark was still a little nervous about dealing with the Sergeant. Mark had been a farm boy who had signed up for military service after being rescued from the man beasts by the warrior in the mountains. The duchess had been impressed by the young man and had asked him to join her staff. Mark had gladly accepted the offer and now worked for her. However, the sergeant still made him feel nervous when he had to question him about the fulfillment of the sergeant's duties.

Sergeant Miller was about to respond to Mark when the door to his office burst open. Several soldiers were struggling with a young teenage farm boy. The teenager was big and strong, and because of that, the soldiers were having difficulty controlling him. In their struggle with the teenager, he had kicked the door to the office open.

Sergeant Miller stood and said, "What is the meaning of this? Why are you men fighting with this boy?"

Everyone stopped struggling, and a corporal said, "Sergeant, this boy came running in here demanding to see you. When we told him he had to wait, he went crazy trying to get into your office. It was while we were trying to restrain him that he managed to kick the door open."

Sergeant Miller looked at the boy and waved to the soldiers to let him go. "Well, young man, you wanted to see me. What can I do for you?"

The boy was visibly relieved that he was getting his audience with the sergeant. The boy became nervous and started talking so fast that he was just rambling and not making any sense. Sergeant Miller said, "Slow down, boy. You're not making any sense. Sit down here next to Mark and start over slowly this time." The boy slowly moved to the empty chair in front of the desk and sat down. He looked at Mark and then turned his attention to the sergeant. Slowly he began to talk. "I live on a farm about a week's ride north and west of Northport. Two days ago, we were attacked by the man beasts. My father made me take our best horse and told me to ride day and night to come here and warn you. I have been riding nonstop since."

"Young man, the beasts are always attacking farms in the countryside. You know that up front when you buy a farm. We do our best to try and protect you, but sometimes the beasts get the best of us," said Sergeant Miller.

The boy said, "You do not understand. This was not just a raiding party of a dozen or so beasts. It was a sea of beasts. There were beasts as far as the eye could see. There were thousands of them, and they appear to be headed to Northport. That is why my father sent me. I did not want to come I wanted to stay and fight. But my father insisted that the lives of all the people of the city were more important than one farming family."

Total silence overtook the office. Finally Sergeant Miller spoke up. "You say there were thousands of beasts."

"Yes, more beasts than I have ever seen," said the boy.

"Then your father was right to send you to warn us. The citizens of the city and the duchess will be grateful. Your sacrifice will not be in vain. Corporal, send out scouts to find the beasts and send back estimates of the size and speed of the beast's army."

Mark said, "Young man, why don't you come with me, and we will notify the duchess of this threat."

Three days later, one of the scouts returned with news of the beasts. The scout reported that the farm boy had been correct. He and the other scouts estimated that there were about three thousand beasts. They were moving slowly and completely devastating everything in their path. The beasts were definitely heading to the city and would arrive within a week. The news made everyone including the sergeant very afraid. If there were that many beasts, then he did not have enough men to defend the city. The garrison was at full capacity, but that meant he had only 2,500 soldiers. This made for some bad news. He sent messengers to Commander Wallace at North Pointe. However, he knew they could not send troops in time to help with this army.

The sergeant decided the best way to deal with this threat was to meet it head on. He would lead his men and take the fight to the beasts. He hoped he could outsmart the beasts, and if they were lucky, maybe even slow them down long enough to allow the city to be evacuated. The sergeant told the duchess he would send back word if the battle went against them, and it would be up to her to evacuate the city. The duchess though refused to accept the word of a messenger. She said if she was going to have to evacuate her home she had to know for herself. She would accompany the army and make the determination to evacuate herself.

The sergeant was not happy about having the duchess with the army. However, he also knew there was nothing he could do about it. He was the military leader of the garrison only. That meant he had no authority over the city or city rulers. Therefore, now here they were within minutes of starting the fight and the duchess was right there next to him. The army had marched hard for three and a half days before they encountered the beasts. The beasts were on the north end of a small valley between the rolling hills northwest of the city.

The duchess, Mark, and the sergeant were on the rise on the south end of the small valley. The two armies were about a mile apart watching each other. Suddenly there came a low rumbling from the north. The beasts were on the move. The sergeant knew the chances of them defeating this army of beasts were very slim; as a result, he convinced himself that today was a good day to die. He tried one last time to convince the duchess to return to the city and evacuate. Of course she would not budge. As the two armies came together, there was a deafening clash. The sergeant bid his farewell to the duchess as he started down the low hill to join the fighting.

The duchess noticed a single rider coming in from the north. The rider was coming in fast and appeared to have two swords, one in each hand. She said, "Sergeant, wait, look over there to the north behind the beasts."

The sergeant stopped, saw a rider, and pulled out his looking glass to get a better view. He said, "It appears to be a man. He is charging the beasts. He is carrying two swords."

Mark asked the sergeant to borrow his looking glass. Mark had an idea as to the identity of the rider but wanted to be sure before he said anything. As he looked through the glass, he began to smile.

The duchess said, "Mark, are you mad? Why are you smiling at a time like this?"

Mark handed the looking glass back to the sergeant and said, "I am not mad, but I believe we now have a very good chance of winning this battle."

The duchess and the sergeant just looked at him, anxiously waiting for an explanation. Finally he continued, "The rider down there is none other than the warrior who has been fighting the beasts in the mountains, the same warrior who rescued me from the beasts."

It took a few moments before the duchess and the sergeant realized the significance of what Mark had just said. With the warrior on their side, the men would have hope. This warrior had been fighting the beasts in the mountains for at least three years. The mere mention of him gave the people hope. The warrior had rescued hundreds, if not thousands, of people from the beasts. Not once had the warrior been defeated by the beasts. For the first time since hearing about this army of beasts, the sergeant thought they might be able to win. He smiled at the duchess and turned his horse toward the fighting and raced away to join the fight.

When Jack woke up, he did not know what had hit him or how long he had been out. He sat up and looked around. He was alone, but what he saw made him feel giddy like a little boy. On the ground next to him was the God Stone Sword, and in the middle of the hilt, the God Stone was as bright red as the first time he had seen it. Jack knew that he was now free to leave the mountains, free to find Linnie and fulfil his promise to her. Jack felt like a massive weight had been lifted off his shoulders. He hoped that she still remembered him and the promise he had made to her. Then he thought about his mother. He was also now free to look for his mother. He hoped she was still alive.

Then he remembered his encounter with the leader of the man beasts. Jack went to his knees and gave a prayer of thanks to the gods. He thanked them for allowing him to survive for the last twenty years, for allowing him the opportunity to keep his promise to Linnie, and for believing in him and giving him their blessing. Finally, he prayed for his mother and her well-being. Then when he had finished, he asked Zephra and Pearl for forgiveness. He asked them not to be angry with him for not accepting their offer. He asked them to forgive him for being simpleminded and human. In his mind, he heard the voices of both the goddesses telling him he was forgiven and they thanked him for having the courage to stand up to the gods for what he believed in.

They thanked him for not succumbing to the whims of two gods who had been acting selfish.

When Jack finished his prayer, he quickly gathered up his things and the God

Stone Sword, mounted his horse, and headed south out of the mountains. It was easy to follow the tracks of the beast army. They left a path of destruction that was half a mile wide and sunken into the earth. After a day and a half of hard riding, Jack came to a point where the trail he was following split. A large number of the beasts had split from the main group and headed west. The force that headed west would most likely head towards North Pointe. At North Pointe, there was a full garrison of soldiers. Jack did not worry about the beasts heading for North Pointe because the city had protection. The larger group of the beasts had continued ahead straight to Northport. Northport did not have a garrison and was not protected. Jack ate a quick and cold meal and was off towards Northport after only a few minutes' stop.

The next day in the afternoon, Jack came over a small hill and there before him was a battle taking place. He estimated that the beasts had more fighters than the soldiers. The fighting appeared to just have started. Jack took both his swords, one in each hand, and charged down the hill. Jack hit the back end of the beast's army that had not engaged the soldiers yet. He ran straight into them, swinging both swords from the top of his horse. Every swing of his swords was fatal. He had killed about one hundred beasts before they realized he was attacking them. Once the beasts made the realization that they were in danger from behind, they concentrated on this threat.

The beasts surrounded Jack and attacked his horse. The horse stood on his hind legs and fought to defend itself. However, there were too many beasts, and he began to fall. Jack suddenly knew that he was in danger, and without knowing why, he jumped off his horse. His reaction happened so quickly that the beasts did not realize that he was no longer on the horse when the horse finally fell to the ground. The horse was dead, and so were the beasts that attacked it. Jack landed on his feet directly behind the attacking beasts and instantly started swinging his swords; the beasts never saw what happened as they died.

The fighting was fierce and had been going on all afternoon long. The soldiers had heard the warrior from the mountains had joined the fight and was attacking the beasts from behind. This news gave the men hope, and they fought harder. Both sides were taking heavy losses. The soldiers knew the beasts were distracted by the appearance of the warrior. The warrior appeared to be unstoppable by the beasts. He was lightning-fast, and every swing of his sword was a killing blow. The beasts were so distracted by the warrior they had lost the edge in the battle. The battle was turning in favor of the soldiers.

The fighting had been going on for several hours, and on several occasions,

Jack knew he was in danger and instinctively made a move that took him out of harm's way. This time he knew he was in serious danger. Somehow he knew he had to stop and drop down to his knees. As he landed on his knees, he also instinctively ducked his head. Jack felt the hair on the top of his head brushed by something. He turned and behind him stood the leader of the beasts. Jack realized that the sword had been warning him every time he was in danger, and the sword was telling him how to avoid the impending danger. The leader of the beasts was stumbling as Jack turned to face him. The beast had swung so hard that when he missed, the momentum had almost knocked him over.

The beast leader recovered quickly, but Jack was just as fast. During the beast's brief stumble, Jack was able to stand up and turn so now they were standing face to face.

The beast leader said, "So, warrior, you left the mountains to try and stop me." As he spoke, the leader started another swing with his axe. Jack stopped the swing by crossing both swords and absorbing the blow. At the same time, Jack kicked the beast in the stomach, and the beast staggered back. Jack wasted no time, and with lightning speed and deadly accuracy, he swung both swords at the beast. With his left hand, he hit the beast in the neck and sliced off his head. With the God Stone Sword in his right hand, he swung at the same time at the beast just above the waist. The God Stone Sword sliced through the beast like a hot knife slicing through butter. The beast fell to the ground in three pieces.

With the loss of their leader, the beasts became disorganized. They fought on fiercely but with no plan. As a result, the soldiers were able to gain even more momentum, and by the time the sun started to set in the west, the battle was over. The scene in the valley was one of blood and carnage everywhere. All the beasts had been killed, and the soldiers had lost about one thousand men. The surviving soldiers had all taken some wounds; some wounds were serious and some not so serious. Sergeant Miller had taken a blow on the shoulder and had been knocked out. He had a broken bone in his shoulder and had his arm in a sling.

The duchess and Mark had watched the entire battle from on top of the rise to the south of the battle field. They had seen the initial tide of the battle go in favor of the beasts. However, as soon as the warrior had joined the fighting, the battle started turning in favor of the soldiers. The realization that the warrior was on the battlefield had made a visible difference to the spectators in the way the beasts fought. The duchess knew without the warrior the soldiers would not have been able to win the battle. She was grateful the warrior had come along when he did, and she aimed to see that he was properly rewarded.

Jack looked around until he found the body of his dead horse. He felt sorrow as he stared at the dead body; the horse had been a gift to him from Jerris and Myra on his birthday. As he stood there, Jack realized all he owned in this world and the clothes he wore were covered in blood and dirt and smelled bad. Soldiers had started to gather around Jack. They did not say anything to him; they just watched him. When Jack finally looked up, the soldiers cheered. Jack smiled, and the cheers grew louder. The line of soldiers opened up, and a young man with his arm in a sling stepped forward.

"I am Sergeant Miller, the leader of the garrison at Northport, and I would like to thank you personally for your help. We could not have won this battle without your help." As he stopped talking, the sergeant stuck out his hand. Jack reached out his hand, and they shook hands and embraced. Jack had been afraid his people would not easily accept him. When the sergeant gave his thanks and offered his hand, Jack was overwhelmed. The cheers started again.

The cheers stopped because someone else came out of the crowd. It was a woman and a young man who looked familiar to Jack. The young man smiled, and Jack remembered his name.

"Mark, is that you!" said Jack.

The fact that Jack remembered his name made Mark swell with pride, and from that moment forward, he would become a strong supporter of Jack's cause. Mark said, "Yes, it is me. After you rescued me, I came straight to the garrison and enlisted. When the duchess heard about my experience, she asked me to join her staff."

"That was almost three years ago, but you knew that, and now he is my right hand and I cannot figure out how I managed without him all those years," said the duchess. "I am Sheila, Duchess of Northport, pleased to meet you." She also offered Jack her hand to shake.

Jack took her hand and bent and kissed it and said, "I am honored to meet you. My name is Jack, but everyone calls me warrior"

While Jack visited with the duchess and Mark, Sergeant Miller gave orders to gather up the wounded and the dead. He started the process of cleaning up the battle site. When he finished he came over to the warrior and the duchess and said, "Duchess, it is late, and I think the men are weary. We will be staying out here tonight and heading back to town in the morning. I think it would be best if you stayed also."

The duchess said, "Absolutely, I agree. We brought our tents. Warrior, I believe we have room in our tents for you if you would care to join us."

Jack smiled and said, "I would love to join you, but look at me. I am filthy."

"Don't you worry about a thing. When we get back to town, I will make sure you get the hottest bath possible, and I'll see to it you get new clothes too. It is the least we can do for the man who saved our city from the man beasts."

Jack smiled and said, "I cannot remember the last time I had a hot bath. Therefore, how can I refuse your offer?"

The leader of the man beasts had given the group of beasts that split off and headed to North Pointe some very specific orders. He had ordered them to be ruthless, to rape, pillage, and burn everything. He did not want anyone to survive. The beasts who headed west took the orders to heart and followed them to the letter. They killed all the people, burned down houses and barns, ate all the food and livestock, and moved on. The beasts were three days ride from North Pointe before a young man who was coming home from town saw the beasts feasting on his family and livestock. The beasts never saw him. He turned his horse around and headed straight to the garrison. He rode his horse so hard that when he entered the courtyard of the garrison early the next morning, the horse collapsed and he was thrown and broke his arm as he landed on it. The boy ignored the pain and blurted out his news.

Commander Wallace immediately gave orders for five thousand troops to prepare for battle and to be ready to leave in one hour. The commander led the troops out one hour later. The commander knew the beasts had been on the move all day long the previous day and were now just two days march from the city. The commander ordered the troops to take lunch on horseback and he marched them for an hour after dark. They made camp, and he sent out scouts to see if they could find the beasts. The scouts came back quickly with reports that the beasts were camped about five miles to the west of their position. The scouts estimated that there were about two thousand beasts.

Just before dawn, the soldiers were up and preparing for battle. As dawn broke, the scouts returned with word that the beasts were on the move. They estimated the beasts would cover the distance in just over an hour. One and a half hour later, the beasts arrived. When they saw the soldiers, they became enraged and charged full force. Since they had a full head of steam and were so focused on the soldiers, they ignored the archers with crossbows on either side of them. As the lead beasts came within range, the crossbows were fired. All the arrows hit a target. Only a few were lethal; however, the purpose was not to kill the leaders but to cause them to slow down or stumble. The archers kept firing, and within a matter of minutes, the beasts started to stumble and fall. The beasts that stumbled and fell caused the beasts behind them to slow down, and soon the beasts were trampling each other to death. With the beasts' attack slowing to a crawl, the commander ordered the attack.

The soldiers charged and caught the stumbling beasts off guard. Half the beasts were dead before they were able to mount any kind of a battle against the soldiers. By noon the beasts had been defeated. For the first time in twenty years of fighting the beasts, the soldiers had only a couple of hundred casualties and injuries. The results of the battle had never been in doubt from the beginning. As was always the case, there had been people watching the battle. The plan the commander had used had been simple because he had not had time to mount a proper defense. However, to the onlookers, that was not how it looked. To them the plan had been brilliant. As a result, word spread of the decisive victory and the military genius of Commander Wallace great commander and would fight for him no matter what. As news of this battle spread, his popularity grew.

CHAPTER 13 - REUNION

It had been two weeks since Jack, the duchess, and the army had been back from the Man Beast War. It was called the Man Beast War because the beasts had attacked both Northport and North Pointe at the same time. Word had come a few days ago that the beasts headed to North Pointe had been defeated by Commander Wallace and the troops from the garrison there. Word had also been received at North Pointe that the even larger army of beasts that had attacked Northport had been defeated because of assistance from the warrior. The news of the warrior spread like wildfire throughout the northern Kingdom. Jack had been trying to leave for several days but had not been allowed to leave for one reason or another.

Jack had spent the first day back mostly in the bath. He had taken the hottest bath he could endure. The duchess had insisted he stay at her home; which he, after encouragement from Sergeant Miller and Mark, reluctantly accepted. Jack was treated like a king. After his bath, the duchess had a seamstress come in and measure him for clothes. The seamstress had made Jack two pairs of pants and three shirts. She had even made an adjustment to the clothes that would allow Jack to carry both of his swords, his regular sword around the waist and the God Stone Sword strapped to his back.

Jack had performed one act of magic with the sword. He had placed a spell on the God Stone to hide it from everyone's view. If you saw the sword, you would see the most beautiful sword ever made. However, on the hilt, the stone was not shining bright like it should be. Everyone saw what looked like a beautiful large ruby on the hilt. Jack did not want anyone to know right away that he was the chosen one. He had prayed about this the night of the battle in the tents. The gods had all spoken to him that night in his dreams, and they had all agreed he should not reveal himself just yet. They told him he would know when to reveal himself to the world.

Given all the attention Jack was getting, he was glad the gods had agreed to let him keep his privacy for a little while longer. The seamstress had refused to tell Jack what he owed for the clothes. She had insisted the duchess had already paid for the clothes. Jack had asked the duchess about paying for the clothes, and she also refused to let him pay. Instead she had given Jack twenty-five gold coins. To Jack this was a fortune; it was more money than he had ever seen. Sergeant Miller had come around with a new horse for Jack. He told Jack the men at the garrison wanted him to have this horse to replace the one he had lost in the battle. The men had seen how much Jack had cared for his fallen horse that they decided to give him a new one. Jack had taken his money, on the rare occasion that no one was with him, and gone into town and bought himself a new pair of shoes.

Jack now had new clothes, new shoes, and a new horse. He was ready to head out to fulfill his promise. Sergeant Miller, Mark, and the Duchess had followed Jack to the city gates. At the gates, the duchess asked, "Where will you be going?"

"First I will go to North Pointe. I have some old friends I would like to see. Then I will go home," replied Jack.

Mark asked, "Where is home?"

Jack smiled and said, "Home is Twin Falls. I have not been home for a long time. I am looking forward to seeing my mother again."

Sergeant Miller brought his horse up close to Jack and reached out with his hand. Jack took his hand in a firm handshake. Sergeant Miller said, "Warrior, if there is ever anything that I or the duchess can do for you just let us know. We owe you our lives, and we would be more than happy to be able to return the favor someday."

The duchess and Mark both agreed with the sergeant. Jack assured them that if he ever needed help, they would be the first ones he would call upon. Then he turned his horse west and headed out of the city.

Jack would have liked to race his horse down the road to North Pointe but decided he would take his time and enjoy the trip. Jack had never seen this part of the Kingdom so he thought he would enjoy the scenery. Jack spent his first night on the side of the road. He was up early the next morning and by mid afternoon had come to a small town. The people were very friendly, and the inn had a vacant room so Jack decided he would stay the night. At dinnertime, the inn got crowded. It was the only inn in town that served hot meals and cold drinks.

Jack was surprised by the number of people in the inn. The innkeeper found him a small table toward the back of the inn. Jack liked this because he could see the entire room from this table. There was lots of noise—people talking, laughing, and singing. However, the topic of conversation was quite easy to pick up on.

Everyone was talking about the warrior from the mountains. Listening to the conversations, the warrior was eight feet tall and the strongest man alive. Jack smiled at the comments he heard. No one could agree on what the warrior looked like, how tall he was or how strong he was. However, they all agreed that he had left Northport and was headed west.

This agreement sparked new speculation as to where he was going. Again no one could agree on where he was going or what he was going to do when he got there. About an hour after dark, when the patrons had had a little too much drink, Jack noticed he was starting to get some strange looks. He decided it was time he left the dining room. Jack went upstairs to his room and went to bed. The next morning Jack rose early and headed down to breakfast carrying all his belongings. The innkeeper already had some breakfast ready and served Jack.

After breakfast Jack settled his account with the innkeeper, and the innkeeper thanked him for the business and asked him his name. Jack looked at the man and smiled and said, "Warrior, which is what my friends call me."

The innkeeper's eyes went wide when he realized what Jack had just said, but he was so stunned he could not speak. Jack smiled and headed out the back door to the stables. He got his horse and rode around the front to head west again. When Jack was in front of the inn, the innkeeper had two gentlemen with him, and he was very excitedly telling them something. When the innkeeper saw Jack, he stopped talking and stared. Jack waved at the man and rode west. The innkeeper could not believe his luck. It was one of the two men with him though that pointed out that the rider on the horse had two swords and one of them had a ruby on the hilt.

The rest of the trip to North Pointe was pretty much the same. When he got closer to the city, however, the conversation changed a little. Now the townsfolk also talked about the military genius of Commander Wallace. Jack knew who that was because Sergeant Miller and the duchess had told him about Commander Wallace. It seemed that the commander had made a name for himself by defending the north from the man beasts. The commander had been gravely injured and yet continued to fight. It was obvious to Jack that both the sergeant and the duchess had tremendous respect for the commander. As a result, Jack was not surprised to hear the children in the streets claiming to be Commander Wallace and some pretending to be the Warrior.

It took Jack ten days to make the trip to North Pointe. When he finally entered the city, he was stunned at how large the city was and how many people there were. The road heading into the town had been crowded with people heading to the city.

Some were going to the market to try and sell their goods, others were going to look for jobs, and some were just visiting. Jack fell in with a small family that was going to town to buy some supplies and whatever else they could find. They noticed the awestruck look on Jack's face and asked him if this was his first time to the city. Jack blushed and said, "Is it that obvious?" The family laughed and offered to guide him around town.

They took Jack with them to the market. At lunchtime they went to a small café and had a nice warm meal, which Jack insisted that they let him pay for. During lunch the family explained to Jack that the duchess was a fine lady and a very astute businesswoman. She and her husband, a Mr. Jones, had been the best thing that ever happened to North Pointe. Jack asked if the duchess was related to the old Duke Winston. The family went silent and stared at him.

Finally the father said, "Son, where have you been living the last twenty years, in a cave? Of course she is related to the old duke. She is his sister. After the duke died, she became duchess. After a few years, she married this Jones fellow. Mr. Jones and his daughter Linda came down from Twin Falls. Mr. Jones started working for the duchess, and shortly after, they got married.

Jack's heart skipped a beat when he heard them mention the name Linda and that they had come from Twin Falls. Jack asked where the duchess and her husband lived. The family told him they were not sure exactly where the estate was but that it was just south of the city. Jack asked where he could find this Mr. Jones. The family gave him a strange look, and he assured them that all he wanted was to ask Mr. Jones for a job. Then they told him that a few streets over from there were the business district and that was the most likely place to find the Joneses. Jack thanked them for their tour and company, but he told them he had to go find a job.

Jack spent the rest of the day just wandering the streets, looking around. He headed in the general direction of the business district, but he was in no hurry. He saw streets lined with warehouses on both sides. He saw merchants of silk, clothes, jewels, weapons, food, and many more. He had never seen another city besides Twin Falls, and he had never really been out of the palace grounds there either. Only when Morten would take him on one of his trips to the mountains to get herbs and things for his magic had he left the palace grounds. As a result, this was Jack's first chance to really see a city. Jack ate dinner that night by buying a sandwich from a street vendor. The bread was warm, and it contained beef; it was quite tasty, and Jack enjoyed every bite and licked his fingers when he was done.

By the time Jack finished eating, it was getting late, and many of the businesses where already closed; the others were in the process of closing.

Jack found an inn that appeared to be quite popular and went inside. He asked the innkeeper for a room; the innkeeper looked at Jack and said, "That will be five silvers paid in advance."

Jack looked around at the clientele and understood. All the inn's customers were well-dressed and properly behaved. This was not the type of inn a wandering stranger would normally frequent. Jack decided this was just the type of place he needed to be at to find this Mr. Jones. Jack reached into his pocket and tossed one gold coin on the counter. The gold coin was worth twenty-five silver pieces. The innkeeper took one look at the coin and smiled and said, "For another silver, it includes a bath and breakfast." Jack nodded his approval and retrieved his change.

That night Jack stayed in his room. Shortly after he arrived, in his room, there was a knock on the door. It was the cleaning lady and a boy carrying the hot water and tub for his bath. Jack took his bath and went to bed. The next morning, he got up and went to breakfast. After breakfast, he asked the innkeeper to hold his room then headed out into the streets. He spent the next two days looking for this mysterious Mr. Jones with no luck. He made a few inquiries but not enough to arouse suspicion. The thing was, Jack could tell that Mr. Jones should be around all the time, but he could not find him. He headed back to the inn. When he entered the inn, he went straight to the bar and asked for a glass of lemonade. When he was served, he turned to scan the crowd. As he scanned the crowd, there was a table of older gentlemen by the window. One of the gentlemen looked familiar to Jack. It took him a few minutes, and then it came to him. The gentleman was Silas the Counter, treasurer to the king. He looked a little older, but Jack was convinced of who he was. Jack became nervous and anxious at the same time. Jack asked the waitress who the men at the table by the window were. The waitress said that they were only the most important men in North Pointe. She said it was the mayor, two local bankers, and Mr. Jones.

Jack immediately ran upstairs, gathered his belongings, and came back down. He settled his bill and started to approach the group. Much to his surprise, the men were already outside. Mr. Jones was getting into a carriage. Jack instructed the innkeeper to have his horse brought to the front. Jack went out front and watched the carriage head down the street. The carriage was about a block away when his horse was brought around. Jack quickly tipped the stable hand and headed after the carriage. It was difficult to catch up to the carriage along the busy streets. It took all his efforts not to lose sight of the carriage. When the carriage finally turned to a wider street, Jack realized they were headed toward the city gates. They were heading south, so Jack decided he would follow the carriage home.

Once out of the city gates, it was easy to follow the carriage. Then Jack began to think. The Counter was calling himself Mr. Jones now. That made sense—not to use his real name. Suddenly, Jack was feeling lucky. If this truly was the Counter, then he would lead him to Linnie. He wondered what name she was using now. For about an hour, Jack followed the carriage south on the main road until it turned down a side road. This road was not as wide and as travelled as the main road, but Jack could tell that it was used regularly. About a mile down this road, the carriage turned into an estate. Jack stopped his horse and stared.

The estate was the most beautiful home he had ever seen. There was the main house, a large barn, a smaller house, behind the main house, and several small houses scattered around the property; Jack figured those were the servant's quarters. The carriage went down the road and stopped in front of the house. The passenger got out and went inside. Jack's heart started to beat faster, his palms began to sweat, and he felt butterflies in his stomach. Jack had to concentrate very hard to get himself under control. He told himself, you have been in worse circumstances than this. Relax, breathe normally, and everything will be okay.

He started down the road again. As he came to the road that headed to the estate, the view took his breath away. It was late fall, and the trees still had all their leaves. The road was encompassed by shade from the trees. There were huge trees on both sides of the road. They were so large that the branches came together at the top and formed a canopy. As he walked his horse down the road, Jack just enjoyed the view. On the left side of the road, there were fields that looked like they had just been harvested and been prepared for the winter. On the right side of the road were pastures. The pastures had several horses and a few cows. As the rows of trees ended, the road split. If you followed the branch straight, the road went around the back of the house over to the barn. To the right, the road went toward the main house and circled back to the road. There were rows of small flowers that looked like a hedge with yellow and red flowers. Jack did not know what they were, but they were beautiful.

Jack tied his horse to the gate pole that followed a row of stones to the front door. He decided to leave his swords behind; after all he still had his knife. He walked up to the front door, took a deep breath, and knocked. He waited a few moments, and when no one came to the door, he knocked again.

This time the door opened; a friendly-looking maid stood before him. She said, "May I help you, young man?"

Jack swallowed hard and replied, "I am here to see the Counter."

The maid said, "There is no one here by that name. I am sorry."

Jack said, "Yes, there is. I followed him here from town. I must speak to him."

"Young man, I have been employed here for decades, and never has there been anyone here by that name,"

The maid started to close the door. Jack placed his hand in front of the door and stopped her.

The maid looked scared but defiant. She said, "I don't want any trouble. Just go away."

Before Jack could say anything else, someone grabbed the door from behind the maid and swung it open. An attractive older lady was standing behind the maid and said, "What is all the commotion about here, Sarah?"

Sarah looked back at her and said, "This rude young man insists on speaking to someone named the Counter. When I told him there was no one here by that name, he became rude."

When Emily heard the name of the Counter, she went pale. Jack noticed the stricken look on her face and asked, "Are you the lady of the house?"

Emily could still not speak; she simply nodded her head yes.

Jack said, "My lady, I am sorry for the intrusion, but it is very important that I speak to your husband."

It took Emily a moment but she gathered herself enough to say, "Very well. Sarah, take him to the study, and I will go get Mr. Jones."

Sarah was surprised at this order and turned around to protest, but she was too late. Emily had already turned her back and was headed down the hall. Sarah turned back to Jack and said, "All right, young man, follow me, but I warn you don't you try anything."

Jack smiled and said, "Sarah is what the lady called you, right? I am sorry about earlier, but it really is very important that I see Mr. Jones. Actually I am quite nervous about this, my mouth is dry, and my hands are sweating. I have not seen him in a very long time. He probably will not recognize me. May I bother you for a glass of water?"

Jack had been rambling and had not noticed that Sarah had led him into a rather large room with a desk and several chairs. She was standing there in the middle of the room just looking at Jack.

When Jack realized he had been rambling and his nervousness showed, he apologized for rambling. Sarah looked at him and decided he was harmless. She said, "Despite my first impression and my better judgment. I think I like you and therefore I will get a glass of lemonade." Jack smiled and thanked her. She asked him to have a seat and wait.

Emily went up stairs to the master bedroom where Silas was changing. As she walked in the room, he looked up at her, and she was white as a sheet.

Silas immediately went to her and said, "Emily, what is wrong? You look like you have seen a ghost."

She looked at him and said, "Oh dear, maybe I have. There is a young man in the study looking for you. He said he followed you here from town."

Silas said, "That is perfectly normal. Who is he that he has caused you to be so distressed?"

She replied, "I do not know who he is, but that is not why I am scared."

"Darling you are not making any sense. Tell me who or what is it," said Silas.

Emily looked at him and said, "He said he had followed the Counter here from town. He said it was very important that he speak to you.

Silas froze when he heard the name. No one had called him that for twenty years. Now there was an unknown young man asking for him by his old profession. Who could this possibly be? He began to get nervous. He took Emily by the hand and said, "No use waiting. Let's go find out what this is all about."

Hand in hand, they went downstairs to see this young man and get to the bottom of this. Before they entered the study, they ran into Sarah. Sarah was smiling and said, "The young man is quite pleasant. I gave him some lemonade and cookies. He is harmless." Silas and Emily looked at each other and relaxed a bit then entered the study.

When Silas and Emily came into the room, Jack stood up and stared at the Counter. Silas came over to him and extended his hand and said, "I am Silas Jones.

I understand that you followed me home from town and need to urgently speak to me. Please have a seat."

Jack reached out and shook his hand. When he heard the voice, Jack was sure that this was the Counter. His heart started beating faster again. He thought, at last I will be able to find Linnie and try to fulfill my promise. I wonder if she is even still alive.

Silas gestured for Jack to sit, and they all sat down.

"Counter or Mr. Jones, whatever you go by these days, what I am about to tell you will be hard to believe."

Silas raised his hand immediately and said, "Young man, I do not know who or what you are referring to when you call me Counter."

Jack continued, "I realize that you are using another name now, but I know that you are Vernon Silas, treasurer to King Phillip. As treasurer, you were called Silas the Counter." Jack could tell by the look on their faces they knew that he was right.

No one said anything for a moment. They just stared at each other. Silas and Emily were pale. Finally Silas said, "What makes you so sure I am this Counter person, and how is it you knew him?"

Jack smiled and said, "Because I was there. I grew up in the palace. I am Jack, Anna's son."

Silas dropped his glass, and it shattered on the floor. Jack and Emily both reacted to the broken glass and started to pick up the pieces.

Jack used his napkin to dry the fluid off the floor. When they finished and sat down again, Jack said, "I told you that it was going to be hard to believe."

In the meantime Linda and Vanessa had come in from their daily horse ride. They had seen the horse out front and were quizzing Sarah about who the horse belonged to. At the sound of the glass hitting the floor and shattering, all three of them ran into the study. As they entered the study, Jack, Silas, and Emily all turned simultaneously to look at the three ladies that entered the room. First to enter was Linda then Vanessa followed by Sarah. They stood still just looking at everyone with an inquisitive look on their faces.

When Linda walked into the room, Jack immediately recognized her. He thought his heart was going to burst. She was the most beautiful woman he had ever met. He just stared at her, and she stared at him. Everyone just stared at them, staring at each other.

Finally Jack stood up and went to one knee and lowered his head. Jack said, "My queen, I have found you. I have come to fulfill my promise. I am at your service."

Linda looked at Silas, and he was dumbstruck. Everyone was stunned, and nobody moved.

Linda reached down and took Jack's face and pulled it up so she could see his face. As she looked at his face, she thought she recognized him. It did look like Jack. Then she looked at his eyes, and she knew for sure this was Jack. Tears ran down her cheek, and she said, "Jack, it really is you!"

"Yes, it is me, and I have come to keep my promise to you if you will let me." Again there was silence.

Emily finally reacted and said, "Wait, first everyone sit down, and let's talk about this."

After everyone was seated, Linda said, "Jack, I do recognize you, but how is it possible? We heard that you were exiled. Your mother confirmed it. You were sent to the desert. How can you be here?"

Jack heard her mention his mother, and tears ran down his cheek. "Is my mother still alive?" he asked.

Emily was the one who answered, "Yes, Anna is alive and well. She still works at the palace for Queen Ariel."

At the mention of Ariel's name, Jack became visibly upset. Jack said, "Ariel is no queen, and she is not my queen. She is a murdering bitch."

Jack looked at everyone. They were all surprised to hear him speak so badly and openly about Ariel. "Let me explain. Counter, after you and Linnie left the palace, I saw everything. Marshall Petrel led the army out to meet the freedom fighters. The battle lasted all day, and in the end, it turned badly for the army of the Kingdom. The Marshall was gravely wounded. About five hundred men made it back to the palace. The next morning, the king ordered all the council into the ballroom. They barricaded themselves in. I went into the ballroom using one of the secret tunnels that apparently only Linnie and I knew about. Eventually the freedom fighters broke into the ballroom. The fighting only lasted a few minutes.

"Ariel ordered all the council members to be gathered in the middle of the room. She forced them to their knees. Then they killed them all. It was cold-blooded murder. I ran back into the tunnel. I was sick to my stomach. For several minutes, I just cried and cried. Then I thought about my mother. I ran to our quarters, but she was not there. I panicked and started running everywhere, looking for her. Finally I went outside into the east courtyard. Ariel was standing on top of some boxes and talking to all the palace staff. I saw my mother in the crowd, so I went over to listen. Ariel said they could all continue to work for her if they would bend their knee to her right there on the spot. Everyone fell to their knees except me. When Ariel noticed that I was standing, she asked me why I was still standing. I said, 'Because you are not my queen.'

"She became furious. She jumped off the boxes and ran toward me. She punched me in the face. I fell back with my eye immediately swelling. She asked me what I had said. I stood up and said again, 'You are not my queen.' She pulled her knife and was going to kill me right there. Boris caught her hand and stopped her. He told her about an ancient custom in the Kingdom. So she exiled me. My mother cried out and tried to run to me. Ariel had her taken away by her soldiers. That was the last time I saw her. I was taken to Bordertown and sent out into the desert on a mule."

As Jack spoke everyone hung on each word. They could feel the pain as he spoke. When he called Linda, Linnie, tears ran down her face. They could see the pain in Jack's eyes and hear the hurt in his voice. Everyone had watery eyes. Linda got up from her chair and went to Jack. She embraced him and he embraced her and they openly cried. For several moments, they cried. No one said a word. There in her arms Jack knew that he had finally come home. He prayed to the Gods and thanked them for letting him find her. In his arms, Linda knew it was her Jack that had come home. She also admitted to herself that she loved him.

Silas cleared his throat and said, "Well, Jack, it is quite clear to us here that you are Jack, the son of Anna. You are a mirror image of her." Everyone shook their heads in agreement. "Let me introduce everyone. I am the Counter. This is my wife, Emily. You know Linda, this young lady is Vanessa, and you already met Sarah."

Jack let out a huge sigh of relief. Linda had taken the chair next to him. She reached out and took Jack's hand and held it in her lap.

Vanessa said, "Jack, that explains why you were exiled, but where have you been for the last twenty years?"

Jack looked at everyone and could tell from the look on their faces that they were all asking the same question. Jack decided he would tell them the whole story. "The soldiers scared the mule so that it would run for a while. Once the fear wore off, the mule stopped. It mistook my struggles, trying to get loose, as my instructions to keep moving. So the mule just kept going west. It was late the first day when I finally was able to get free. I stopped and ate some cheese and bread, drank some water, and gave the mule water also. I was tired so I stayed there for the night. I had to use the mule to keep me warm that first night. The next day I started walking again heading west. I was too scared to turn around. I thought they would kill me if I went back so I kept going west. I quickly realized that I had to walk at night and sleep during the day.

"So I slept during the day and walked at night. I made the bread and cheese last for a week. After two days of no food, I started to eat the roots of cactus. Then I caught and skinned small lizards and ate them. I just kept heading west. Without proper nourishment, I slowly became weak. The heat of the sun burned my skin, and I was generally degrading health-wise. Throughout the entire time, I prayed to the gods for the strength to survive. I prayed for my mother, and I asked the gods to keep Linnie safe so that I could find her and keep my promise to her. I prayed to the gods for guidance in this matter. I asked if my promise was just the foolish wish of a child I would accept their judgment.

"I felt the gods were listening to my prayers because every time I thought I could no longer go on, something would happen that would renew my strength and my will to go on. For example, about a month into my track I was exhausted. The sun was taking its toll on my skin, and my punched eye was infected and almost swollen shut. My strength was gone. I thought I was going to die. I tripped over something and passed out. When I woke up, I had a headache and no willpower. I looked up and saw water. At first I thought it was my mind playing tricks on me. I saw palm trees, water, and shade. I decided to try to get to the water. When I reached for the water, much to my surprise and delight, it was real.

"I jumped in the water and drank till I was no longer thirsty. The mule had died about a week before. I had skinned it and made some shoes and clothing. I washed the clothes and my eye. I cleaned and cleaned it until it was pink in the reflection. Then I climbed the palm trees and picked coconuts and ate them. I thanked the gods for this miracle. I knew that the gods had to be watching over me because the oasis was very small I walked right to it. From that day forward, I began to give a prayer of thanks for every day I survived. Along with the thanks, I prayed for my mother and a chance to live long enough to fulfill my promise.

"I stayed at the oasis for several days. It was my prayers that made me realize that I had to keep going if I really wanted to fulfill my promise. So I took the mule skin and made sacks for water. I still had plenty of jerky meat from the mule so I continued west. After about a month, I came across ruins in the desert. There was a broken statue and some tumbled pillars. At the time I had no idea how they had gotten there. Now I know that they were remains from the War of the Gods. While I was there, a severe sandstorm came in. I had already been through several storms, but this one was more intense, and the winds were stronger than the others. When the storm finally broke and I came to, I was covered in sand up to my chin and only my knees and head were above the sand.

"I dug myself out of the sand. Unfortunately the wind and sand were so strong that it ripped my water and food bags to pieces. Once again I was left with no food or water. However, I was confident the gods were looking over me otherwise I would not have survived the storm. That night I headed west again. I caught small lizards and drank from the roots of whatever plants I found. The wind and sand had also ripped my skin. The sun quickly took its toll on my skin. My entire body became infected. Every evening when I would get up to start walking, I would break open the wounds so they never healed.

"I went on praying and heading west. Once again my strength began to dwindle until I was no longer fast enough to catch the animals. I was left to eating and drinking from the roots of plants in the desert. I went on for several weeks like this until one morning I could no longer walk. I fell to the ground. I thanked the gods for allowing me to survive this long, and I asked for forgiveness for not being strong enough to fulfil my promise.

"I do not know how long I lay there on the ground. All I know is the next time I woke up I was in a tent and a lot of the pain was gone. At first I thought I was dead. I heard voices, and they sounded strange but familiar. I thought maybe I had wandered south and been captured by more freedom fighters. Then I realized I was still alive. I was in and out of consciousness. One day I noticed I felt much better. Most of the pain was subdued, and I could clearly hear people talking around me. At first I could not understand what they were saying. I concentrated on their words, and I was able to understand them. They were speaking the same language just with a strange accent.

"I decided to listen for a while before opening my eyes. I had to open my eyes to see them because what they were saying made no sense at all. They were saying that I was not Rumalian, meaning that I had to be from the desert. They argued that I could not be from the desert and that if I was not from the desert I had to be from the other side of the desert. At this point I could not stand it anymore I opened my eyes. There was a girl standing over me and watching me. When I opened my eyes, she screamed.

"I told these people that I was from the Kingdom. I asked them what direction the desert was from there. They said the desert was to the east. I told them that the desert was to the west of the Kingdom. That meant that I had crossed the entire desert. I told them about the war and my exile. Then they told me about themselves. They were Rumalians. They called themselves the Claw tribe. They said there was a total of seven tribes the Arians, Coho, Rumans, Bore, Wolf and Crete tribes. They lived on the plains of Rumalia. Every summer they headed north to the foot of the Rumalian Mountains. In the fall, they returned back to their home campgrounds. They trekked back and forth every year. The seven tribes would get together at the end of the summer when they were ready to head back south. This was called the Gathering. There were games and trading, and the tribal chiefs had a meeting. The gathering was hosted by a different tribe every year.

"The tribes spoke of another people that lived in the mountains. They called them the Horde. The Horde was the enemy of the tribes. The entire culture for both races is based on defending themselves from the other. At the gathering that year, the chiefs' council voted to accept me as a member of the Claw tribe. The girl who screamed when I opened my eyes turned out to be the daughter of the chief of the Claws and the one who found me in the grass. Anjie, that is her name, took it upon herself to teach me the customs of the Rumalians and their way of life. The tribal healer, Jerris, and his wife Myra, the chief's sister, took me in and raised me as their own.

"After the gathering, on the way south, I realized there were no wagons. I asked why nobody had a wagon. Everyone looked at me like I was crazy. They did not know what a wagon was. The plains people of Rumalia are a simple people. For example, to get married, the couple tells their parents they want to marry. The parents agree and make a public announcement, and the couple is considered married. If the couple cannot make a living together, all they have to do is have another public announcement that the matrimony is terminated and the marriage is over.

"When we reached the home campgrounds, I taught the Claws how to make wagons. At first nobody thought it was possible, and they said the sun in the desert had affected my mind. I ignored all the criticism and kept working. Soon the entire tribe got involved, and everyone was helping to make wagons. When we finally completed the first one and tied a team to it, the Claws thought it was a miracle from the gods. They then asked me what I could do with it. I had to show them what a wagon was used for. Once everyone saw the usefulness of a wagon, it changed the way of life on the plains. Everyone wanted a wagon. We built enough wagons for every tent in the tribe. The next summer, we gave a wagon to each tribe and taught them how to build their own.

"The wagons made me a folk hero. After that I could pretty much get anything I wanted. The Claws taught me how to fight with a knife. They taught me how to hunt with a bow and arrow. Finally they taught me how to fight with a sword. I was the youngest hunter allowed to go on hunts. I made some kills on my first trip with the hunters, and again I was a folk hero. When I turned fifteen, I was turned over to the warriors, and they taught me how to be a warrior. This training was exactly what I wanted. Throughout the years, I never stopped praying for my mother and to someday be able to keep my promise.

"When I was sixteen, I was introduced to the other people of Rumalia, the Horde. We had been having problems with a mountain lion that summer. At the gathering that year, it attacked many of our people. The lion was smart and only attacked when the odds were in its favor. It would not come out of hiding when we sent large hunting parties out looking for it. So we had to send out small parties of two or three. I was in one of those parties. Jessica and I found a trail that took us into the mountains. We followed the trail for two days when we finally caught up with the lion. It jumped at us from a ledge at least fifteen feet above us. This gave me time to notch an arrow and fire. The arrow struck the lion straight through the heart, and it was dead by the time it hit the ground.

"We tied our prize to a pole and were carrying it back down the mountain when they hit us. A small hunting party of four Horde hunters caught us by surprise. The first shot got me in the thigh of my right leg. I fell and immediately came up firing my bow. The lion fell on Jessica and pinned her to the ground. I killed two of them with arrow shots and a third with a knife throw. I thought it was over and turned to help Jessica, and she warned me just in time for me to avoid the fourth hunter. After a brief struggle, I was able to kill him also. Jessica had to help me all the way down the mountain. Jessica made me out to be a great warrior when in fact I had simply outsmarted my attackers, and that was why I had been able to defeat them.

"After that encounter with the Horde, they began a series of raids on the Claws that continued until the day I left. The Horde are brutal killers and tough fighters but without discipline. When they attacked us, they always had superior numbers, but we defeated them every time.

I explained to the Claw warriors that if we remained disciplined when the Horde attacked, our archers could wreak havoc on their numbers. Sure enough when they attacked, our archers were able to decimate their numbers. The Horde simply charged, and we stayed in formation and the archers shot arrow after arrow. When they were totally rattled and disorganized, we attacked with our warriors. We taught this tactic to the other tribes, and soon the Horde started suffering heavy losses.

"Since this fighting technique had so thoroughly worked on the Horde and it was my idea, I was quickly becoming a well-respected warrior. I became co-leader of the Claw warriors. The other co-leader was Dar. Dar is the man responsible for making me the warrior I am today. My ideas of the wagon, my hunting exploits, the episode with the lion and the hunters, and now the archers made me somewhat of a legend not only among the tribes but also among the Horde. The Horde became so caught up with me that they made it their personal goal to defeat me.

"During that winter, the Horde discovered they could protect themselves using shields. When they attacked us with shields, we were caught by surprise. Fortunately for us, the Horde were not sure how or if the shields would work. They did the first time, but they sent so few warriors that we were able to prevail. They would abandon their shields when they got close enough that the fighting was hand to hand. They attacked us like this all summer long. One time we were ready for them, and we ambushed them just as they came out of the forest.

When the fighting was over, a voice came from the forest taunting and laughing at me. The voice asked if an ambush was my response to their shields. This was how we discovered the Horde were fixated on me.

"In reality, my response was to make a better shield and to teach our warriors how to use them in hand to hand combat. We made a lightweight shield much like those the royal guard carried. I gambled with our lives and bet that the Horde would make one final attack on us with a large force. The other warriors were afraid when they heard the Horde was coming with about 250 warriors and they wanted to use the shields. I managed to convince Tanner, chief of the Claws, that the ambush was a better plan than using the shields. As it turned out, I was right. Two weeks later, the Horde attacked with about 1,500 warriors. We were outnumbered two to one. However, we used our shields and our men were trained on how to use them in hand-to-hand combat, so once again we easily defeated them.

"When I turned eighteen, Anjie and I got married. We were together all the time. We had been together since she found me in the grass. We grew up together and became best friends. When we became of age, we started exploring each other's bodies, and one thing led to another. All the other kids our age that were our friends had already married, so it seemed like the thing to do, and we got married. However, as it turned out we were only physically attracted to each other and not in love. I will explain later.

"As the years passed, the Horde continued to attack us, and every time we held them off. Finally, the last year I was there, they attacked us with over three thousand warriors. We had been expecting a major attack from them, so we were prepared. We set traps in the forest at the base of the mountain. When the Horde entered that part of the forest, they sprung our traps. We made it so they had to keep going forward. They were surrounded by traps and every time they sprang a trap me and some of our warriors would attack and quickly retreat back into the forest. The Horde had no choice but to keep going. By the time they cleared the forest, they had lost about two-thirds of their army. Dar led the warriors at the edge of the forest and were able to get most of the Horde as they were coming out in the open. I led the team that had harassed the Horde in the forest, and we trapped the Horde in the middle.

"Over the years, we always allowed the Horde who survived to return to the mountains. This time they called a retreat, and we followed them up the mountain. We followed them for over a day and caught up to the leaders of the group that had attacked us. I had wounded them in the fighting, so they knew who I was when Dar and I, followed by five other warriors, trapped them in a cave. However, instead of killing them, I delivered a message. I told them that the tribes wanted peace and that we would not attack them unless they attacked us. I had allowed both these men to live intentionally when we had fought in the past. I told them that if they attacked us again I would no longer spare their lives.

"As we turned to go, Dar spotted five trunks in the cave. He said they were of a design that was used long ago by the tribes. The Horde warriors said they had been stolen in a raid many years ago. I instructed our men to steal them back. That theft would be the answer to my prayers. Throughout the years, I had continued to pray to the gods. I prayed every day and thanked the gods for allowing me to survive another day. I asked them to keep my mother safe and for me to find a way home so that I might fulfill my promise.

"The victory was such a huge success that I was given the five trunks. A few days later, I started to go through the trunks. In them I found old jewelry, clothes, and the item that set me on a course home. In one of the trunks, I found an old map. The map showed Rumalia, the Crystal Desert, and the Kingdom on the same map.

As I studied the map some more, I realized that on the map the desert ended somewhere to the north because there were mountains all across the north. I cleaned the map off, and there on the map were the words "NORTHERN PASS." I became very excited and cleaned off the rest of the map. When I finished cleaning the map, I thanked the gods for showing me the way home. All I had to do was head north along the edge of the desert until it ended. Then I could turn east through the Northern Pass. Once I reached the other side of the desert, I could head south into the Kingdom.

"During the entire time I was with the Claws, I made no secret of my desire to return home and fulfill my promise. I had even asked Anjie to come with me when I found the way home. The topic always caused an argument between us. When I told her about the map, which is in my bags outside, I told her I had to come home. She became furious and told me she would not hold me back. She said she understood my need to return home but that she would not be coming with me. The next day we went to tell her parents and Jerris and Myra. I told them that I had found the map in the trunks. I showed it to them and explained that the map was the answer to my prayers because it showed me how to get home.

"When I told them I was going to leave in a few days, they were shocked. Then Anjie shocked all of us. She told everyone she and I had decided to terminate our marriage so I could come home. We had never discussed such a thing. This made me angry, but I did not say a thing. Tanner, as the chief of the tribe and father of the bride, had to make the public announcement. The tribe was shocked at the news. They were further shocked when they heard I was leaving. On the day I left, the entire tribe lined up outside of my tent. I walked my horse between the two lines until I came to the end of the line. I said my good-byes and mounted my horse and headed north.

"The trip north and through the Northern Pass was relatively easy. I had only one incident. I came across a very hungry black bear. The bear charged me and spooked my horse. I was lucky to land on my feet. However, the bear was just as fast, and he caught my shoulder with his paw. I still have the scars. I managed to climb on a rock, and as the bear came at me, I jumped as high as I could. And when I came down, I hit the bear in the head with my sword. After that the bear was dead but fought on for a few moments before he completely died.

"When I reached the Northern Mountains, I headed south. From out of nowhere, I heard a woman screaming. I followed the screams and found a small boy and a woman being held captive by the man beasts. I charged in and caught them by surprise. I was able to kill the beasts and save the woman and boy. As I led them through the mountains to safety, we came across several more groups of beasts with captives. The freed captives told me how the beasts would kidnap them and bring them here to the mountains. When I reached the plains of the Kingdom, I set the captives free and headed back to the mountains.

I decided to free all the human captives or die trying. I prayed to the gods for guidance in this decision. That night I swear the gods spoke to me in a dream and told me that if I tried to free all the humans they would protect me and allow me to live through it so I could fulfill my promise.

"For three years, I fought the beasts and freed human captives in the mountains. Then one day, I saw a trail the beasts left heading south out of the mountains. Again I could swear the gods told me the time had come for me to leave the mountains and follow these beasts. So I followed the trail. I came to a point where they split up. The larger group of beasts headed to Northport and a smaller group towards North Pointe. I knew there was a garrison at North Pointe, so I followed the larger group towards Northport. I caught up to them the next day just as they had started to fight with Sergeant Miller and his men form Northport.

In that battle, the beasts killed my horse. The men of the garrison gave me another horse. The Duchess Sheila insisted on taking care of me and that I stay at her home. I stayed there for two weeks. They treated me like a king, but I finally told them I had to leave. I told them I was going to visit some friends in North Pointe and then go home to Twin Falls. It took me about ten days to reach the city. I had never seen this part of the Kingdom, so I enjoyed myself. A small family helped me when I got to the city. They gave me a brief tour of the city and told me all about a certain Mr. Jones and the duchess. I figured I should find this Mr. Jones and start my search there. I spent several days looking for this mysterious Mr. Jones.

"I was about to give up on this line of search when I spotted four men in an inn. One of the men looked familiar to me, but I couldn't quite place him. So I went into the inn, which happened to be the inn I was staying at. I went to the innkeeper and inquired about the four men. I was told it was the mayor, a couple of local bankers, and Mr. Jones. When I heard the name Mr. Jones and I looked at you, it hit me as to whom you were. I realized that you were a little older, but I was sure it was you. So I followed you home, and that is how I came to be here right now."

Everyone was stunned by Jack's story. They hung on his every word. As he spoke of his ordeals, they could see the pain and hurt in his eyes. They could see his determination to come home and keep his promise. One by one, they all accepted Jack and decided that they would do everything they could to help him. As Linda listened to Jack tell his story, tears came to her eyes. She wanted to reach over and hold him to let him know it was over now and he was home safe. She looked around the room, and everyone's eyes were shiny with unshed tears. When Jack told them about Anjie, she thought her heart would break. It took all her strength to control herself. She was crushed. Jack was married. Then when he told them how Anjie had terminated the marriage, her heart filled with joy. This time she could not hold her tears, but no one else could either. Tears ran down everyone's face. Even Silas had watery eyes. Jack won their hearts over with his true story.

When Jack finished, they all came to him and hugged him and together they all cried. It was Silas who finally said, "It is late. Jack, we have a spare bedroom upstairs where you can stay."

Emily said, "Please, Jack, stay here with us."

Jack was emotionally wrung out. He gladly accepted the offer. Then Silas said, "In the morning, we will fill you in with what has happened since you've been gone. I think you will be pleased with some of our news."

When Silas said that he looked at Linda and winked at her, and he brought Emily close and held her tightly. Both women understood his meaning. He meant the plan they had started twenty years ago was now ready to be put into motion.

When Jack was alone in his room, the first thing he did was drop to his knees. He thanked the gods for allowing him to find Linda. He thanked the gods for keeping his mother safe. He asked them for the strength and courage to be able to fulfill his promise. He told the gods he knew the road ahead would be difficult, but he was willing to do whatever was within his power to right a wrong that had been committed twenty years ago. When he finally finished praying, he went to bed. For the first time in twenty years, Jack slept and rested.

CHAPTER 14 - ADJUSTING

Jessica had become worried about Anjie on the trip up the mountains after the Claws had surrendered. The entire tribe was pushed into caves and locked in. The Horde then proceeded to have a celebration. They celebrated the end of a war that had been going on for thousands of years. Sam gave a speech from the ledge and praised the bravery of Gar and Karn. He credited them with the execution of a plan that not even the desert warrior could overcome. Sam's speech made the entire valley of the gathering erupt in cheers. Nicolas of the elders spoke also. Nicolas told the people that the real credit for this victory belonged to Sam. He explained to the people that it had been Sam's plan from the beginning. He explained it was also Sam who had convinced the council to entrust the execution of the plan to Gar and Karn. The crowd cheered and began a chorus of "SAM! SAM!"

Jessica and Anjie were sitting together watching the festivities. Anjie said, "This is all Jack's fault. If he had not left, this would not have happened. If he had not left, we would still be free living on the plains. Instead, we are captives locked in a cage like animals." This attitude, more like anger, that Anjie had taken toward Jack was why Jessica was worried about Anjie.

Jessica replied, "Anjie, Jack had nothing to do with this. If you listened to the speeches, they said it was a plan to overcome Jack. This would have happened to us regardless of whether Jack had stayed or not. If Jack had stayed, the Horde would have killed him. At least this way he is still alive."

Anjie could not believe what she was hearing. She did not care; she knew better, and she made a promise that someday she would make Jack pay.

The celebration lasted for about one week. After the celebration ended, the tribesmen were divided among the various clans, and the clans went to their individual mountain homes. All warriors were put in chains before they were allowed to leave the caves. The Claw warriors were kept in small groups of no more than ten per clan. The Horde considered them the most dangerous because it was from this tribe they had been humiliated by recently. Dar and his family were kept with Tanner and Jerris and their families. It was Sam's clan that had taken them as slaves. As a result Gar and Karn could keep an eye on Dar, and Sam could keep an eye on Tanner and Jerris.

One day Anjie was walking along a trail in the camp when she was joined by Faithe. Faithe wanted to know what it was like having been married to the Desert warrior. Anjies' response was to inform Faithe that the Desert warrior had a name, and it was Jack. She also told Faithe that unless she referred to him by his name she would not answer any questions. As a result of this reprimand Faithe gained a lot of respect for Anjie. As the ladies walked and talked, they started forming a friendship. As the days turned to weeks and the weeks to months, Anjie and Faithe became good friends.

It was on one of their walks alone that Anjie told Faithe it had been Dar who had taught Jack how to fight. She told Faithe how hard Dar had been on Jack. The only way Jack had survived the training was to get better fast, and that was why Jack had become such a good warrior. Faithe told her that in the eyes of the Horde, Jack had been the greatest warrior they had ever faced. She explained about the elders' council and how they passed on the history of the Horde through the council. The council members all agreed that never in the known history had the Horde encountered a warrior like Jack before.

Faithe went straight to Karn and told him everything Anjie had told her about Dar teaching Jack how to fight. Karn in turn spoke with Gar and Sam and told them he wanted to have Dar teach him how to fight. Gar and Sam agreed, but Gar was to be taught also. One day Dar was called out of his daily exercise routine. Sam, Gar, and Karn had Tanner and Jerris with them, and they wanted to talk to Dar.

Sam said, "Dar, we have learned that it was you who taught the desert warrior, ah, I mean Jack, how to fight." Dar looked at Tanner and Jerris, and they both nodded approval for him to answer the question.

Dar replied, "I do not know how you found this out, but it is true."

Sam said, "Then we want you to teach Gar and Karn how to fight like Jack."

All the tribesmen were surprised at this request. It was Tanner who spoke up. "If you don't mind my asking, why do you ask this of Dar?"

Sam said, "Gar and Karn are the best warriors of the Horde, and your Jack easily defeated them on more than one occasion. This not only insulted their personal prides but it also showed our people that we have many things to learn about fighting. We wish to be able to defend ourselves should your friend decide to come back one day. We wish to be able to have a chance to win."

Jerris said, "If you wish to learn from Dar, I warn you, you will come to regret it."

Tanner said, "If after that warning, you still want to be taught, then it is up to Dar if he is willing to teach you."

Everyone turned to Dar and awaited his response.

Dar looked at everyone and then looked around. Spotting some warriors training, he said, "Before I answer, I would like to see what I have to work with. Let's go over to those warriors training and borrow their training weapons."

Sam said okay, and they all went over to the training warriors. Sam stopped the training and asked the warriors to give their wooden training swords to him. Sam gave one to Dar and one to Gar. The men faced off and began to spar. In less than a minute, Dar had Gar on the ground with his sword tip on his throat. Dar stopped and took the practice sword from Gar and gave it to Karn.

Karn was a bit stronger than Gar but not much better at fighting. Dar had Karn in the same situation as Gar in the same amount of time. Both Karn and Gar were breathing heavy, and Dar was not even winded.

Dar said, "As easily as I defeated you is how easily Jack can defeat me, not because I am not a good fighter or because he is stronger than me. Jack became a great warrior because he was determined to be the best warrior he could be. He devoted his entire life to being a great warrior. If you wish to learn to fight like Jack, you will have to forget everything you know about fighting and dedicate yourself to becoming a great warrior. You must also agree to obey my every command without question. Jack became a great warrior because he never gave up no matter what the situation. Are you willing to make this commitment? "

Gar and Karn looked at each other and together they said yes. Karn said, "When do we start?"

Dar said, "Not so fast. We will need an appropriate training area." Dar told them what he needed, and Sam gave orders to have the training area fixed to meet Dar's request. It took the Horde five full days to finish the training area to Dar's liking.

When the area was completed, Dar called Gar and Karn over to him. He said,

"We will start training tomorrow, if you are sure that is what you want. However, I will tell you now it will not be easy and there will be times when you will hate me and you are going to want to kill me. You will be hurting so bad you will not be able to move. You will continue no matter what because it is at that point when your mind tells your body you cannot take anymore that you will begin to become a great warrior. Are you prepared for this?"

Both Gar and Karn told Dar not to worry about them. They received their instructions for the next day and went to have dinner with their families. Karn was upset because of Dar's attitude. He told Faithe he would show this tribesman what it meant to be a Horde. When Gar and Karn arrived at the training grounds the next morning, a small group of onlookers were already there waiting to watch the training. Sam, Nicolas the Elder, Faithe, Anjie, Jessica, a young warrior named Elan, Tanner, and Jerris were all there to watch the training.

Dar began by saying, "I told you that you would have to forget everything you knew about fighting, and I meant it. The key to fighting is not being the fastest or strongest. It is about balance. A warrior must always keep his balance."

Gar and Karn just looked at each other and laughed.

Dar continued, "In all your battles with Jack, did you ever see him unbalanced or out of control of his body as he fought?"

Karn stopped laughing as he realized that in all his battles with Jack he had never seen him lose his balance or not be in control of the fight. Apparently Gar had made the same realization because he had stopped laughing also.

Dar continued. "In order to learn how to fight like Jack, you must first learn to balance yourselves. You must be able to keep your balance regardless of the situation you are in. That is why I had these logs set up like this. Before I teach you any combat moves, you will learn how to balance yourself."

Dar explained how the balance routines worked and began the training. After an hour, the watchers were laughing so hard at the two warriors that it was making them mad. Both men had fallen so often they were beginning to get bruises all over their bodies. After two hours of training, Dar gave them their first break. Both men were exhausted and ached all over.

After only a few minutes, Dar made them start the training again. Just when one of them appeared to be getting the hang of the current balance routine, Dar would change the routine. He kept them off balance; this way they had no idea what was next. When they broke for lunch, Dar received another surprise. The young warrior named Elan, who had been watching, asked if he could join the training. Sam said it was up to Dar. However, before Dar could answer, Faithe, Anjie, and Jessica together made the same request. The men were against training the women. It was not until Dora, one of the elders, came and sided with the women that the men agreed to allow them to be trained. As a result after lunch, Dar had six students instead of two.

Dar recruited Sam, Tanner, and Jerris to help him administer the balancing exercises. By the end of the first day, all six students were so tired and bruised they had to be helped back to their homes. Before they left, Dar told them he expected them back the next morning at the same time and they should be prepared to face another day of the same routines. Dar knew he had not accomplished much today with Karn or Gar, except he had managed to make them mad at him. He could see the anger in Karn's eyes. He could feel the frustration and embarrassment the two Horde warriors were feeling.

The next day, everyone showed up for training as they were supposed to. Each of the students had bruises and was very sore. The pride of each of them made them come to training. The second day of training went much like the first, with everyone falling and getting bruised. As the days turned into weeks, the training continued; the men were starting to get frustrated with Dar because they felt they were not learning how to fight. Dar reminded them he had told them in the beginning they would not like the training and that they had agreed to obey his every command without question.

After about one month of balance routines, Dar surprised everybody by having some practice swords waiting for them one morning. He explained that first he was going to show them a series of combat routines then he would start with Karn and work with him one full day. The next day he would work with Gar and on down the line; the others would spend the mornings working on balancing and the afternoons on the combat routines. They would pair up with each other and practice the routines.

The first routine Dar taught the students was a defensive maneuver. He took Karn aside and worked closely with him all morning long until Karn thought he was ready to learn the next routine. At this point, Dar told Karn they were going to spar, if Karn could stop him from touching him then and only then was he ready to move onto the next routine. As it turned out, Karn found out very quickly he was not even close to being ready to move onto the next routine. Karn had managed to block the first swing, but after that, he was too slow with the flow of the defensive routine. As a result, Dar was all over him, and Karn took hit after hit. By the end of that day, Karn was badly bruised and could barely move.

None of the other students fared any better than Karn had. All the students walked away badly bruised and barely able to move. Dar had not given the women any special treatment, and they too were battered and bruised. When it was Faithe's turn to spar with Dar at the end of the day, she called Anjie over and asked her, "Your Jack went through this sort of training also?"

Anjie smiled and said, "He went through worse because he had to come back every day and suffer the same beating on a daily basis. He did that for weeks until he started being able to defend himself."

After each of the students had their first day of sparring, they developed a new respect for Jack, his ability as a warrior and the dedication and commitment it had taken to learn how to fight. It took several more weeks for everyone to master the defensive maneuver. Dar realized this training was going to take a very long time. However, he was impressed by the women and their willingness to learn to fight. Dar felt that the women were making faster progress than the men. He was especially impressed with Anjie's determination and fierceness. Dar guessed that having been with Jack all those years had paid off for her, and some of his desire to learn had rubbed off on her.

Prince Willard had been deeply crushed by his mother's visit. The only two people he really cared about were disappointed in him. He had to get their respect and admiration back. He had always admired his father's ability with sorcery and wizardry. He coveted the fear and respect his abilities gave him. He knew not everyone liked his father, but they were all afraid of him. If people lied to him, he would know so everyone always told him the truth as a result; he always made the correct choices and decisions. His mother did not have magical abilities, but people were afraid of her also. Ariel was decisive and acted on her decisions. For this reason, people admired and feared her. The prince wanted people to look at him the way they looked at his parents. He wanted to see the look of fear, respect, and admiration in the eyes of his subjects. Up until now, he thought because he was heir to the throne he automatically would get the respect that came with the position. How wrong he had been. His position had not given him anything he wanted. In fact it had only given him grief. And now he had alienated his parents.

After thinking on the subject and talking with Master Tam, the prince decided the only way he could gain back the respect of his parents was with his magical abilities. He decided to apply himself diligently and work extra hard on all his lessons. By applying himself to his studies, he discovered Master Tam was not so mean after all. The master would not push him as hard because he was pushing himself. He realized themaster was actually a very smart and kind old man. He decided he liked him, and he would get the respect of Master Tam also.

Master Tam was pleased with not only the changes in the study habits but also the change in attitude of his student. He was impressed with the new determination and newfound desire to learn. As a result, the prince was actually learning faster than he had ever expected him to be able to learn. The master was reluctant at first to move on to new lessons so quickly, but he felt he had no choice because the prince was ready to move on. The prince not only learned how to perform each task but he wanted to understand the theory behind what he had just been able to do. By doing this, the prince was able to get a complete understanding of sorcery. The prince did not appear to have his father's ability with wizardry. However, he made up for that with the strength of his abilities in sorcery. Whenever the training was complete, Master Tam had no doubt that the prince would be stronger in sorcery than his father.

Prince Willard had begun to notice a strange sensation when he was practicing his lessons. At first he thought it was nothing, but as he learned more, the stronger the sensation became. He had learned his sorcery was within him, and he could reach for it at any time. Lately when he reached for it and began using it, he felt it reaching out or calling him to it. He was beginning to get scared because the more he practiced, the stronger the reaching was. He tried to fight the feeling, and that worked for a while. However, the reaching feeling always came back, and it came back stronger every time.

The prince thought he was losing control of his ability. He thought this was why many untrained sorcerers killed themselves because they could not resist the reaching sensation. One day while he was practicing, he had a horrifying experience. He was working on a comprehensive exercise Master Tam had assigned him. The routine would require him to draw on his powers because he had to cast multiple spells and perform various tasks simultaneously. He was confident he could do this because the master had told him all he had to do was draw on more of his power whenever he needed it.

As the prince was going through the routine, he began to pull on his power more and more. He had never pulled on so much power before. After working for over an hour, he was tired, and he found himself stretching his abilities to the limit. It was at this point that the reaching sensation hit him and hit him hard. The pulling sensation was not only reaching for him; it was coming to him. The prince became very scared because he realized he did not have the physical strength to resist. He began to panic and started losing control of the spells and tasks he was performing. His ears began to ring, his head started pounding, and his heart was beating so fast he thought it would explode. At the last minute, he thought to put up a barrier to protect his mind. As he cast the spell, everything went dark, and he passed out.

Master Tam had been closely watching the prince's progress from his reading chair in the library. The prince was doing very well so he decided to take a quick nap. He fell asleep very quickly in the chair. Suddenly he was awakened by a jolt of power that knocked the chair over. Immediately he knew something had happened to the prince that had caused him to lose control of his routine. The master got up and quickly went to find the prince. When he reached the practice room, the prince was in the middle of floor passed out. He was flat on his back and breathing very slow and low.

Master Tam moved the prince to his room and began trying to put together what might have happened. The master tried tracing the patterns of sorcery left behind in the practice room, and nothing appeared to be wrong. He could not understand what had caused the sudden jolt of power. The prince had now been unconscious for two days, and he was beginning to worry. The master thought the prince may have drawn on too much power and burned himself out. However, if that had happened, he should be able to detect the residue of power.

There was nothing; he was concerned.

Finally, on the morning of the third day, the prince opened his eyes. Master Tam breathed a sigh of relief and asked the prince if he was okay.

At first the prince did not respond; he only stared. After a few moments, he said, "Yes, I am fine."

Master Tam said, "Thank the gods. You had me worried there for a while. What on earth happened?"

The prince decided to tell the truth. He swallowed and took a deep breath and began to speak. He said, "Master Tam, for some time now, I have been feeling this strange sensation every time I draw on my power. It only occurs when I need extra power, and I reach down for more power. At first I thought it was me losing control of my gift. I was being stubborn and resolved not to let that happen. No matter what I did, there was the sensation. It pulls at me, draws me to it. The more power I use, the stronger the pull from it became.

"Things were going so well with my studies that I did not want anything to get in the way of my progress. I also thought this was happening because of my late start in training. When I was going through the routine you gave me, I needed more power so I reached for it. Every time I reached for more power, the sensation reached for me also. The more power, the stronger the sensation/pull was. When I blacked out, I threw up a shield to protect my mind at the last minute, and then everything went black. The next thing I know, I wake up here in my bed, and you tell me it has been almost three days."

Master Tam just sat there thinking. Then he asked the prince several questions about the pulling sensation and about the accident. After more than an hour of questioning, he said, "Prince, I think you have the makings of a master sorcerer. The pulling sensation is your gift reaching out from within you. If you can allow it to take you and control it, you will have taken your first step at becoming a master. Your father and I tried very hard to get him to this point, but he never felt the pull from within. It was during these attempts that we discovered his ability with wizardry. Then he learned to use both sorcery and cast a magic spell using wizardry. We gave up trying to get him to master status and concentrate on fine-tuning his natural abilities.

"Now with you it seems you have no magical abilities but have the opportunity to become a master. I say opportunity because it is your choice whether or not to become a master. Before you decide, you must know most sorcerers that try this are killed in the attempt. The moment at which you let the pull take you over and you try to control, it is at this moment when you can be killed. Only the strongest survive and become masters. Therefore masters are very powerful and are to be feared and respected. If after knowing this you decide to try to become a master, I will help you as much as I can."

The prince was not fully recovered yet so he told Master Tam that he would have to think about it while he rested. It did not take him long to decide that he wanted to be a master. Unfortunately for him, his head had other ideas. His head was still pounding, and he could barely move. The headache persisted for two more days before it started to subside. On the morning of the third day, the headache was gone, and the prince was able to get out of bed without any pain. He was still weak, but he was getting better.

The prince went in search of Master Tam. He found the old master in one of his rooms working on one of his many experiments. The master was glad to see him up and around.

"I have decided to try to become a master," said the prince.

"I thought you would. I must say I am pleased with your decision. Now we must prepare you both physically and mentally. You must be prepared to endure the most intense pain you will ever know. The pain will be so great your mind will not be able to believe you can endure such pain. If your mind convinces you that you cannot endure the pain, then you will die."

For the next several days, the prince rested and recovered his strength. It was not until a week after the accident that Master Tam began preparing him for his attempt at being a master. First he worked on the mental aspects of the preparation. He made the prince concentrate on some tiny insignificant item while he bombarded him with unseen attacks. This was meant to make him keep his concentration. Then he started jolting him with electric pulses to cause him some pain. At first the physical attacks angered the prince, but he realized it was not intentional.

The training had been going on for two weeks when Master Tam decided he had done all he could to prepare the prince. "I believe there is nothing else I can do to prepare you for what is to come. You should go to your room and rest tonight. In the morning, we will go to the main training chamber. There you will begin your concentration. Once you are ready, you will reach for your power. Once you begin drawing on your power, the sensation will return. First you must give in to the power then you must take control of it and master it."

The next morning, the prince was ready. He felt nervous, but he was ready. He went to the central training room where he found Master Tam waiting for him. The master had laid out a blanket on the floor and placed a pillow on one end. He instructed the prince to lie down and begin. The prince lay down and began his routine. He decided he would go back to the basics and work his way through a progression of routines, each one more difficult than the previous one. As the routines became more difficult, he would need more power. He would draw on his power and slowly build on the need for more power; that way he could control every step of the process.

He began with a small light then he made it bigger. He went through all the routines the master had taught him from the beginning. Only he did not stop one routine to start the next. He kept the routine going and started the next. This way he would be forced to concentrate and draw on his power. After what felt like an eternity to the prince, he began to feel the pull of the sensation reaching out to him.

At first he resisted because he was a little scared, but as he pulled on more power, the harder it became to resist the pull of the sensation. Slowly he began to give in to the sensation. When he started to give in to the sensation, it was slow to take over him, and he felt a little pain but nothing that was devastating. This gave him courage, and he opened himself up and gave into the sensation. All at once, the power rushed in and assaulted every inch of his mind and body. Suddenly there was intense pain; he felt like he was being stabbed by hot knives all over his body. He began to panic, not sure what to do.

The prince was shocked at the intense pain. He could feel his heart pounding, and it felt like it was about to burst. He felt his heart was a hot sword and the pain was the blacksmith's hammer and the hammer was coming down harder and harder. He was totally lost; he had no idea where he was or what was happening to him. The pain was too much; he could not take it anymore. He was going to pass out from the pain. Then he remembered. No, I cannot pass out. If I do, I will die. I must endure.

The pain was too much that his mind was losing control; he was having trouble telling himself to breathe. He was having problems thinking. His thoughts were erratic and all over the place. He felt himself losing his cognizant abilities. He thought, I am going to go crazy. This pain is too much. No one can endure this much pain. No one can, no one…

For a brief moment, the prince lost consciousness; but somewhere in the recesses of his mind, his concentration exercises kicked in. In his subconscious, he remembered to concentrate on one thing. That one thing he had placed in the back of his mind was a little light. It was that little light that reminded him to stay awake and not pass out or he would die.

But the pain was too much; he could not understand how anyone could endure so much. He began to think of his parents, and he wanted to run to them and have them hold him like when he was a child. He was crying from the pain and the loss he was feeling. He had lost everything, his parents, his chance to be king, his attempt at being a master, his life. His mind was about to break from the pressure of the pain. His mind slowly began to tell him to let go; no one can endure this much pain. Nothing is worth suffering this much.

The prince felt overwhelmed by the pain and his mind had started to shut down and he was about to give up his life. Just when he was about to give up on life, he understood. Everything became clear to him. The reason a master was given this title was because each master had to endure this pain and not only survive but overcome the pain and control it. Once you did that, you would no longer feel pain; you would only feel the power, the purity, and the ecstasy that came with the power.

With this realization came hope; with the hope came courage. The prince found his light and concentrated on the light. Slowly he made the light grow larger and larger. He realized that as the light grew, the pain lessened. The bigger he made the light, the less pain he felt. This gave the prince more courage, and he made the light bigger. Finally he was feeling no more pain. He felt the pure power pulsating through him. It was still dangerous, and he was not in the clear yet. He needed to control the power now. It was so much power and seemed to be endless.

As he thought about what to do, he remembered his training and how the master had told him to look for certain things of the power. He began looking at the power itself. As he concentrated, he began to make out strands. The power was made of strands. The more power he drew on, the more strands appeared. He realized he could use these strands to take control of the power.

Slowly one by one, he reached out with his mind and took a strand. Then he pulled them together and tied them into a knot. He kept pulling on strands and making the knot bigger. When the knot became too big, he started a second knot then a third. When he had several knots, he took them and tied them together. As he did this, he noticed that the individual strands fused into one. He kept on going, pulling more strands together and fusing them into the large strand.

As he was pulling the strands, another realization came to him. These strands that he was pulling together were the power that he would be able to pull on when he needed it. The more strands he could fuse into the large strand, the more power he would have. Everything made sense to him now; all the training skills he had hated so much were in preparation for this. Every sorcerer began his training with this as his ultimate goal. Those boring repetitive drills had a purpose and were essential in the training of a sorcerer.

The prince mentally chided himself for being so resistant. Now he understood the need for all the training and wished he had been a better student from the beginning. All this time he just kept gathering strands and fusing them together. Finally, the prince realized it was getting harder to grab the strands and maintain the fused strand under control. He kept pushing himself and continued to fuse the strands. When he finally could not control anymore he knew he had mastered the sorcery.

For two days and two nights, Master Tam sat there and watched over the prince. The prince's body would twist and turn and stretch and twist some more. The body became hot and started to sweat. He noticed that the prince was becoming feverish. This made him worry. Normally this was the first sign the sorcerer was losing the fight. Usually within a day, the sorcerer would be dead after they became feverish. However, the prince's fever had gone down some, and he continued to twist and turn and stretch.

After another day, the fever broke, and the body started to return to normal. The twisting, turning and stretching also started to subside. Master Tam knew the prince had managed to master his sorcery. However, he had been under too long. Four days was the longest any one had ever lasted under the pain. He did not know what effect this would have on the prince. On the fourth day, he noticed the prince's body started to mature before his eyes. He grew a couple of gray streaks from the roots to the end of his shoulder-length hair. The prince no longer looked like a teenage boy. He looked like a middle-aged man.

As the prince lay there, Master Tam was able to feel the power building within him. He was shocked at the amount of power the prince would be able to wield. He would be the most powerful master ever if he survived.

On the morning of the fifth day, the prince opened his eyes. He looked at Master Tam, and they both smiled.

CHAPTER 15 - SCAPEGOAT

In the town of Bartersville, law enforcement was provided by the local garrison. Of course, the garrison was manned by troops loyal to Ariel. Over the years, the number of soldiers stationed there had dwindled. Now there were only three hundred soldiers stationed there. However, they only patrolled the streets and acted as policemen. There was a liaison between the garrison troops and the city council. The liaison was the city constable. It was the responsibility of the constable to oversee all investigations and determine if anyone arrested was due a trial. As a result of these duties, it was the constable's responsibility to conduct the investigation into the attempted murder of the queen.

The constable had been serving in this capacity since the George Long ordeal. Therefore, he knew every criminal, thug, and pickpocket in the city, yet he was clueless as to who had tried to assassinate the queen. He was worried that if he did not find this person soon it would cost him his life. He had just left a city council meeting where the councilors had grilled him on the investigation. The queen had sent a message a few months back asking for a status report. This message had the council concerned because they knew what the queen was capable of doing if she decided to take matters in her own hands.

The council had questioned his ability to continue on as constable, saying that maybe he had grown too old for the job. He knew he was not too old for the job. He had harassed every gang leader and petty criminal in the city, and no one had any idea who was responsible for the attempt. He knew they were telling the truth because he had tortured them, and he had threatened their families and their very existence. Yet after all this, he did not have a single clue or suspect. As he had told the council, it was not because he was not trying to find the responsible party; it was that whoever had done this had planned the perfect crime. If not for the protection spell that Boris had placed on the queen, the assassin would have succeeded.

The constable knew none of the local thugs had the skill required to fire two quick arrows with the precision required to succeed in the attempt. Yet there had not been any new talent in the city. The constable had locked the city down a week prior to the arrival of the queen. This was a precaution he always followed when the queen was coming to town. This time had been no exception. No one had been allowed to leave the city for months after the attempt. So he knew the would-be assassin had not left the city. Everyone coming into or leaving the city since then was thoroughly questioned and searched. Still nothing, so he knew the would-be assassin was still in the city. If only he could figure out a way to trap him. No matter how hard he tried, he could not come up with a plan that had merit, much less a chance to succeed.

The constable was totally engrossed in his thoughts that he really was not paying attention to his surroundings as he walked. He knew the city like the palm of his hands so he was not worried about getting lost. He was so engrossed in his musings that as he turned a corner he never saw the young girl until they were both lying on the ground due to the collision.

Jenna had not left the surroundings of her home for months. Only once since her failed attempt at killing the queen had she ventured more than a couple of blocks from her home. She was very afraid she would get caught. Only one time had she tried to leave her immediate surroundings to go fishing because she was tired of being cooped up at home. As she reached the area around the city gates, she saw the line of people trying to leave the city.

She asked some of the folks why there was a line. The answer she got scared her to death. The soldiers were still questioning everyone who entered or left the city in an attempt to find the assassin. Jenna had panicked, not knowing what to do. Finally she slowly backed up and turned around and slowly started to walk away. As soon as she was around a corner, she ran as fast as she could all the way home. Since then she had not left the safe confines around the few blocks of her house.

Her mother had asked her why she had not gone fishing or hunting lately. She explained to her that it took too long to get out of the city and that she did not have time to get a good spot before she had to turn around and head home. Her only other option was to spend the night out, and she did not like doing that. Her mother accepted her explanation and did not question her about it anymore.

Jenna, however, was not a person to sit back and let life pass her by. Lately she had been getting irritated, and it seemed that everything bothered her. She knew it was because she was restless and had no way to release any energy. All this time spent at home had finally started to get to her

In order to help her through this difficult time, she had started praying to the goddess Pearl. She had not forgotten her encounter with the goddess. The goddess had been the most beautiful woman Jenna had ever seen. Also, she had been thinking about what the goddess had said to her. The goddess had told her that someone would come along and complete what she had started. This person was someone who had suffered more than she had. This person had been asking the gods for help and strength to do exactly what Jenna had tried. She said the gods had heard his prayers and were going to give him the chance because he had been asking for help and guidance for longer than Jenna had been alive.

Jenna wished she knew who this person was. She prayed to the goddess that she might meet this man, and if possible, she would like to be there when he got his chance. These thoughts always came to her no matter how she tried to avoid them. These thoughts always made her feel guilty, and she would pray to the goddess asking for forgiveness.

In the last few weeks, she had also started to remember that the goddess had told her if she made it home she would be safe. She had made it home with the help of the goddess. Jenna had always thought that the goddess's words meant she had to stay home in order to be safe. However, now she was thinking that the goddess did not mean for her to stay home for the rest of her life. She felt she had meant if she made it home that night she was safe.

Getting home that night had not been easy. She had encountered dozens of patrols looking for the assassin. She had had to take a very long way around in order to get home that night. At times she was not sure she was going to make it home. It seemed the soldiers were everywhere. Several times she had to turn around and find alternate routes. She had even had to hide in dumpsters for several minutes at a time. After hours of out maneuvering the soldiers, she had finally made it home. It was this accomplishment that Jenna thought was what the goddess had meant.

All this time, she had taken it to mean she had to stay home in order to be safe. This new thought process had not occurred to her until she started praying to the goddess. As a result, today she had decided she would go out and walk around the city to test her theory. It was late afternoon, and Jenna had been all over the city without incident. She had even gone by the garrison and spoken to a couple of soldiers. She was so happy that finally she had her life back.

Jenna was starting to get hungry, so she decided to head back home. She had not eaten anything since breakfast. She was so happy she had started to skip and hum as she went along. She was so engrossed in her humming and skipping that she never saw the constable until they were tangled on the ground after they had collided turning a corner.

At first Jenna was dumbfounded and embarrassed that she had tripped this man, and she was apologizing. The man looked familiar to her, but she could not place him. When the man finally had gathered himself together and faced her, his eyes went wide. He grabbed her and said, "You. You are the one. You will come with me." The man was bigger and stronger than her, and no matter how hard she tried, she could not escape his grip.

Jenna panicked. She could not imagine what was going on. Then it came to her who the man was. He was the constable. That could only mean one thing; he knew that she was the assassin and was taking her to be handed over to the queen. This realization scared her more than ever, and she began to struggle even more. The constable heaved her up against the wall of a building they were walking by. He slapped her twice, once on each cheek. He said, "Young lady, you are guilty of trying to assassinate the queen. For your crime, I am going to send you to Twin Falls in a cage. First I will take you to the city council so they can see that I have found the criminal."

Jenna said, "I did no such thing. You cannot prove anything."

The constable just smiled and said, "I do not care if you are guilty or not. You are the only person in this city with the skill to make those shots. Therefore, your guilt or innocence is irrelevant. As far as the council or I are concerned, you're guilty, and the queen will be grateful to us for finding you. Bumping into you like this has saved this city from the wrath of the queen. So you see, what you say does not matter."

Jenna tried to squirm away but could not. She tried hitting the constable and kicking him. All he did was laugh. He took off his belt and wrapped it around her tying her arms, so she could not move them. Then he simply pulled her along.

The city council was still in session as the constable stormed in the room with Jenna in tow. The mayor immediately jumped out of his chair and demanded an explanation. The constable smiled and said, "I have solved the mystery as to who tried to assassinate the queen" as he pointed to Jenna. The entire council started talking at once. He let them all jabber until they finally controlled themselves.

The mayor finally spoke. "Constable, you expect us, and therefore the queen, to believe that this little girl tried to kill her."

The constable just smiled and said, "Let me explain. Who has for the five years won every archery contest in the city? Who is stronger last and runs faster than most boys her age?" He just smiled and pointed at Jenna. "No one in the city has the skill required to deliver two bow shots so fast and accurately, except her."

The mayor looked at her and asked, "This is a serious accusation. Did you commit this crime?"

Jenna replied, "No I did not. If I had I would have succeeded."

The constable said, "Of course she is going to deny it. However, you heard her. She has the skill required to accomplish the task. Of course, if you gentlemen do not believe she is guilty, then we will have to tell the queen that we have failed in our investigation. If you men replace me, that will send the same signal of failure to the queen and she will take matters into her own hands. We all know what she will do to the city. I fear the city will not survive. At a minimum, no one in this room will survive. The choice is yours. I give you the only person in our city with the skills to commit the crime. What you do now is up to you."

The room was silent. The mayor looked around to every councilor one at a time. Each one reluctantly nodded their head, giving approval. Each of the councilors was more concerned about their own hides than the guilt or innocence of one girl.

The mayor cleared his throat and said, "Constable, on behalf of the council, I would like to congratulate you on solving and apprehending the person responsible for the attempt on the queen's life. If you would please deliver her to the commander at the garrison, we can close this matter."

Jenna screamed, "Cowards, you spineless bastards!" She tried to squirm out of the belt, but it was too tight.

The constable bowed to the councilors and headed out of the room, jerking Jenna along. Once outside he punched her in the gut, knocking the wind out of her. He said, "Now girl, you will come along peacefully or do you want me to knock you upside the head and carry you? The choice is yours. It does not matter to me."

Jenna said nothing, but as he started walking, she followed along like a dog on a leash. Jenna's mind was reeling. She could not believe this was happening to her. She looked up to the sky and prayed to the goddess for forgiveness. She apologized for her arrogance and for not listening to her. She silently began to cry.

At the garrison, the constable went straight to the commander and told him that Jenna was the person responsible for the attempt on the queen's life. The commander laughed out loud and heartily. The constable let him have his laugh then he reminded the commander of who had won the city's archery contests for the last five years. He reminded him that his own archers had competed in those contests. He told him that Jenna had bested most of the archers in the garrison; therefore, if he wanted to laugh then explain how this little girl had managed that. He also reminded the commander that Jenna was not so little; she was after all seventeen years old.

The commander thanked the constable for his service and duty to the queen. He called the guards and had them take Jenna to a cell. He told Jenna that first thing in the morning she would be headed to Twin Falls to receive her punishment.

Jenna was numb with fear. She could not understand why this had happened now after all this time. She cried and sobbed until she fell asleep. While sleeping she dreamed about the night she tried to kill the queen. The goddess again appeared in her dreams. The guards woke her when they brought her breakfast. Jenna ate her breakfast and recalled her dream. She thought how real the dream felt and how real the presence of the goddess had seemed. Then she remembered the words the goddess had said. The goddess had not told her that if she made it home she would be safe. Instead the goddess said, "Do not be scared, and instead have faith."

Jenna knew then that the reason the presence of the goddess had seemed so real was because she had been there again. However, she could not see how she was going to get out of this mess. Then she began to doubt that the goddess had been there. She reasoned that the words had been changed because that was what she wanted to hear.

At about midmorning, the soldiers came for her. They took her outside. They had a cage on a cart waiting to put her in. There were three cages of prisoners' altogether. However, she was the only one in her cage. The other prisoners gave her ugly looks and shouted, "Queen killer, murderer" at her.

It was apparent to her that her arrest and story had gotten out into the city. The small caravan headed out of the garrison. As they came out of the garrison, Jenna's mother was at her cage crying and asking her why. Jenna did not have a chance to answer because the soldiers grabbed her by the hair and pulled her away.

Jenna was devastated; she knew her life was over. She knew she could not escape, so she just sat down and cried. The soldiers would occasionally come up to the cage and kick her through the bars and tell her to stop her balling. She ignored them and cried more.

During the trip, all the prisoners were allowed to get out of the cage and walk around at the end of the day before the evening meal and before bedding down for the night. All the prisoners except Jenna— she was fed in the cage and not allowed to come out ever. At night when everyone was asleep was the only time she could privately take care of her bodily functions. She would be given a fresh batch of hay every day for that purpose. She would take care of business and throw the hay out through the bars.

On the night before they arrived at Twin Falls, Jenna was restless and could not sleep. Suddenly a bright light appeared in her cage. The light was so bright she had to hide her eyes or be blinded. Then she heard the voice: "Do not fear, Jenna. Open your eyes and look at me." Jenna slowly looked up and noticed the light had faded. Standing there in the cage with her was the goddess Pearl.

Jenna immediately went to her knees and began kissing the feet of the goddess and begging for forgiveness. The goddess laid her hand on Jenna's shoulder and let her cry a little bit. When the goddess placed her hand on her, Jenna immediately began to feel safe and secure. She stopped crying. Then Jenna looked around to see if anyone had seen or heard them. The goddess said, "Do not worry. They cannot hear or see us. They see you still sleeping in the corner of the cage."

The goddess sat down beside Jenna and laid her head on her shoulder and comforted her. After a few short minutes, she said, "I have come to you tonight to tell you that in order for me to protect you, you must have faith. You must stick to your story the way you did with the city council. You will be questioned by Kain in front of the Queen and Boris. Tell them the same thing you told the city council. Boris has some truth spells he will use on you to determine if you are telling the truth. As long as you stick to your story, his spells will not detect our deception. They will have no choice but to let you go."

Jenna woke suddenly when the soldiers starting moving around. She was puzzled at first. The soldiers misunderstood her confusion as fear or realization that today she would receive her punishment. Jenna did not remember when the goddess had left or how long she had been there, but she knew it had not been a dream.

Jenna swallowed her breakfast and even asked for more. She felt rested and invigorated. When the small caravan headed out, Jenna looked back to the campsite and saw the goddess standing there waving at her. She saw her throw her a kiss and wave. Then she heard the voice of the goddess say, "Have faith and all will be fine." Jenna threw a kiss back at the goddess and watched as she disappeared. Jenna sat down with her back to the back side of the cage. She wanted to see everything around her. She felt blessed.

The guards had tossed the prisoners some bread and cheese for lunch. Shortly after lunch, Jenna caught the first sight of the city. Twin Falls spread out like a blanket on the ground. The city was humongous; it was larger than she had imagined and beautiful. One hour later, they entered the city. A messenger had been sent ahead to announce that the assassin had been caught and was being brought to the palace. The soldiers at the gate had made a sign that read ASSASSIN. When Jenna's cage passed by, they attached the sign to the cage.

Anna had put out the word in the streets to have people line the streets and curse the assassin. As usual the people did as they were told. Word got to the palace that the caravan had entered the city and that the citizens were cursing the assassin. This news lifted the spirit of both Ariel and Boris, and they headed to the palace front door to wait for the assassin.

The story about Jenna had also been sent ahead—how she was a young girl and how she was an expert with weapons. These stories had made Jenna a folk hero to the citizens of Twin Falls. They admired her for having the courage to try what they had all thought about.

As the caravan entered the palace grounds, only Jenna's cart headed to the front of the palace. When the cart reached the front of the palace steps, Boris and Ariel rushed down to the cart. Boris looked at Jenna and said, "I hear you are quite the archer, young lady."

Jenna looked him straight in the eyes and said, "Give me a bow, and I will show you."

Boris laughed and ordered that she be let out of the cage and signaled for a soldier to come forward. He told the soldier to give his bow and one arrow to Jenna. He looked around. About 150 yards away, a supply wagon was being unloaded. A palace servant was standing in the middle just in front of a keg of rum. Only the brim of the keg could be seen over the top side of the wagon. Boris told Jenna, "See the brim of the keg on the supply wagon? Can you hit it?"

Jenna looked at the wagon and noticed a soldier on the other side talking to one of the palace maids. She saw that he was leaning on his sword. She looked at Boris and said, "I can do better. Look through the wagon wheel. See the sword that soldier is leaning on. He is about to fall down." Without warning, Jenna brought the bow up, notched the arrow, aimed, and fired. While she was doing this, she said a silent prayer to the goddess.

Before Boris could say anything, the arrow hit the mark perfectly, and the oldier fell down. As Jenna fired, she spotted a large tarantula walking across the ground about thirty feet away. Again without warning, she picked the knife from the soldier who had given her the bow and threw the knife. The knife struck the spider dead center of the body and pinned it to the ground. It happened so fast that no one had a chance to react before she threw the knife. When the crowd saw the knife in the spider, a round of applause went around.

Boris, with a stern look on his face, said, "Well, young lady, your reputation does you no justice. You indeed are a very dangerous girl." Turning to the soldier, he said, "Put her in shackles and take her to our private audience room." To another soldier he said, "Find Kain and tell him to meet us there in an hour." Turning to Ariel he said, "Come, my queen, we must prepare."

Just like that the crowd disbursed, and Jenna found herself in chains. She was rushed up the stairs into the palace. She was amazed at the size of the palace. She had never seen a building this large. She did not even know that a building this large could be built. She wished the soldiers would slow down so she could get a better look around. Instead, they rushed down the various hallways without concern for their prisoner. After about ten minutes of walking through hallways, they came to two large double doors. The handles looked like they were made of solid gold. They were molded into the design of a rose. Jenna found this unusual because she knew the rose had been the family emblem of the Martin family for hundreds of years. Obviously Ariel did not know this or she would have had the handles changed.

The soldiers pushed open the huge double doors and led her in. The room was small in comparison to the palace but large compared to any room Jenna had ever been in. At the center of the far end was a small platform that stood about a foot higher than the rest of the room. On the platform was a table that looked to be made of solid mahogany. At least Jenna thought it was mahogany because of its deep dark red/ burgundy color. The legs were made to the shape of the paws of a lion. This made the table look menacing. Behind the table were two large thrown-like chairs. The walls on the left were decorated with beautiful carpets that hung from the ceiling almost to the floor. The carpets were various colors and had designs of trees on them. The wall to the right had large battle scenes drawn on them. Behind the platform at the far end, the wall had been painted with the Twin Falls the city was named for. This was the most beautiful room Jenna had ever seen.

While Jenna was admiring the room, a tall man with a beard had walked in. He came over to Jenna and said, "I hear you put on quite a show outside. I am Kain. As soon as Boris and the queen arrive, I will be your interrogator."

Jenna looked at him straight in the eyes. She did not want him to think he intimidated her. Under normal circumstances, this man would intimidate anybody. However, Jenna knew she was protected by the goddess Pearl. She thought, Go ahead, Kain. Do your worst.

A short time later, Boris and Ariel entered the room through a door in the middle of one of the battle scenes that Jenna had not even noticed. They went to the head table and sat down. Ariel looked at Boris who nodded his head; she then looked to Kain and said, "You may begin." Kain pulled Jenna to the center of the room and started his interrogation.

For what seemed like an eternity, he drilled her. He hit her and slapped her; he even kissed and fondled her. Through the entire process, Jenna never changed her story. She was hurting; she briefly considered confessing if it would make Kain stop. By the look in his eyes, Jenna knew he would not stop until he was forced. Instead, she formed a picture of the goddess Pearl standing at the campsite waving and throwing a kiss to her. When Kain kissed her, she immediately spit in his face. This only managed to anger him, and he hit her harder.

Through the whole process, Boris and Ariel just watched. They never said a word. Occasionally they would look at each other and raise an eyebrow. Finally Boris placed his hand on Ariel's arm and nodded. She said, "Enough, Kain. Take her to a cell and have her looked at by the physicians."

Kain went to the doors and let a guard in. He gave him instructions, and they carried her away. As the guard picked her up, Jenna turned to Boris and Ariel and said, "You know if I had tried, I would have succeeded."

When the door closed, Kain said, "Never have I seen anything like this. She truly believes she is telling the truth that she is not guilty."

Boris said, "She is telling the truth. According to my spells, every word she said is true, including her final statement."

"Is it possible that she has convinced herself she is innocent and therefore is able to trick your spell?" asked Ariel.

Boris replied, "My spell does not work that way. It not only considers her words, but the way she says them. Her tone, her thoughts, everything. While you were questioning her, I cast a second spell. The spell I used on Commander Wallace to read his memory. There was no memory of her committing the attempt. The only explanation is that she is truly innocent."

No one spoke for a few moments then Boris continued. "I received a private letter from the commander at the garrison in Bartersville. He said even though this girl has the skills required to have committed the crime, he is not convinced she is guilty. He says he has never had any trouble with her. Everything being said about her skills is true. However, he thinks the city council is afraid because they have not found the guilty party. He thinks they have sent her as a means to protect themselves."

Kain said, "I questioned her for over five hours. If she was guilty, she would have confessed. I am sure of that. However, she never once wavered one iota from her story. Most people would have confessed just to stop the inquisition."

Ariel added, "Based on this questioning and the letter from the commander at the garrison, I think he is right. This Jenna has been given to us by the city council as a scapegoat in an attempt to save themselves."

Boris nodded his head in agreement.

Ariel stood up and went around the table. Kain could see the concerned look on her face. She said, "We have made a serious error with this girl. However, this is one that is easily corrected. In three days, we will have a public hearing. Kain, I want you to put out the word that in three days at high noon in the city square Jenna's fate will be announced. I will wait three days to give her time to heal. Kain make sure she gets the best attention available. At the hearing, we will tell the people the truth. We will tell them she is innocent and that the city fathers of Bartersville have tried to fool the entire kingdom. For this, they will pay with their lives. I want you to send a messenger to Bartersville as soon as you leave this room. Have the city council and constable arrested. Tell the commander what has happened here and instruct him to arrange for the election of a new city council and constable."

When she finished talking, Kain bowed and left the room. She looked at Boris, and he said, "This is the right thing to do."

Jenna had passed out as soon as she had made her final statement before she was carried out of the audience hall. She had been tortured for over five hours. She thought for sure she had some broken bones. She felt like her entire body was broken. The doctors had given her an elixir that was supposed to stop the pain, but so far it had not worked. It was dark in the room she guessed it was around midnight. A bright light appeared next to her bed. Jenna knew it was the goddess; she closed her eyes until the goddess told her to open them.

The goddess said, "You did well today," and laid a hand on Jenna. As she touched her, Jenna felt a sudden tingling all over her body. For a few seconds, she shook then she was healed. She said, "I have healed you. You will still be sore for a few days but you will be fine. Do not worry you will get your vengeance on those who have made you suffer this day. Sleep."

With that the goddess left, and Jenna was sound asleep.

CHAPTER 16 - ANOTHER TEST

In the days since Jack had come to the Winston estate, he and Linda had renewed their friendship. Everyone noticed how happy the two of them were together. Jack had also joined Linda and Vanessa on their daily horse rides. As a result, the three of them were becoming very close and were bonding into an inseparable trio.

It was early winter, and the weather was starting to change. In his mind, Jack knew it was too late in the year to launch a campaign against Ariel. So he decided not to bring up the subject until later. He was enjoying his time with Linnie and Vanessa. In his eyes, they were the two most beautiful women he had ever met. He realized just how much he had missed Linnie and how much he loved her.

Every chance they got, Jack and Linnie would sneak off alone to be with each other. During these brief moments, they would kiss, hold each other, and talk about the last twenty years. Today was no exception. Vanessa woke up with a severe headache and was not able to join them on the daily horse ride. Alone, Jack and Linda went riding through the estate. The countryside was quiet and peaceful. Jack enjoyed both the serenity and a chance at being alone with Linnie.

Every day on their rides, Linnie and Vanessa would show Jack a new area of the estate. Today was no different. Linnie took Jack to a small lake a couple of miles from the estate. Linnie told him this was one of her favorite spots. She liked the tall trees around the lake and the peacefulness. There was one large tree whose trunk was so large they could both sit with their backs to it and the trunk was still wider.

They had tethered the horses and were sitting at the trunk of the tree. They looked at each other and saw the same loving and longing look reflected in the other's eyes. They began to kiss. The kiss became long and passionate. They began caressing each other both over and under their clothes. Before long they were lying on the ground naked.

They kissed and explored every inch of each other's bodies. For hours they just enjoyed each other and made love time after time. They finished by telling each other "I love you." It was then they first realized how cold it was and that a light snow had started to fall. They laughed, got dressed, and headed back to the estate.

When they reached the estate Jack noticed a horse tied to the front gate of the yard. He said, "Linnie do you recognize that horse?"

Linnie said, "I think that is Commander Wallace's horse. It is about time for his quarterly report. If he is not here to report, then he has created an excuse to come here to see Vanessa. He is crazy about her. She likes him too, but I think she is playing hard to get. Actually, I think she does not want me to be alone, and that is why she has not accepted one of his proposals. Commander Wallace has been proposing to her for the last several years every time he sees her."

They stabled their horses and went in the house. Jack was curious to meet Commander Wallace. He had heard a lot about him. When Jack and Linnie walked into the study, Silas, Emily, Vanessa, and Commander Wallace all rose. Vanessa immediately noticed that Jack and Linnie were both glowing, and she suspected she knew why. She did not say anything; instead, she turned to Commander Wallace and said, "Commander, this is Jack, the young man we have been talking about."

Jack walked over to the commander and shook his hand. "Commander, I am pleased to finally meet you. I have heard many good things about you from many different people including those present."

Commander Wallace replied, "Jack, I am honored to finally meet the warrior who rescued all those people from the man beasts. Plus, I cannot thank you enough for your assistance in Northport. I have read the reports from both Sergeant Miller and Duchess Sheila. They both agree that if not for you all would have been lost."

Jack replied, "Thank you for the kind words. However, the stories of my contribution at Northport have been overstated I think. After all I am only one man. The sergeant and Duchess do not give themselves enough credit."

Silas and Emily asked everyone to sit. The commander noticed the looks and smiles between Jack, Linnie, and Vanessa. This made him jealous and caused him to not like or trust Jack. He said, "Jack, Mr. Jones and the duchess were just telling me about how you managed to survive the Crystal desert and live among the Rumalians. I must say it is quite an incredible story. In fact I find myself trying very hard to believe it. It just seems impossible for a small boy to survive such an ordeal."

Jack looked at the commander and knew he did not trust Jack. Jack knew that he was going to have to prove himself to the commander. As he thought about it, he decided it would probably be a good idea that way everyone would realize he was trustworthy. Jack said, "Commander, I can understand your hesitation. After all, out of nowhere, I have shown up with a story that is very hard to believe. However, I can assure you it is all true. I know I was aided by the gods, and that is the only way I managed to survive the ordeal."

The commander said, "Jack, I do not mean to be disrespectful, but since I do not know you, your assurances do not mean much to me."

The conversation was making Linnie angry, and she said, "Commander Wallace, you may not mean to be disrespectful, but I assure you that you are being very disrespectful not only to Jack but to everyone else here. Not to mention the rudeness of your behavior."

Before things got out of hand, Silas stepped in and said, "Before this gets out of hand, let me first say that in my opinion there is no question that Jack is who he says he is. Also the old wizard Morten and I had many conversations about the geography of our land. He was convinced the desert did end somewhere and another land existed. He based this opinion on research and stories he had heard while growing up. I do not need to remind you that the old wizard was over three hundred years old."

At the mention of Morten's name, Jack fondly remembered the old wizard and the brutal murder of him and the royal court. He decided he would end this needless argument and said, "Please, everyone, let's not argue about this. I am not offended by the commander's distrust, and I admit I have been expecting someone to react exactly like that. Therefore, I ask the commander to test me in order to prove my trustworthiness, loyalty, and heritage."

For a moment, no one said anything. Finally, the commander said, "Jack, I apologize for my behavior. I must say I am not questioning that you are who you say you are. After all by looking at you, I swear I am looking at your mother. But everyone should remember I am a lifelong military person. It is this military training that has made me a bit skeptical." He paused for a moment, considering his next words very carefully. He said, "Since you have volunteered to prove yourself, then I suggest we do just that."

Everyone else in the room began talking all at once. The commander's request had not fallen well with anyone. Linda and Vanessa were visibly very angry. Emily was appalled the commander would even suggest such a thing, and she was berating him. Silas was trying to calm her down.

Finally, it was Jack who restored order. He clapped his hands several times to get everyone's attention. When all was quiet, he said, "There is no need for all this hostility. The commander's request is very practical, and it was my idea. Therefore, I say name your test and I will pass it. However, I think the test should be something that after I complete it no one will be able to doubt my allegiance."

Silas said, "I think for the benefit of everyone we should do this. However, right now I think we should have a nice peaceful lunch. During lunch we can each think of a test that will accomplish the goal." He looked at everyone, one at a time and each nodded their agreement. "With that agreed on, let's go eat. I am famished."

Everyone stood and headed to the dining room. Jack and Linda walked hand in hand. Vanessa turned to Linda and gave her a sly smile, telling Linda she knew what had happened earlier that morning. Linda smiled and turned red. The commander noticed the looks and smiles and became even more jealous.

During the meal, everyone was pleasant, and conversation was polite. The earlier hostility seemed to disappear. After the meal, everyone slowly went back to the study. They all sat down and relaxed without saying a word. It was Jack who finally broke the nervous silence and said, "Since I have been away for so long I cannot make a suggestion as to what the test should be. Therefore, I think one of you will have to make the suggestion. Whatever it is, I will agree."

Throughout the entire meal, an idea had started to form in the commander's mind. He was not sure how everyone would take his suggestion, but he knew it was the only way he would be able to completely trust Jack.

He said, "Since Jack has asked us to make the test so it leaves no doubt, the test will have to be difficult not only in scope but also to accomplish. As a result, I believe I have just the test. There is an individual I think we can all agree the world would be a better place without around." He looked at everyone to make sure his point was getting through. By the looks on their faces, he could tell his meaning was indeed understood. He continued, "This individual would be Kain the Butcher. Therefore I say the test should be to have Jack kill Kain."

Jack did not know who this Kain was, but by the looks on everyone's face, he could tell this would truly accomplish his goal. So before anyone had a chance to say anything, Jack said, "I agree. I do not know who this Kain is, but by the looks on everyone's face, I can see he deserves to die. Therefore, I will do it."

It was Silas who spoke next, "Jack, before you agree to this you must know who Kain is. Kain is Ariel's personal hitman, assassin, or investigator. He lives in the palace at Twin Falls. Next to Ariel and Boris, he is the most powerful man in the Kingdom."

Jack said, "Based on what you just said, that makes this the perfect test. After I kill him, I think all doubt about me can be erased." Jack looked at the commander, and he nodded his head in agreement.

For the next hour, they discussed how to accomplish the test in a manner that would satisfy everyone. The commander wanted an eyewitness; he did not want to hear about how someone had killed Kain. Everyone seemed to agree this approach would be best. The problem was who the eyewitness should be. Many different names were mentioned, but the problem was none of them really knew who Kain was or what he looked like. Neither did they know their way around Twin Falls well enough to guide Jack through the city. Everyone agreed the city had grown too much for Jack to remember his way around the city.

Finally Vanessa said, "The solution to this problem is easy. We need someone who can not only identify Kain but also someone who can guide Jack through the city and whom we all can trust. There is only one person who can satisfy all these conditions. That person is me. I will go with Jack."

Commander Wallace immediately objected. Not because the idea did not make sense, because it really did, but because his jealousy jumped to the forefront of his feelings. No one else was arguing the idea.

Finally Silas said, "Commander, we all understand your hesitation given your feelings for Vanessa. However, this truly is the best solution. You will not have to worry. Jack will make sure that nothing happens to Vanessa."

Although he hated the idea of Jack being alone with Vanessa, the commander could see the truth of the situation. Vanessa was the best person to fit the requirements. So he reluctantly agreed. They spent the rest of the day planning how to get Jack access to Kain and an escape route. They realized much of the plan would have to be formulated once they arrived in Twin Falls.

Jack did not say much while they were planning. He only occasionally asked questions. He was considering the situation and knew this was going to have a harsh outcome for him. He did not care though because he knew it was necessary. So while everyone was planning, Jack began praying to the gods for strength and guidance through the upcoming ordeal.

It was decided that Jack and Vanessa should leave as soon as possible. Since winter had already arrived the weather would only get worse and make it hard to travel. Two days later, Jack and Vanessa were ready to leave. It was midmorning as they made the final preparations to leave. Commander Wallace pulled Vanessa aside and said, "Vanessa you know how I feel about you. It is because of my feelings for you that I do not like sending you off with a man I do not know on this very dangerous trip. I must ask you to be careful, and will you marry me?"

Vanessa smiled and said, "I would be a liar if I said I do not have feelings for you. When we get back, I will give you the answer to your question. In the meantime, do not worry I will be fine, and besides I think we will both like my answer." The commander stood there stunned, not knowing what to say to her. Vanessa smiled, kissed him on the cheek, and went back to her horse.

They left shortly after Vanessa had spoken with the commander. They set a steady pace. They talked about anything and everything. Vanessa told Jack that Linnie had told her about their escapade under the tree. Vanessa just smiled a wicked smile at Jack because she knew she had embarrassed him. Jack then asked her why she was playing hard to get with the commander. He said it was obvious to everyone that she cared for him. Just as Linda had suspected, she replied she did not want to leave Linda alone and therefore she was delaying the inevitable. However, she explained maybe she did not have to delay it anymore, again giving Jack the wicked smile she knew embarrassed him.

Unfortunately for them, that afternoon, the weather turned bad. The first winter blizzard hit, and it hit hard. To make matters worse, they were nowhere near a town or village where they could find shelter. They decided to find a place that offered some shelter where they could put up their tent. They found a small copse of large trees that would provide small shelter from the wind and snow. It was here they setup their tent.

The tent was a small tent that was really designed for just one person. As a result of that, they had to lie down on their sides facing each other. In order to stay warmer, they decided to hug each other to take advantage of the combined body heat. Vanessa was a beautiful woman and to have her in his arms in such tight quarters made Jack feel a little uncomfortable. Jack being the man he was could not help but react to having a beautiful woman next to him. It seemed to him that Vanessa was reading his mind because she just looked at him with that wicked smile.

After a few minutes, Vanessa could no longer ignore the pressure of Jack's manhood against her. She reached down with her hand and grabbed it. She squeezed it hard and rubbed it gently. All the while she was looking at Jack with that wicked smile. She continued to caress him. Finally Jack could no longer ignore her, and he looked at her.

Vanessa said, "I was wondering how long you would be able to resist. I am glad to see it did not take long."

With that, Jack reached down and kissed her. One thing led to another, and before long, they were both naked and making love. They made love off and on all night long. The next morning, the storm had passed, and they resumed their journey. The next night they stopped about an hour before nightfall because they were in a small town, with an inn, and the next town or village was several hours' ride away. They took a room at the inn. When they got to the room, Vanessa again looked at Jack with that wicked smile. This time they had a bed so they were able to fully enjoy each other. Again all night long, they made love, this time taking their time to kiss and explore each other's bodies.

It took them eight days and nights to reach Twin Falls. Every night they stopped in small towns with an inn. Every time they got to the room, Vanessa had that wicked smile on her face and Jack knew what she wanted. They spent every night in each other's arms.

When they finally made it to Twin Falls, Jack was shocked at how much the town had grown since the last time he had been there. The entire city was a buzz about a public hearing in the town square the next day. Apparently it had something to do with an attempted assassination on Ariel. Vanessa was able to find out that Kain would be at the hearing. Therefore, they decided Jack would simply have to find a place to shoot from. They spent the afternoon finding a suitable spot.

After they found what they thought to be the best spot, they took a room at an inn located only two blocks from the square. When they got into the room, Jack sat Vanessa down on the edge of the bed and reached back behind his back and drew the God Stone Sword. He said, "I want you to hold this for me tomorrow. No matter what happens, good or bad, do not give this sword to anyone. Do not allow anyone to touch it. If anyone besides you touches it, they will die. You can touch it because I have told the sword you will be its caretaker for a while. This is a very special sword filled with magic. It is the magic within the sword that makes it so dangerous."

"If something happens to me tomorrow, just keep the sword until someone comes to you and asks you for the sword. Do not worry. You will know that they should have the sword. I know this sounds mysterious, but I cannot tell you more at this time. If I survive and make it back to North Pointe, I will explain it all.

At midmorning the next day, Jack and Vanessa went to their spot. They were about seventy-five yards from the platform. They agreed that Vanessa would identify Kain to Jack and then get lost in the crowd and they would meet back at the inn later after the commotion died down.

People had already started to gather in the square. Right at noon a procession of troops arrived and took their place forming an isle for the rest of the procession. Ariel and Boris were the first to walk up on the platform. When Jack saw them, he froze. He immediately recognized them as the two people who had caused him all the hardships in his life. He started to feel nervous, and for the first the time, he was a little unsure of himself. He said a quick prayer to the gods.

When he opened his eyes, Vanessa was staring at him, and she could see the hatred in his eyes for Ariel and Boris. Jack looked back at the platform, and Boris and Ariel had been joined by a tall muscular man and a young girl. The girl was in chains and being pulled by the tall muscular man. Vanessa told him the muscular man was Kain. Jack acknowledged her and told her to leave. She left and mingled into the crowd.

Ariel stepped forward and told how this young girl was accused by the city fathers of Bartersville as the individual who had tried to kill her. However, after interrogation, it was obvious that the girl was innocent. She signaled for Kain to bring the girl forward.

When Jack saw Ariel, he was tempted to shoot her instead, but he knew he had to wait; this was not the time or place for this to happen. So when Ariel called Kain forward, he knew this was his chance. Before anyone around him could notice what was happening, Jack took out his bow and two arrows. He notched the first arrow, raised the bow, aimed, and fired. As soon as the arrow left the bow, Jack notched the second arrow and fired.

The first shot entered Kain through his left eye and exited out the back of his head. Just seconds later, the second arrow hit him in the throat. That arrow also went all the way through and stuck out the back of his neck. Kain fell back and was dead before he hit the ground.

Soldiers spotted Jack and immediately attacked him. The soldiers were well-trained and good fighters. However, they were no match for Jack. Jack easily parried their attacks and killed them. In a matter of moments, a dozen soldiers lay dead on the ground around Jack. The number was growing rapidly. It was obvious to anyone watching the fighting that Jack was going to be able to escape. The fact did not escape Boris, and he decided to act.

Boris conjured up his magic and fired a bolt of lightning at Jack. Jack felt the magic and tried to find the source. The bolt would have struck Jack fully in the chest if he had been standing still, and as a result, the bolt struck right behind him. The bolt caused a thunderous explosion, and Jack was tossed a dozen feet into the air. When he landed, he bumped his head hard and passed out.

Anna did not know why this public meeting was different from the others. She very rarely attended any of these types of gatherings. She told herself it was because Ariel and Boris were actually going to do the right thing for a change that she decided to attend. She was standing at the edge of the platform between the isles of soldiers. Anna jumped when she saw Kain hit the floor of the platform dead. She noticed the commotion on the far side of the square, and she climbed a few steps up to the platform.

When Anna was high enough on the steps to see what the commotion was all about, she saw a man easily killing the soldiers. Her breath caught in her throat; she thought her heart would burst. Not because Kain was dead but because she immediately recognized the man fighting the soldiers. It was Jack, her son Jack. She remembered the visit from the goddess Athena three years ago. The goddess had told her that Jack was alive and she would see him again. She also remembered the goddess had told her that he had become a great warrior. And now there he was fighting like the greatest warrior she had ever seen.

When the bolt of lightning flew across the square and exploded next to Jack, Anna screamed. Everyone around thought she was screaming from fear of what was going on.

Jack was aware that he was being carried somewhere. When he fully regained consciousness, he was being tied by the soldiers on the platform. In front of him stood Ariel and Boris.

Ariel said, "First let the girl go. She is free." Then she looked at Boris and stepped back.

Boris came forward and asked him, "Who are you and who sent you? Are the one who tried to kill the queen in Bartersville?"

Jack looked at him and said, "I am nobody, and nobody sent me. I killed the one I came here to kill."

Boris was furious and began to punch Jack. First he punched him in the face then the stomach. He called a guard over and ordered him to remove Jack's shirt and he began to whip him. Boris struck Jack repeatedly with the whip. He struck with all his might. He did not stop until he became tired. He went around in front of Jack and noticed that Jack was still breathing and conscious. He ordered two big soldiers to continue the torture. They beat Jack with their fists all over his face, chest, stomach, and back. Then they each took a whip and whipped his legs. One of them whipped the back of his legs while the other whipped the front of his legs.

Jack's entire body was striped with whip marks. His face and chest were bruised from the brutal beating he had taken. Finally Boris stopped the soldiers to take a look at Jack. Jack was unconscious but was still alive.

Boris said, "Enough. Let him die slowly over the rest of the day and night. Hang him over the edge of the platform and leave him there. In the morning come see if he is still alive. If he is still alive beat him some more and leave him hanging. Keep coming back until he is dead."

Anna could not believe what she was seeing. When Boris told the soldiers to hang Jack over the platform, she stepped down to the ground and walked away from the platform. When she had cleared the soldiers, she began running. She ran all the way back to the palace and went straight to her quarters. She made sure to avoid anyone. She would not be able to talk to anybody right now. When she made it into her rooms she began to cry.

She cried and cried no matter how hard she tried not cry and to bring herself under control she could not stop crying. She could not believe that Jack had survived all these years only to end up dying at the very hands of the people he hated most. She knew that Jack had to hate Boris and Ariel. Then she remembered the goddess and what she had told her. She began to pray asking why the gods would be so cruel to her. After all these years why should she be allowed such a small glimpse of her son?

That thought gave her some comfort. She realized that the goddess Athena would not be so cruel and that this glimpse could not have been what the goddess meant when she had said she would see her son again. Suddenly Anna felt someone's arms around her. She looked up and it was the goddess Athena who was holding her. At first the goddess did not say anything she just comforted her.

Athena let Anna cry for a few moments more. Then she began to speak. "Your son took this burden upon himself voluntarily. He knew this was the only way he could convince certain individuals of his allegiances. He began praying for strength to complete this task regardless of the consequences to him. He understands he cannot bring down Ariel and Boris by himself; he knows he needs help to do that. He needed to prove his intentions to those who would help him. He could not come up with a better way to prove his loyalty. There is more at stake here than just your son's life. And you are right to think that this short glimpse is not what I meant when I told you that you would see your son again. Take heart my dearest child your son will live through this and he will get the opportunity to right not only the wrongs that have been done to him, but wrongs that have been done to countless others. His slaying of Kain today is only the beginning of his opportunity."

Athena kissed Anna on the forehead and disappeared. Anna was now able to control herself. She washed her face and returned to the palace and her duties.

Jenna was shocked at the sudden turn of events. She was free. She could not believe the skill required to have shot two shots so accurately from such a distance. If she had not witnessed it, she would not have believed it. Then the skill with which this man fought. Never before had Jenna seen anyone fight like this man had fought. He had killed close to thirty men by himself in a matter of moments. He would have escaped if Boris had not used magic against him. She was even more amazed at the courage with which he had resisted the torture. The torture he had received was far worse than what had been done to her.

The torture of this man was done with the intent to torture him, to cause pain. What had been done to her was planned and not done with malicious intent. This, however, was done with the intent to kill. Yet this man had survived and still defied the authorities. She knew it was this defiance in the face of death that had angered Boris so greatly.

Jenna wondered if this was the man the goddess Pearl had meant when she told her another would come along and fulfill what she had attempted. For some reason Jenna could not shake the thought from her mind. Finally it came to her. If this was the man the goddess meant, then he was still alive and would not be dead in the morning when the soldiers came to beat him some more. Jenna knew in her heart she had to do something to help this man.

Vanessa was mingling in the crowd and had made it almost to the front. She was careful not to get to close in because someone on the platform might recognize her. When Ariel called Kain to the front with the girl, she knew this was when Jack would strike. Sure enough she saw the arrows hit their mark perfectly. She smiled because she now knew Linnie had been right about Jack all along. Linnie was the only one who had never wavered in her belief about Jack and his loyalty.

She watched until Kain hit the platform dead. Then she heard the cling of metal on metal and turned to see what was happening. A tall man was telling everyone what was happening. Based on the awestruck look on the tall man's face as he described what was happening, she knew these people had never seen anyone fight with the skill Jack possessed. When she saw the lightning bolt fly across the square overhead, she panicked. She held her breath waiting to hear what had happened. Then the people started to part to allow the soldiers through.

The soldiers were carrying Jack to the platform. They carried him right in front of her. She saw that Jack was unconscious. She watched him as they carried him. When the soldiers reached the bottom of the platform, she saw Jack begin to move as he regained his consciousness.

When they tied Jack up and Boris began to torture him, Vanessa felt guilty. She felt this was her fault. This was hers, Commander Wallace, Silas, and Emily's fault because they had not truly accepted Jack. As the beating continued, she felt as if each stroke was being racked against her very soul. She felt ashamed and embarrassed. When the beating finally stopped and she heard the instructions, she along with the rest of the crowd turned around and walked away.

Vanessa went back to the inn and the room they had rented. She cried for hours. She did not know what to do. She was beginning to panic; she had to do something she could not just leave Jack hanging there. At mid afternoon it came to her, and she knew what she had to do.

First she had to find a different form of transportation. She found a livery stable and traded their horses for a small wagon and team of horses. She knew she had paid too much for the wagon and team, but that did not matter. Next she went to one of several animal markets in the city. She found a merchant that sold small chickens usually sold for laying eggs. She bought twenty-five small chicks. The merchant even had small bottomless wire cages he sold. She bought one of them as well. The cage fit perfectly in the back of her wagon. The merchant recommended she buy some hay to spread on the bottom of the wagon. He told her where there was a merchant that could sell her the hay.

She went to the hay merchant and when she pulled up and he saw what was in the back of her wagon he knew exactly what she needed. She bought two of the odd-sized hay bales from the merchant. The merchant told her that one was all she needed. She explained that it was a long way home for her and she wanted to be sure she had enough. Actually she wanted to be sure she had enough to hide a body below the hay.

It was almost dark by the time Vanessa made it back to the inn. She ate a quick meal and went upstairs to their room. She packed up all their belongings went downstairs and settled their bill. Then she took the wagon and went around the corner from the inn. From there she could see the city square and Jack's body hanging. Now all she had to do was wait.

Vanessa waited until three hours after midnight. She wanted to be sure no one would be awake to see what she was about to do. She slowly walked the horses and wagon to the square. She looked all around to make sure it was safe before continuing. Once satisfied it was safe, she walked the team to the platform. She was extremely nervous, her hands were sweating, and her heart was pounding so hard she thought it was going to burst out of her chest.

She maneuvered the wagon so that Jack's body was hanging directly above the bed of the wagon. When she went to the back of the wagon she saw movement in the shadows. She immediately took a defensive posture with a knife in her right hand. The shadow came closer and said, "Do not be afraid I am here to help. My name is Jenna, and I am the girl they released this morning before he killed Kain."

Before Vanessa could say anything, she noticed that Jenna had tensed up and also took a defensive position. Vanessa turned to see another movement in the shadows. As the figure came closer, she recognized that it was Anna. She said, "Anna what are you doing here?"

Anna walked up to the wagon so she could she who it was that had recognized her. When she saw Vanessa everything became clear to her. She smiled and said, "Did you think I would not recognize my own son?"

Vanessa noticed the tears in Anna's eyes. She said, "Anna I am sorry but we do not have time for this right now. I cannot explain but rest assured that everything will be okay."

Anna looked at her and said, "Oh, I think I know exactly what is going on here. I also know if my son is involved then it is a good cause. So let's get to work before someone sees us.

Jack was feverish and in and out of consciousness. However, he knew he was being moved, but it was still dark and the soldiers had been told to wait until morning. Jack felt himself being lowered down onto what felt like hay.

Between the three women, they cut the ropes that held Jack and lowered him into the wagon. Jenna went inside the chicken cage and covered him with the hay. Before Jenna completely covered him, Anna went to Jack and said, "Jack, my dear boy." She was crying and her tears fell on his face.

Jack felt the tears on his face and heard a voice that sounded familiar but how could it be. He thought he heard the voice of his mother. He tried as hard as he could to open his eyes but could not all he could do was say a single word: "Mother". Anna being so close to him heard him speak and knew Jack was aware she was there. She kissed him on the forehead and let Jenna finish covering him up.

Anna looked at Vanessa and said, "He burns with fever. You must hurry and take care of him."

Vanessa looked at her and said, "I will."

Jenna immediately said, "We will."

Vanessa did not know what to say to Jenna. However, she knew that because of Jack's condition, she would need help. She really had no choice; besides this girl was risking her life to help her. Jenna noticed the look of hesitation on Vanessa's face and said, "Look, I have no money, no horse, nothing. I am from Bartersville, but I have no way to get there. Besides after everything that has happened, I doubt the city fathers will allow me back in the city. I have nowhere else to go. Please, I need to do this."

Vanessa looked at Anna, who nodded her approval and she made up her mind. She said, "Very well, but you must do exactly as I say, when I say it, and no questions asked."

Jenna grinned and said, "Agreed." With that, they said goodbye to Anna and headed to the city gates. Vanessa drove the wagon slowly so they made as little noise as possible. By the time they made it to the city gates, the sun was just starting to rise; it was dawn.

Vanessa wanted to be out of the city before the soldiers came and found Jack's body missing. As a result, they were the first in line to leave the city that morning. The guard was not fully awake, and as he was yawning, they pulled the wagon up to the city gate. He looked at them and in the back of the wagon. Since it was dawn, the young chicks were coming awake and were very active and noisy. Vanessa was glad to hear the chicks making all that noise because earlier she had heard Jack moaning. She was hoping the noise of the chicks would cover up any moaning that Jack made.

The guard said, "Chicken farmers, huh?"

"Yes, and we have a hard day's ride to get home, and our father will not tolerate us deviating from his schedule. So we have no choice but to leave early."

The guard replied, "Your father is correct to not allow any leeway. He is obviously a good man." He barked out orders to the other gate guards to get up off their lazy asses and get to work. He told them to open the gates and start letting people through.

Vanessa thanked the guard and guided the team out the gates and away from the city. Silas had told her about some trails that sprouted off the main road. He recommended they take these trails on the way back. It would take them closer to the mountains but away from the main road. The main road would be watched once they realized what had happened. Two hours after they left the city, Vanessa took a trail that headed north towards the mountains

As they got closer to the mountains, the trail started turning west. Vanessa then thought the trail was going to circle the mountains toward the west. At midmorning, they came to a stream. Vanessa pulled the wagon over as close as possible to the stream. She told Jenna that they had to clean Jack's wounds. Since they had the chicks in the back if anyone were to come along it would look like they were getting water for the chicks.

It was after lunch before they finished cleaning all the wounds on Jack. Jack was still feverish and in and out of consciousness. They left several wet rags on his forehead, around his neck, and chest. They ate some cheese and bread before continuing on.

The ladies had not talked much until now. Jenna was very curious as to where they were going. She said, "Vanessa, where are we going?"

Vanessa realized she did not know anything about Jenna and yet she was trusting her with everything by bringing her along. She decided to only tell Jenna enough to answer her questions and to get to know her better. She said, "I will tell you where we are going then I want you to tell me about yourself. We have a long trip ahead of us so we might as well get to know each other."

Jenna smiled and said, "Okay."

Vanessa said, "We are going to North Pointe. My family has an estate there. We will be safe once we get there. However, until we get there, we must be very careful."

Jenna's eyes went wide with amazement at what she heard. She needed to tell someone the truth about herself. Considering the fact that Vanessa had just stolen the body of a criminal in the eyes of the queen, she felt she could trust her and decided to tell her everything. Once she began to tell Vanessa her story, she could not stop. She told her everything from the beginning. She told her how she was the illegitimate daughter of George Long. She explained that her mother had raised her to hate Ariel and Boris and that was why she had tried to assassinate her.

Jenna noticed the confused look on Vanessa's face when she admitted to having tried to kill Ariel. She explained about how the goddess Pearl had visited her and helped her trick Boris and his magic. Jenna told her how she had planned the attempt on Ariel's life. She explained every detail of what had happened. She even told her what the goddess had told her about someone coming along who had suffered more than her and who would be given the opportunity to finish what she had tried.

When Jenna mentioned the words of the goddess, Vanessa knew meeting Jenna was more than a mere coincidence. She was positive that the person the goddess had referred to had to be Jack. She relaxed about Jenna and decided she could be trusted.

By the time Jenna finished telling her story, it was well after dark. They came to another stream, and Vanessa decided this was a good place to spend the night. Once again they cleaned Jack's wounds. The weather was cool so that helped to keep Jack cool. It took them three days to skirt around the mountains. Vanessa knew they now had no choice but to get on the main road. Vanessa found a trail that headed north and took it. Around mid afternoon, they came to the main road. Fortunately for them the weather was cold, and there was not much traffic on the road.

They spent the night in a livery stable in a small town. They pretended not to have enough money to pay for a room in the inn. The story worked, and they were able to spend the night in the barn of the livery stable. The next morning, the owner of the livery stable felt sorry for them, and he fed them a hot breakfast of eggs and bacon. They thanked him for his kindness and headed north again.

The farther north they went, the colder and worse the weather became. Two nights later, they found themselves in the barn of a small farm. A winter storm had hit, and they had no choice but to find the first shelter they could. This farmer had agreed to let them stay in his barn. The farmhand that worked at the farm had to stay in the barn also because the weather was too bad to allow him to go home. The farmhand told them about how a great warrior had killed Kain the Butcher and over thirty soldiers before being trapped by Boris's magic. Then he told them how someone had stolen the body.

The farmhand told them this had made both Boris and Ariel very angry. He told them rumor had it there was an elite troop of warriors going around killing important people in the government. He said it was one of them who had tried to kill the queen in Bartersville. It was them who had stolen the body of the warrior who had killed Kain. Vanessa and Jenna just looked at each other with a knowing nod. Vanessa was glad to hear there were rumors being spread because the more outrageous the rumors were the less anyone would suspect that three women had stolen the body. It was even less likely they would believe that two of them had the great warrior and were heading north with him.

It was midday the next day before the storm let up enough that the ladies could continue their trek north. They thanked the farmer and the farmhand and headed north again. It was mid morning of the eleventh day when the team entered the driveway of the Winston estate in North Pointe.

Jenna had never seen anything as beautiful as this estate. She was interrupted in her amazement by four figures running toward them, in the snow, from the house. Vanessa stopped the team and jumped down and ran to meet Emily. She embraced her and cried. Linda, Commander Wallace, and Silas were all there. They all had tears in their eyes as they greeted each other.

Jenna gave the impromptu family reunion a few moments then drove the team up to the house. Vanessa said, "Everyone, this is Jenna and don't worry she can be trusted. If not for her, I could not have made it. We have to hurry. Jack needs medical attention." She walked over to the back of the wagon and had the servants remove the cage, the chicks, and hay. There lay Jack trembling with fever.

Commander Wallace and Silas carried Jack into the house and upstairs to the room he had been staying in. Emily immediately sent one of the servants to town to fetch the doctor. In the meantime, she said, "You two look half-dead. We need to get you a good hot meal and cleaned up. Linda while Sarah makes a hot meal you help Vanessa and Jenna get cleaned up."

By the time the girls were cleaned up, the meal was ready. Everyone ate. Vanessa and Jenna ate till their hearts content. As they finished the meal, the doctor arrived. They all followed him upstairs to Jack's room. The room was large enough to accommodate everyone, and there was still enough room for the doctor to work on Jack.

The doctor said, "This young man is lucky to be alive. Honestly, I do not know how he could have survived such torture. With the medication I have given him, his fever should break by morning. If that happens, then he will be all right. It will take time for some of those wounds to heal. He has a couple of broken ribs, and some of those cuts are very deep. If he makes it until morning and the fever breaks, he will survive." His job being done, the doctor left.

After the doctor left, Vanessa asked Jenna to tell everyone her story. She said, "Tell them everything just like you told me." Vanessa explained that Jenna's story had bearing on what happened to Jack.

Once again Jenna told her story. She told them everything just like she had told Vanessa. She told them about her father, the goddess, the assassination attempt, how she with the help of the goddess had fooled Boris and his magic. She told them about the public hearing at which she was freed. Then she looked to Vanessa who told them the rest of the story.

Vanessa told them about the two perfect shots Jack had hit Kain with. She told them of how he had fought the soldiers and how easily and quickly he had killed about thirty of them before Boris had struck with a lightning bolt. Then she told them of how they tortured Jack and how she had to stand there and witness it all. She was crying out of control by the time she finished telling about the torture. Linda came to her and they cried together.

After a few moments, Vanessa continued her story. She told them how she met Jenna and Anna at the platform that night. She told them how they had made their getaway. When Vanessa finished talking a bright light appeared in the middle of the room. The light was so bright that everyone had to hide their eyes. After a few moments, the god Ator said, "Uncover your eyes, my children."

Everyone looked up and saw five individuals standing around Jack's bed. They all recognized the gods and immediately went to their knees. Again Ator spoke, "I am Ator, father of the gods. Rise, my children." Everyone rose, and Ator signalled for them to take their seats.

Ator then continued. "We have come here today first to dispel any doubts anyone of you may have about Jack and his allegiances. First Jack is loyal to us the gods. He has proven this to us time and time again. Second he is loyal in his love for you Linda and his mother. Third he is loyal to the fulfilment of his promise to you Linda. He is loyal to whatever it takes to accomplish that promise. We the gods had given up hope on the human race. It was my daughter Zephra who convinced us thousands of years ago that the human race was still worthy and deserved our support. It was because of her faith in the human race that we made the prophecy of the chosen one.

"We are here today to tell you that the prophecy has come true. This young man, Jack, who lies here near his death, is the long ago promised chosen one. Vanessa the sword he asked you to hold for him is the God Stone Sword." Everyone looked at the sword that Vanessa had leaned against the wall. The God Stone was shining in its full brilliance.

"Jack placed a spell on the stone so it would not shine like that. It was this little boy's plight across the desert that brought our attention to him. Everything he has told you about his trek is true. There is more that he has not told you. Let me assure you Jack's heart is pure. You are correct, Commander Wallace, in thinking that an eight-year-old boy could not survive such a trek. However, because of his faith and prayer to us we helped him when he needed it. We only gave him the extra strength he needed to keep going and we did not let him die. We also tested him at every opportunity we had. Throughout his life, we have tested him. Maybe someday he will tell you about those tests. Every time we tested him he came through stronger than before. Never once did his faith waver. Never once did he stop praying for you, Linda, to survive. Never once did he stop praying for his mother, and never once did he stop praying for the opportunity to fulfil his promise to you Linda.

"When we allowed him to find the way home, we decided to test him one final time. We asked him to spend three years in the Northern Mountains fighting the man beasts. He had ample opportunity to leave the mountains, but he never took it. He remained faithful to his test. His three years in the mountains were very hard on Jack. Not since the battle with my brother Zultar has the earth seen battles such as the ones he fought in the mountains."

Pointing to Pearl and Zephra, Ator said, "Jack even forsook the love of not one but two goddess. My daughters came to him and offered him an eternal life as a god and promised him their undivided love. He turned them down because his heart belonged to you, Linda. For these reasons and many more, he is the long ago promised chosen one."

Commander Wallace upon hearing all this was internally berating himself for letting jealousy not allow him to trust Jack.

Ator, knowing the commander's thoughts, said, "No, Commander Wallace, do not berate yourself. Jack knew your plan was the only way to eliminate all doubts from everyone. While all of you were planning the trip to Twin Falls, Jack already was praying to us for strength and guidance in this ordeal. He prayed for the strength he would need for the torture he would suffer if he got caught."

"Do not worry. Jack will survive these wounds. He will be given the opportunity to correct the many wrongs that have been done to him and many others." Ator then turned to Jenna and said, "Yes, Jenna, this is whom Pearl was referring when she told you someone would come along that had suffered more than you, and would be given the opportunity to right the wrongs of Ariel."

When Ator finished, the bright light returned, and everyone had to cover their eyes. When they were able to uncover their eyes, the gods had left. Linda rose from her seat and went to Jack's bedside took his hand, kissed it, and said, "I always knew I could depend on you. Even back at the palace when we were kids, I could always count on you."

Emily said, "Linda, I always thought you clinging to that promise were a childish dream on your part. I thought it was your way of not wanting to let go of what had happened to your parents. I see now how wrong I was."

Silas spoke next, saying, "Well now that we know the truth about Jack what is our next step?"

To everyone's surprise, it was Commander Wallace who answered the question. "The next step is to allow Jack to heal so that in the spring he can lead us against Ariel." Everyone nodded in agreement.

CHAPTER 17 — REVOLUTION

The next day when Jack finally opened his eyes, it was about noon. Linda was in the room with him. Her face was the first thing he saw when he opened his eyes. She smiled and kissed him and said, "I love you."

Jack smiled and said, "I love you too."

Linda told Jack they had arrived the previous afternoon. She explained about Jenna and told him how the gods had come to them and told them he was the "chosen one." Jack tried to sit up, but he was in too much pain. Linda went to the door and hollered, "Everyone, Jack is awake."

Vanessa was the first one in the room; with her a young girl Jack did not know entered. Vanessa noticed the non-recognition on Jack's face and introduced Jenna to him. Emily and Silas came in, and they spent the next several hours just talking about the killing of Kain and the visit of the gods. Everyone was full of questions for Jack. They all wanted to know about how he had been selected by the gods to be the chosen one. Jack would have loved to keep talking with everyone, but his strength ran out.

For the next two weeks, he was in and out of consciousness. Finally he had enough strength to sit up and eat on his own. After that the healing process was faster. Jack had to first work the soreness out of his body, then he was able to start retraining his body to get back into fighting condition. It took most of the winter and lots of hard work, but when spring came around Jack had regained his conditioning and was ready to move on with their plans.

As soon as spring came around, Commander Wallace came to the estate to make his report and to see how Jack was doing. He was very surprised to find that Jack had already made a full recovery. The commander took Jack aside and apologized for doubting him and having caused him all the pain and suffering. As he expected Jack told him not to worry about it that everything had happened for a reason and was necessary.

After lunch everyone gathered in the study and began to discuss what to do next. It was Jack who finally made a suggestion that everyone agreed on. Jack said, "I think we should invite the Duchess Sheila and Sergeant Miller here and present them with the facts and our plans. We should give them the opportunity to join us."

Commander Wallace then added, "I think Linda should address all the troops. She should tell them who she really is and see if they will support her legal and rightful claim to the throne of the Kingdom."

Everyone agreed with the plan. Emily and Silas planned a small dinner party. They sent out invitations to the mayor, a few key merchants and businessmen around town. In addition they sent an invitation to Duchess Sheila and Sergeant Miller. Their invitations had a short note that stated they were needed to discuss a matter of the utmost importance. The note was Linda's idea to make sure they would attend.

Linda spent all her free time thinking about what she would say to the soldiers. She wanted to be honest with them and at the same time instill a sense of justice. She wanted them to join her not because of who she was but because it was the right thing to do. She did not want anyone to help her with the speech. She said she needed to do this on her own. As a result, when she went off on her own, everyone left her alone.

On the day of the dinner party, everyone was a little nervous. The guests started to arrive a little early. In truth it was only Sergeant Miller and Duchess Sheila who arrived early. They visited with everyone and were very surprised to find the warrior at the estate. They asked how he had come to be there, but the only answer they got was that his presence would be explained later when all the guests arrived.

Finally all the guests arrived and the dinner party got under way. First everyone enjoyed some drinks and hors d'oeuvres. The main course was brought out, and everyone sat around the dinner table and ate. It was finally Duchess Sheila who could not stand it anymore, and she blurted out, "Emily, my dear friend. While seeing you and your family and other honored guests is truly a pleasure, I doubt you invited us all here to socialize."

Emily and Silas looked at each other and smiled then they both turned to Linda. Linda nodded and stood up.

Linda said, "You are correct, Duchess. We did not invite you all here to socialize. You are here tonight because I have to tell you a story and then ask for your help." She looked around at all of them before continuing, "This story starts twenty years ago, and I must warn you it will test your patriotism and loyalty to the Kingdom. At the height of the war between Independent City and the Kingdom, King Phillip, realizing that all was lost, sent his daughter away from the palace. He did this in order to have the royal line saved just in case a victory was managed. He sent her out under the care of the royal treasurer. A man named Vernon Silas. Together they came here to North Pointe and settled in. Today you know them as Silas and Linda Jones."

She paused to let her words sink in. Again she looked at each of the guests and made sure she made eye contact with them all. Then she continued. "When our employer, the Duchess Winston, connected the pieces and discovered the truth, she brought Commander Wallace here, and we had a long discussion. It turned out that both Duchess Winston and the commander had no love for the usurper Ariel. We made a plan to recruit an army that would be loyal to us and not to Ariel. In order to hide our true intentions, we devised an entrance/ recruitment questionnaire that would allow us to determine the true loyalty of each new recruit. Only those that would be loyal to our cause were allowed to join. In order to accomplish this, we had to bring Sergeant Miller in on our plan." Turning to the sergeant, she asked, "Do you recall these events?" Sergeant Miller immediately answered, "Yes, I do, and I would like to add that I am still in favor of such a plan."

Linda smiled at the sergeant and continued, "We all agreed that in order for our plan to succeed we needed 20,000 troops. Today between North Pointe and North Port we have 22,500 troops. Given these numbers and the Sgt's earlier answer I think you can guess why we have asked you here today. We have brought you here to ask you if you will support me in my effort to regain the throne of the Kingdom; a throne that rightfully belongs to me." She then stopped talking and looked everyone directly in the eye.

For a moment, there was silence, and each of the guests just looked at each other. Finally it was the mayor who spoke up, "Young lady you took a big chance in bringing us here tonight and telling us who you really are and your plans. I have to assume that Emily, Commander Wallace, and you Silas are all in favor of this plan or we would not be here. However, I still have one question." Turning to Jack he said, "We still have not heard your story or involvement in all this. I understand now that you are the warrior that has saved us from the man beasts but other than that we know nothing about you."

Jack looked at Linda then to Silas. They both nodded their approval for him to tell his story. For the next half hour, Jack told them his story. He told them about how he had watched as Ariel and Boris murdered the royal council. How he was exiled for not bowing to Ariel. He told them about his ordeal in the desert and how the Rumalians had found him more dead than alive. He told them about how he grew up and his training as a warrior. He told them about the Horde and the constant battle between the plains tribes and the Horde. He told them about the pulling sensation he had and about the last battle with the Horde and the trunks he found.

He told them about the map and his trek north to the Northern Pass. He told them he had stayed to fight the man beasts because they were an abomination and insulting to the gods. He explained about his promise to Linda and his faith in the gods. He explained how throughout the twenty years of his exile he always prayed to the gods. He said the gods rewarded him by giving him the ability to fight, stay alive, find his childhood friend, and finally giving him the opportunity to fulfill his promise to her.

When he finished, it was the Duchess Sheila who asked, "If we decide to join your cause. How can we fight against Boris? He is a wizard."

Jack answered, saying, "I will take care of Boris the same way I took care of Kain." This surprised the guests, and everyone fell silent. Commander Wallace explained how he had tested Jack by asking him to prove his loyalty and abilities by killing Kain.

Finally Jenna stood up and told the guests her story. She told them everything including who her father was and the appearance of the goddess Pearl. She told them what the goddess had told her and instructed her to do in order to fool Boris's mind probe sorcery. She told them how Jack had killed Kain, on the day of her being judged and set free. She told them how Jack had in a matter of minutes killed over thirty men before Boris hit him with his lightning.

Upon hearing this, the Mayor said, "Jack, we all know you are a great warrior and possess the greatest fighting skills we have ever seen or heard of. But your fighting skills are no match for magic."

Jack rose from his chair and said, "On the day I killed Kain, I was fighting without this." Reaching behind his back, he grabbed the God Stone Sword, which no one had noticed there before, and stuck it in the floor. Everyone just stared at the sword and the shining bright red stone in the middle of the golden handle.

After a few moments, Jack asked the guests, "Do any of you recognize this sword?"

It was the banker, Lord Emory, who replied, "I like to study ancient artifacts, and unless I am wrong, that would be the God Stone Sword. But if this is the God Stone Sword then the only way you could be carrying it is if you are the long ago promised chosen one." Jack replied, "Lord Emory you are correct on both counts. This is the God Stone Sword and I am the promised chosen one."

He then proceeded to tell them how he came to get the sword. He told them about how he had to spend three years in the mountains killing the man beasts as his final test in order to receive the full power of the sword and the blessing of the gods. Then Emily told them how the gods had come to them when Vanessa and Jenna had first returned with the injured Jack.

It was Sheila who first spoke and said she would support the cause. Then one by one each of the guests joined the cause. Sheila then stood up, went before Linda, kneeled, and pledged her loyalty to the rightful queen of the Kingdom, Linda Martin. The rest of the guests did the same.

Once the formalities were over, Linda began to speak again, "The next step is for me to face the troops and tell them who I really am and ask Commander Wallace has arranged for the entire garrison here to be present to allow me to speak to them. After we speak with them and they make their choice, we will send for two thousand of the troops at North Port. We will give them the same option. Then we will leave two thousand troops here in the garrison and take the remaining twenty thousand and march on Twin Falls." She knew these numbers might change if not all the men chose her cause. She continued, "Once we have all the men I will send a letter to Ariel telling her I am the rightful queen of the Kingdom and that on the first day of spring I will march my army and take my place on the throne."

Everyone was surprised by Linda's announcement of sending a letter to Ariel. This announcement caused a big stir, and everyone was talking at the same time. Finally young Jenna shouted, "Everyone please shut up!" When everyone was quiet, she turned to Linda and asked, "Why do you want to send this letter to Ariel?"

Linda smiled and said, "I am the rightful queen of the Kingdom. As the queen, it is my duty to notify anyone acting against my crown to cease such behaviour. From all the reports we have, Ariel has about five thousand troops in the palace that are from Independent City, the remaining 2,500 are citizens of the Kingdom. Given the odds she may leave without a fight. I am not so naïve as to believe she will do that in fact she will most likely send for more troops from Independent City. However, I feel this is the right thing to do."

For several minutes, no one said anything until Lord Emory broke the silence. He said, "Your Highness, while I admit it is a bit unorthodox to send this letter given the circumstances, however, if you feel this is the right thing to do then can I help you write it."

Linda smiled and said, "Lord Emory, thank you for your offer. I will write the letter first then I would like for you and everyone here to read it and give me your thoughts." Everyone nodded their agreement. They continued planning long into the night. When they finally retired for the night, Silas told Emily, "That young lady became a queen tonight."

Two days later, all the guests of the dinner party, except Sergeant Miller were at the North Pointe garrison. Sergeant Miller had returned to North Port to deliver the message to the troops there and return with them to North Pointe. Commander Wallace had called a general assembly of all troops stationed at the garrison. Just outside the main gate, he had the troops build a small stage. Then he had the soldiers' line up in front of the stage. It was a beautiful display of discipline and pageantry watching them get into place.

As they watched, Linda realized they had a problem. There was no way she would be able to speak loud enough for everyone to hear her. She turned to Jack and told him her concern. Jack explained, "I will amplify your voice so everyone can hear you. Then while you are speaking I will lift you into the air. This will allow you to explain they have no need to fear Boris's magic. All you have to do is speak normally and do not panic when you feel yourself leave the ground." Linda agreed but expressed her concern about being lifted into the air. Jack then explained to the others on the stage what he was going to do. Everyone was shocked and not sure he would be able to do what he said he would do.

When the troops were all lined up, Commander Wallace turned to Linda and indicated it was time for her to begin. She stood up cleared her throat and began to speak. To her and everyone else's surprise, when she spoke, her voice carried to everyone and all could hear her. She said, "I am sure you are all wondering why the Commander has called this assembly and why the mayor and all these dignitaries are up here on this stage with me. I will explain. You all know me as Linda Jones, the daughter of Silas Jones. Well, today I want you all to know my real name. My name is Linda Martin, and Silas's real name is Vernon Silas."

"If you do not recognize these names, I will tell you who we really are. Vernon Silas was the royal treasurer for King Phillip Martin. I am the daughter of King Phillip and Queen Elizabeth Martin. Twenty years ago my father sent me away in the care of Vernon Silas in hopes that one day I might regain the throne and continue the royal line. Ariel and Boris are murderers. I can say this because I have an eyewitness. When the war was over Ariel and Boris gathered the royal council in the great hall of the palace at Twin Falls. They personally ordered the death of the entire council. Not only did they order these deaths, they participated in the killings themselves.

"They are guilty of conspiracy against the crown of the Kingdom and of murder. This makes them common criminals and usurpers." After she said that she paused for a moment, and Jack took advantage of her pause to lift her into the air. Jack mentally reached out to the sword, told it what he wanted to do, and then the sword carried out the instructions. Slowly Linda rose into the air about fifteen feet. When she stopped rising into the air, she began to speak again.

"Therefore, I am here today to ask you to support me in my cause to take my rightful place on the throne of the Kingdom and to join me in bringing justice to Ariel and Boris. I know you are thinking about Boris's magic and wondering how are we going to fight against it. As I think you can see, we have some magic of our own. The warrior on stage is the not only the man who helped save us from the man beasts but is also the man who killed Kain. It is his magic that is allowing my voice to be heard by everyone here and his magic that has lifted me into the air. It is his magic that will fight the magic of Boris. It will then be up to you to fight the soldiers of Independent City. I know you can easily defeat them because you will be fighting for justice and freedom."

Jack stood up at that point and drew the God Stone Sword. When he did, the stone on the hilt shone its brightest over everyone there. What Jack was doing was casting a protection spell on everyone there. All those that were covered by the light of the sword were now protected against magic. When the spell was finished, Jack sheathed the sword and slowly lowered Linda back down to the stage.

When Linda was firmly back down on the stage, she said, "As you can see, I have the support of your commanding officer and the city leaders. Now I am asking for your support. I am asking you to fight for me, not because you are ordered to but because you want to fight for me. I ask you to fight for me because I am the rightful queen. I ask you to fight with me for justice. What do you say?" As soon as she finished speaking, the entire assembly erupted with a chant saying, "Long live Queen Linda." The soldiers kept chanting it over and over.

Linda said, "Thank you, gentlemen, for your support. Commander Wallace tells me the best time to march on Twin Falls is on the first day of spring. Therefore in thirty days we will begin our crusade for justice."

The soldiers began to chant "Justice, Justice."

Linda stepped down from the stage and went out among the soldiers, shook their hands, and thanked them for their support. This single act of kindness on her part won the hearts of those twenty thousand men, and they were ready to fight to the death for their rightful queen. Following her example, everyone on the stage stepped down went among the soldiers and thanked them for their support. On that morning they became a united army of the Kingdom.

As the assembly broke up, everyone returned to the city. As they were returning, Jack and Linda were stopped by people and asked about what was going on at the garrison. Linda told her story to each group that asked. At first it was small groups or families but the closer to the center of town they got, the larger the groups became. By the time they reached the city square, it was full of people. When Jack and Linda entered, the crowd opened and let them through. At the center of the square, Jack once again lifted Linda into the air. From twenty feet in the air, Linda told her story to the citizens of North Pointe.

By the time they left the square word had spread to the entire city that Linda was the rightful queen, daughter of the late king and queen. As Jack and Linda rode through the city on their way home chants of "justice" or "long live the rightful queen" would erupt from the people who saw them. The support of the soldiers and now the people brought tears to Linda's eyes. By the time they made it back to the estate, they had laughed and cried together. That day they became the true king and queen of the Kingdom.

CHAPTER 18 - REDEMPTION

It was the middle of the afternoon, and Ariel and Boris were in the Great Hall listening to grievances between merchants. This was a practice they had been doing for about a year. They thought this would bring them closer to the people and show them that they did indeed care about them. Suddenly the doors burst open wide and in walked a soldier and another individual.

Ariel immediately stood up but before she could say a word the soldier spoke up. "Your Highness, forgive the intrusion, but this person has been hassling my guards for hours trying to see you. He claims that it is very important," said the soldier.

The man stepped forward and said, "In fact I would recommend that you clear the hall."

Ariel was furious now. She said, "How dare you come in here and interrupt me like this? Who do you think you are?"

The man said, "I apologize for my behavior. I am a messenger, and my news is indeed dire for you."

Ariel noticed an air of bravery in this man, and she turned to Boris and nodded her head. Boris then gave the order to clear the hall. As soon as the doors were closed, Ariel said, "All right, now tell me your dire message." The man reached in his pocket and pulled out a letter. He then walked up to her and handed it to her. Ariel rudely snatched the letter from him and opened it.

The letter read:

To the Usurpers Ariel and Boris:

My name is Linda Martin. I am daughter of the late King Phillip and Queen Elizabeth Martin. Therefore I am the rightful queen of the Kingdom. I thank you for running my home while I became of age. However it is now time for me to take my rightful place as queen. If you will be so kind as to leave the palace as soon as you receive this letter there will be no need for any bloodshed.

Ariel was shocked by the content of the letter. She went pale and sat down without saying a word. Boris could not understand what could possibly be in the letter that would leave Ariel speechless. He took the letter from her and read it. He too was taken aback by the letter. However his reaction was anger. He looked up and the messenger and said, "You go back to this child and tell her that me and my army will be waiting for her. We will then crush her army and kill her and all her supporters. Now leave before I change my mind and kill you too."

That was enough time for Ariel to recover. So as soon as the messenger closed the doors behind her, she ordered for a messenger to come to her. She then said to Boris, "We must send for more troops from Independent City. We do not have enough men here. How many do we have here?"

Boris replied, "We have 7,500 counting the palace guard. However 2,500 of those are not from Independent City. We will need to send the messenger via the river and have the men return the same way."

The messenger was dispatched immediately to Independent City. He took with him a letter to Governor Bran explaining the situation and orders for General Lott to bring all the men he had available as quickly as possible. Boris and Ariel were shocked at the stupidity of this young lady and the audacity to announce her intentions. By announcing herself she eliminated any chance they ever had. Now Boris had time to gather his army. Surely she had to know that Boris was a sorcerer and a wizard and that most likely he alone could defeat this so called army.

Ariel was furious, how could both duchesses be against her. They were her friends, her allies. She told Boris that now everything made sense. It was this rebel who had made the attempt on her life in Bartersville. It was also this rebel who had sent the assassin to kill Kain. They decided that they would teach this child a lesson and use her as an example to the rest of the Kingdom. After they finished with her no one would dare challenge her again.

News of the rebellion by the northern cities spread through the palace like wildfire. Everyone was talking about it. Anna was especially curious about the rebel leaders. She knew in her heart that Jack had survived the beating and was part of this rebellion. Anna was so nervous and apprehensive about it that people were starting to notice her odd behavior. That night Betty came to her quarters to ask her about it.

Anna was sitting at her table when someone knocked on the door. She went to the door and opened it; it was Betty. She let her in and led her to the table. Betty wasted no time; she said, "Anna, what is wrong with you. You are acting more nervous than Ariel and Boris. People are starting to wonder, and they are starting to say things. Now I want to know what is going on with you, is it true, the rumors that you are somehow involved in this rebellion."

That question stunned Anna, and she decided she needed to tell someone her story and thought Betty was the best and only person she could really talk to. So she decided to tell her the truth everything from the visit of the goddess to Jack's visit. Once she started talking, everything came out in a rush. It just flooded out of her, Anna had no control anymore. For twenty years, she had kept in the hurt, anger, and hatred and it just came bursting out. Anna told her everything she held nothing back

Anna went on for the better part of an hour. When she finally stopped talking, she cried; she could not stop the tears. Betty just held her and let her cry. Betty was in complete shock, she did not know what to say so she was glad that Anna was crying and she did not have to talk. Finally the tears stopped and they began to talk. They decided that they needed to determine how the palace staff stood on this rebellion. Would they support Ariel or Linda? They came up with a plan to begin asking the staff that very question.

It took three weeks for the army to arrive from Independent City. When they arrived, they arrived eighteen-thousand strong. Ariel and Boris were very happy with the number and were more than sure that they would easily defeat the rebels. It was one week before the first day of spring so they were making plans to defend the city. They knew that if they stayed in the city they could not defend it there was no city wall therefore they had to march out to meet the approaching army. Boris sent messengers to keep an eye out for the invading army. He wanted to know when they left, how many they were and how fast they were moving.

It was ten days after he had sent out the messengers when the first one returned. The news was that the army from the north had indeed marched on the first day of spring and they were twenty-thousand strong. The number surprised Boris; he found it hard to believe that all the men would turn against them. How was this possible? It did not make any sense. Then something in the back of his mind clicked, and he remembered the entrance questionnaire that the garrison at Northpointe had implemented all those years ago. He ordered for his staff to bring him a copy of that questionnaire.

A few hours later, they had managed to find one, and it was delivered to him. He read the questions, and at first look, there was nothing suspicious. Then he thought if I was planning rebellion and needed to recruit soldiers that were loyal to me how would I do it. After that revelation, he read the questionnaire one more time and realized how devious the author of the questionnaire had been. He told Ariel of his findings. He was astonished at the audacity of the plan. The patience required to implement.

They had been very careful and very thorough. That also meant that the real leaders of the rebellion had to be the Duchess Emily, Commander Wallace, Sergeant Miller, and Silas Jones. They had to be the master minds behind this rebellion. Boris was impressed with the ability of the commander to have been able to hide his true feelings from him when he had read his thoughts and memories of the battles against the man beasts. That meant that these people were determined and if all things were equal they might have something to worry about. But since the rebels seemed to forget about Boris's capabilities they would be no match for him.

After the first messenger arrived, then the messengers were arriving on daily basis. They reported progress of the approaching army and were surprised to hear that the people along the way were embracing them and helping them. They decided that the best place to meet the invaders was at the base of the mountain on the west side before they reached the road to Twin Falls. With that plan in mind one week after the first messenger arrived, the Freedom Fighters once again marched to battle. They were twenty-five thousand strong. They were leaving only five hundred men behind; of these one hundred were from Independent City and the rest were recruits from Twin Falls.

The days and weeks following the great meeting, as it was being called now, were filled with preparations for war. The plan was rather simple—Jack would take care of Boris, and the army would take care of the Freedom Fighters.

Both the Duchess Sheila and the Duchess Emily, along with Linda and Vanessa, the mayor of Northpointe, and a couple of the larger merchants would be going with the army. Vanessa was true to her word; she had promised Commander Wallace an answer to his proposal when she returned from Twin Falls with Jack. Vanessa knew the day would come when the commander would ask for her answer. One week after the great meeting, the day came when the commander wanted his answer. Vanessa did not hesitate, she said yes immediately. The commander was on cloud nine; of course everyone agreed that the ceremony would have to wait until after the war.

For Jack and Linda, the days and weeks after the great meeting were filled with them riding to the various villages, towns, and farms around Northpointe. They were spreading the word of the rebellion but mostly they were telling their story. Linda told them who she was and Jack told them about his promise to Linda and his exiling and survival. The story was so compelling that no matter where they went and how many people they talked to everyone loved them and joined their cause.

Every day Jack thanked the gods for allowing him the opportunity to fulfill his promise. He asked for the strength and knowledge of the God Stone Sword, so that he would be able to defeat Boris. Jack knew that the entire rebellion's success was dependent on his battle and defeat of Boris. If this was a normal battle with swords, he had no fear of Boris; it was the magic that worried him. Jack knew that the sword had the ability to defeat Boris if the wielder knew how to use it.

One day Linda noticed the concern on Jack's face and she asked what was wrong. Linda said, "Jack, I have noticed a look of concern on your face for a few days now. Tell me what is bothering you."

Jack just said one word: "magic." She looked at him with a puzzled look, and he continued. He said, "I have been praying to the gods for the knowledge of the sword that I will need to defeat Boris. This will be my first battle with magic. It has me a little nervous that is all." Linda looked at him and took his chin and lowered him to her height and kissed him on the lips.

Then she said, "Jack, I love you, and I have faith in you. You are the little boy that would not kneel to a murderer. You are the boy who survived the Crystal desert. You are the young warrior that time and time again defeated the Horde. As a man you are the warrior who decimated the man beasts and saved the northern cities. You have conquered every foe and situation that has ever been presented to you and you are afraid of a little magic. I am not worried, I have no doubt that you will prevail over Boris." Jack was looking straight into her eyes and he could see the conviction in her eyes as she spoke. He knew that she meant every word. He thought with this kind of support how can I lose.

The first day of spring finally came and the army began their march south. There was 20,000 soldiers and 2,500 doctors, surgeons, cooks, blacksmiths, and everyone needed to support the army. In addition, there were wagons of food, cattle, goats, extra horses and camp followers.

As the entourage travelled south, they discovered that word of the rebellion had spread. Every town and village was waiting for them. The people were all behind the rightful queen. Whenever Linda rode through the towns and villages, the people would shout "Long live the rightful Queen! Long live Queen Linda." Getting the support of the local towns and villages was a great booster to Jack and Linda. The soldiers also were in good spirits and confident because of all the support.

After three weeks of marching, they came to rest at the turning point of the road that headed west to go around the mountains. It was here that the scouts managed to capture an enemy scout. After a long interrogation, the scout told them what they needed to know. He told them the enemy was twenty-five thousand strong and that they would reach the enemy base in less than three days' time. That night all the leaders of the rebellion (Jack, Linda, Commander Wallace, Sergeant Miller, the Duchess Emily and Silas, the Duchess Sheila, the mayor of Northpointe) all got together to discuss the final battle plans.

Everyone agreed that Boris would strike first and quickly thinking he would be able to end the rebellion before it got started. Jack explained to them that he had cast a protection spell over everyone at the great meeting. He warned them though that the protection was only against assured them that he was ready for anything that Boris could throw at them.

Jack felt confident in making that statement. He had practiced his fighting skills and physically he was in great shape. He had also practiced using the power of the sword. He also had prayed to the gods for the strength and ability to defeat Boris. He knew the gods had given him the opportunity to fulfill his promise and now it was up to him to keep it. It had taken him twenty years but finally he was only days away from his destiny.

On the morning of the third day, the two armies stood one mile apart. Boris was about quarter of a mile to the west of the army. Behind him were Ariel and a few aides and guards. Ariel rode up to him and said, "Finish this quickly." He got off his horse and walked up about one hundred yards. There he began his attack.

When Jack saw Boris walking away from the others, he knew the battle was about to start. He turned to the commander and said, "It begins." Then he turned and started walking his horse west to meet Boris. Jack had not gone thirty yards when he sensed the magic. He had no time but to extend the protection shield around the army out.

Boris launched two lightning bolts at the rebels. Much to his surprise, the bolts were blocked several hundred feet in the air in front of the army. When the soldiers saw this, they cheered. It seemed that Jack was going to be able to deal with Boris. Boris was surprised at the results of his first attack. He launched an onslaught of several fire balls. This time Jack was ready he grabbed the God Stone Sword and held it up over his head. All the fire balls were redirected to the sword and it shattered them as they touched the sword.

Boris was taken aback with the ability of this wizard. He knew he had a battle on his hands. He turned to the messengers with Ariel and told them. Signal the troops to attack if in one hour I have not finished with this young wizard. It will be up to them. Boris tried to sound confident but Ariel could see the concern on his face. This slight delay gave Jack the time he needed to ride away from the army and prepare to face off with Boris.

When Boris turned back to Jack, he was only about one hundred yards away. Boris looked at Jack and smiling said, "You're brave lad, but foolish." Boris wasted no time and started his bombardment of Jack. Jack stood there with the sword in one hand using it as a shield and with his other hand launching a few blows of his own.

Boris thought back to his battle with the old wizard Morten and the strength draining spell he had used to defeat him. With a smile on his face, he fired a lightning bolt and fireball at Jack; it was the fireball that had the draining spell. When the fireball hit Jack's sword, it exploded back toward Boris and knocked him back several feet. Jack saw the look of shock on his face and said, "The wizard Morten was a very personal friend of mine. You did not think that I would fall for that old trick." Indeed Jack had prepared for that exact spell and casting a spell that would repel and destroy the spell.

For the first time since he first heard of this rebellion, Boris realized that maybe he should have taken the threat more seriously. Every time that Jack parried an attack from Boris, the rebels would celebrate with shouts. When Boris fell back a few steps, the rebels were elated; not only did they cheer but they also jumped and hugged each other. This made Boris angry and determined to show them just how powerful he was.

Boris recovered quickly and started another attack on Jack. The force with which the attack came surprised Jack. In fact the force was so strong that Jack staggered back a few steps. When the freedom fighters saw Jack stagger a bit they erupted in cheers. For the next hour Boris kept up his forceful attack. Jack took each blow and returned one of his own. Boris finally stopped his attack and turned back to Ariel and gave her the signal for the troops to attack. Immediately the freedom fighters started forward; they were very well-disciplined and made for an impressive sight as they lurched forward.

Commander Wallace saw the signals from Boris to his generals and immediately gave his orders to start the army forward. With both armies on the move, the battle was on.

Commander Wallace said to one of his aides, "Well, Jack is doing his part. Now it is our turn." The ground shook with the pounding sound of the two armies racing toward each other. When the two armies clashed it was so loud that it sounded like a thunder storm.

Both military leaders (Commander Wallace and General Lott) were very good at war craft. Every time one issued an order to try and take advantage of a perceived weakness the other one would counter with the perfect defense. Neither army could get control of the battle. The soldiers on both sides were very well-prepared and ready for a fight. With the skill of the soldiers, there were not many fatalities at the beginning. There was a lot of fighting and lots of nonfatal wounds, which caused blood to burst out on the battle field. Therefore, it did not take long for the battle ground to become a bloody mess.

As Linda and her party watched Jack battle with Boris, they were quite impressed at how well Jack was dealing with Boris. Even though none of them had said it out loud, they were all concerned about Boris and his magic. It was finally Silas who broke the silence. "I must say that Jack is doing much better than I expected. I know how powerful Boris is and I have not had the chance to see Jack in battle or much of his magical capabilities."

It was the Duchess Sheila who replied, "Silas you have not seen anything yet. Wait until he starts fighting hand to hand. He becomes the harbinger of death with a sword in each hand. I have never seen or heard of any warrior that can fight like him."

After that everyone started talking and commenting on what was going on between the two magicians. Then suddenly when the action stopped for a moment everyone became silent and watched without taking a breath. Then suddenly the armies started marching towards each other.

The mayor said, "Well, so far the plan is going exactly as Jack said it would. He is dealing with Boris, and now it is up to Commander Wallace to take care of his end."

Vanessa replied, "I am worried because Jenna is down there somewhere in that mob of humanity."

Linda, seeing the concern on Vanessa's face, said, "Don't you worry about Jenna. I saw her practicing with the soldiers, and she beat most of them and held her own with those she could not easily handle. She will be fine. In fact I was thinking of putting her in charge of my personal guard after this mess is over." After that they all turned back to silently watching the battle as it unfolded before them.

As Ariel turned her horse and rode back to her party, she was sure that Boris would be able to quickly end this fiasco. In her mind she was already thinking about the proper way to punish the leaders of this rebellion— and punish them she would. She was personally devastated that Emily and Sheila were part of the rebel leader group. These ladies had been her friends; she had made a real connection with them. She thought of Emily as a sister and Sheila as a daughter. That was why this betrayal hurt her so much. That was why she would show them no mercy and she swore to herself that she would never again be so foolish as to care for someone and let them in to her heart. No one would ever hurt her again.

It was the sound of the magical explosions that snapped Ariel out of her mental musings. She reached her party and immediately turned to watch Boris decimate the enemy. However, what she saw was not a massacre instead all of Boris's magic was being defeated or at least blocked. She was shocked, and then she saw Boris stagger back a bit and for the first time since she had received the letter she took the threat of this rebellion seriously. Then when Boris turned back to her and his aides and instructed them to prepare the army to strike in one hour if he was still engaged she saw the worry and concern on his face and she became afraid.

As Ariel watched the magic flow back and forth between the two wizards, she thought where could this young and handsome wizard have come from? As she looked at him, she thought he is handsome and also looks familiar. This seemed odd to her. How could he seem familiar? The more she thought about it, the more she became convinced that she knew this young wizard. Then she remembered this wizard was the same warrior that had killed Kain and took a shot at her. Now everything fell into place for her. The killing of Kain had been a distraction, and she had been the real target. She thought no wonder the city leaders of Bartersville could not figure out who had tried to kill her. He had used his magic to conceal the truth. Since he had been able to conceal the truth he was obviously a very powerful wizard.

This also meant that Boris's idea of the rebellion being a long time plot was correct. These rebels had tried to kill her and maybe get lucky and take over the Kingdom without having to fight. It was them who sent this magician to try to kill her at Bartersville and then again at Twin Falls. Now she understood the enormity of the plan and the audacity of the leaders to come up with such a plan. This gave her a new respect for Emily and Commander Wallace. She knew they had to be behind this they were the real leaders of this rebellion.

Ariel realized that they had made a mistake in not taking this rebellion seriously. It was this realization she had seen on Boris's face when he had turned and given the order to prepare the army. For the first time in twenty years, she realized just how sensitive her crown was. For the first time she considered the possibility of losing her crown. She also wondered how many other people who were at the palace might be involved. Who else had been betraying her? As she watched the two wizards doing battle she realized that they were evenly matched and that meant that Boris could lose this battle. She was afraid.

Jack and Boris had been at it for a total of three hours now. Jack was starting to get tired. However, he noticed that Boris did not seem to be getting tired. His attacks seemed to be coming with the same force now as they had early this morning. Jack had spent all morning defending himself and then sending a response to the attack. Jack knew he had to change this pattern or he would lose this battle. He could not lose this fight; a loss meant many horrible things would happen to the people he cared for and he was not going to let them down.

Boris was tired and surprised at the ability of the young wizard. It seemed to him that the young wizard appeared to be getting tired. The young wizard's defense was still solid, but the responses to his attacks were not as forceful as before. Thinking he was starting to get the upper hand gave Boris hope and he pressed his attack even more.

Jack could not figure out what he was doing wrong. How could this be happening to him? He was determined and just as he was about to give his last bit of strength into an attack on Boris it hit him. Instead of using the power of the sword Jack had been relying on his personal strength. Quickly he cast the strongest protection spell he knew about himself. Then safely within his protective cover, he closed his eyes and mentally reached out to the God Stone on the sword. In his mind's eye he saw a bright light. He walked toward it. The closer he got, the brighter and warmer the light became. Within a few steps, he was totally engulfed in the light. He could see nothing but pure white light. He knew that now he was mentally connected to the God Stone itself.

Jack knew that now he would be able to think of a thing and have it happen. Now he truly had the full power of the stone at his disposal.

Quickly Jack returned his mind to the current situation. He thought of ridding his body of the fatigue and instantly he felt refreshed. For a few seconds Jack just relaxed and enjoyed the feeling of having the power of the sword run through him. Jack knew that from now on he would feel this power any time he wanted to or needed it. With that he immediately returned his attention to Boris and the current fight.

Boris noticed that the young wizard had created a protective bubble around himself and that he was no longer returning fire to him. Boris thought, I have him. He is tired. All I have to do now is break his protective shield. This once again gave him hope and once again launched a vicious attack on Jack with all his power.

While this exchange was going on, both men had started walking closer to each other. When Jack mentally came back to the battle, he was surprised to find that he was standing only about fifteen feet away from Boris. With his mind, Jack released his protection spell and immediately started attacking Boris. First he simply fired some lightning bolts at Boris. He fired them rapidly in order to get Boris in a defensive mode.

When Jack thought that Boris was doing more defending than attacking, he struck. Reaching for the power of the sword Jack grabbed as much of the power as he could handle and formed a large fireball. With the full strength of the sword, he shot the large fireball at Boris.

Boris saw the protective shield vanish and thought he had destroyed it. With renewed spirit, he quickly launched bolt after bolt and fireball after fireball at the young wizard. Unfortunately for Boris, the young wizard blocked every shot without any problems. Then suddenly Boris had to defend himself; the young wizard was on the offensive, and it was taking everything he had to defend himself. Just when Boris thought the attack was over, it hit him. The fireball was the largest Boris had ever seen and it hit him with more force than he thought was possible. He instantly blacked out.

Jack saw the fireball hit Boris and blow him back about ten feet. When Boris landed, he had landed badly on his left shoulder and arm. A sharp pain shot up his arm and Boris knew it was broken. In addition he felt a burning pain all over the left part of his body. His left side ached from his feet to his head. He was having problems breathing. Boris could feel the life draining out of him. He was finished and the pain kept getting worse.

Jack walked over to Boris and saw that his left shoulder and arm appeared to be broken. In addition, his entire left side was burned badly. He could see the bone in many areas. He was about to drive his sword through him when Boris asked him, "Who are you?"

Jack smiled and said, "I am a small boy named Jack that you had exiled twenty years ago. I have come to right a wrong that you committed twenty years ago. I watched you murder King Phillip and Queen Elizabeth and the entire royal council. Now I render judgment and sentence you for that crime."

Boris's eyes went wide as he remembered back all those years to the day they had conquered the palace and tried to remember the little boy. It came to him—the boy refused to kneel to Ariel and acknowledge her as queen. Now this boy had finished him.

As Jack finished talking, he took the God Stone Sword lifted it up and drove it straight into the heart and chest of Boris. Boris died instantly. Jack retrieved his sword and looked around until he saw Ariel. She was crying covering her face. She looked at Jack and made eye contact and immediately turned around and jumped on her horse and left the battlefield.

As Ariel watched the two wizards doing battle, it appeared to her that the young wizard was getting tired. She thought that Boris had noticed this also because he increased his attack and started walking toward the other wizard. Then the young wizard quit firing and had built a shield around himself. Ariel's heart skipped a beat as she thought that Boris was about to kill this young wizard. A few seconds later, she saw the protective shield fall apart. Boris increased his attack again, but something was wrong; the young wizard was not dying.

In fact the young wizard was blocking every one of Boris's shots very easily. Suddenly she saw the young wizard go on the offensive, and Boris appeared to barely be deflecting the attacks. Then from out of nowhere, the young wizard launched the largest fireball that Ariel had ever seen. It hit Boris hard, and Boris was blown off his feet high into the air and then fell to the ground. Boris was motionless.

Ariel screamed and began to cry. Her entire world was shattering right before her very eyes. She ordered her aides to bring her horse. Then she saw the young wizard walk up to Boris. They appeared to exchange a few words and the vile young wizard killed Boris. Boris was dead. Her world was falling apart. She realized now just how much she had grown to love Boris. Now he was gone. Then she realized that she was staring straight into the eyes of the young wizard. She shouted turned around and mounted her horse and raced back to the palace.

CHAPTER 19 - A PROMISE FULFILLED

Linda and the other dignitaries would watch the armies for a few minutes then turn their attention to the wizards' battle. They were getting frustrated because neither the army nor Jack appeared to be winning. In fact in the last few minutes, it looked like Jack was starting to lose the fight. Linda thought Jack must be getting tired because he did not appear to be responding as quickly and as strong as before. She thought Boris had noticed this too because he seemed to be attacking with more frequency and stronger.

Then Jack quit fighting and created a shield around himself. Linda let out a whimper as she started to cry. The others turned to see what had made Linda cry. They were all in shock at what they saw. The two wizards were standing fifteen feet apart, and Jack was not fighting. Boris was attacking with such intense ferocity that they knew Jack was about to die. In the blink of an eye, everything changed. Jack's shield apparently shattered but not from the attacks of Boris but because Jack let it shatter. Jack then launched a fury of rapid and extremely strong attacks.

They saw Boris go from aggressor to defender, and then Jack threw the largest fireball they had ever seen. He threw it straight at Boris with extreme force. The fireball hit Boris and knocked him high in the air. He landed awkwardly, and it was clear to everyone watching that he was badly injured. Linda jumped with excitement. Just a few seconds ago, she thought all was lost and now Jack was about to avenge his banishment and turn the entire battle in their favor.

They watched as Jack walked over to Boris. They appeared to speak to each other briefly before Jack sank his sword through Boris' chest. other, cried, and hollered. They also noticed that as soon as Boris died, Ariel mounted her horse and headed away from the battle. She seemed to be heading back to Twin Falls.

When Jack saw Ariel leave, he fell to his knees and prayed. He thanked the gods for giving him this victory. He asked the gods for the strength and ability for him and the army to defeat the freedom fighters. He thanked them for allowing him to come one step closer to fulfilling his promise to Linda. When he finished praying, he stood and turned to Linda and the others and raised his arms up in victory. Then he started toward the fighting armies.

The armies had no idea that the magic battle was over. They were locked in a very tight and even battle of their own. When Jack reached the battle, he took out his regular sword and with a sword in each hand charged the ranks. At first the freedom fighters thought that the rebels had tricked them by splitting their army and the rest of them were attacking from behind.

It was General Lott who first looked over to where the wizards had been fighting. To his surprise, he saw the dead body of Boris. Then he realized that the rebels had not split their force. It was the young wizard, by himself, which was now attacking them from behind. With a sword in each hand, every swing of his swords dealt a deadly blow to his unfortunate opponent. The general knew he had to kill that wizard because he was single handedly turning the battle from an even match to an advantage for the rebels.

The general gave orders to have his best fighters leave the battle and go after this new threat. There were five of them. One by one they charged Jack. Jack easily dispatched all five of them and then again joined the battle. When the freedom fighters saw how quickly and easily this warrior defeated their best they became afraid and demoralized.

Commander Wallace noticed that the freedom fighters had suddenly fallen apart and the fight had gone out of them. He quickly gave orders to take advantage of the situation. Within the hour, the freedom fighters were finished. However, they refused to surrender, and they were forced to kill them all. Even their officers and the general himself made them kill them. When the battle was over, every single freedom fighter was dead.

Linda and the others watched as Jack joined the fighting armies. They watched as Jack took out his other sword and watched him transform from a victorious wizard to a one man killing machine. They were speechless as they watched the skill and ability of Jack as a warrior.

It was the Duchess Sheila who spoke first. "See that, Silas, like I said you had not seen anything until you saw Jack fight with two swords."

Silas said, "I, uh, I am amazed at his speed, accuracy and skill. He has in a matter of moments turned this battle from a stalemate to a slaughter. I can honestly say that I am grateful to have him on our side."

As the battle was coming to an end, Linda and the others gathered their belongings and headed toward Jack and Commander Wallace. When the fighting stopped, Jack looked around, and the soldiers all cheered him.

He walked over to Commander Wallace and shook his hand and said, "Congratulations, Commander. Job well done."

The commander replied, "It is I who should congratulate you." The commander was cut off by a commotion coming behind them. It was Linda and the others.

Jack was covered in blood, but that did not stop Linda from jumping off her horse and running to him and jumping in his arms and kissing him on the lips. When the soldiers saw this, they fell more in love with their new queen. They began to chant "Long live Queen Linda, Long live King and Queen."

Jack and Linda ignored it all as they were lost in each other. The entire army saw that these two were truly in love with each other.

By now it was mid afternoon, and they decided that they would wait until the morning before they marched on Twin Falls. As a result a massive celebration followed.

Anna and the sergeant who was in charge of the palace guard had sent out messengers to let them know how the battle was going. If the battle was going in favour of the rebels, they were going to take the palace. Of the five hundred soldiers there, only one hundred were loyal to Ariel, and that was because they were from Independent City. The plan was to take the palace and hold it for Linda.

It was shortly after lunch when the messenger arrived and gave the signal that he needed to meet with the sergeant and Anna. The plan had been made that when the messenger arrived they would rendezvous in the ballroom. Since Ariel and Boris were both gone, no one would go in the ballroom. When Anna arrived in the ballroom, the messenger and the sergeant were already there. The messenger looked at them and smiled and said, "Boris is dead."

Anna asked, "This is very important. Are you sure?"

"Yes," said the messenger, "I saw the battle myself. As soon as he died, Ariel mounted up and is headed back here. I took short cuts through the goat trails at the foot of the mountains. I estimate that cuts about three hours off the trip. Ariel will be here in a few hours."

With that Anna and the sergeant dismissed the messenger and went into action. The sergeant had placed his men around the palace so that they could easily overwhelm the freedom fighters in the palace. It only took an hour for them to kill or capture all the soldiers loyal to Ariel. The next part was critical to the plan. They had to convince Ariel, when she arrived, that everything was okay. That way they could get her away from the guards she had with her and they could be overtaken and Ariel captured.

As soon as Ariel mounted her horse, she set a fast pace. She had two aides and ten guards with her. Therefore, it was easy for everyone to stay together and move fast down the road. Ariel was glad to be moving so fast because that way no one would try to talk to her. She was in no mood to talk to anyone. In fact she was panicked. She had no idea what to do. Maybe she should just keep riding straight to Independent City. Once there she could rebuild her army and retake the Kingdom.

She knew her son was a wizard, and according to the last letter they had received from Master Tam, he was going to be a master himself. That meant that Willard would be able to deal with this murdering young wizard. The longer they rode, the more she realized that she could not go straight to Independent City. She had too much to lose by not going back to the palace. She decided she would return to the palace and wait for the messengers to return with news of the battle. Once she was certain they had lost, she would take the few hundred men at the palace and return to Independent City.

Ariel was pleased with herself. Even in the middle of this heart breaking event, she was able to still think clearly and could still make plans. She thought that this proved she was a true ruler, a true queen. Realizing that she was going to kill the horses, she slowed the pace a bit. She knew the animals could not keep that pace all the way to Twin Falls. She could feel the sigh of relief from her entire party when they noticed that she had slowed the pace. She called her two aides forward and went over her plans with them. They agreed that it was a good plan.

It was late afternoon when Ariel and her party entered the city. It only took a few minutes for Anna and the soldiers to prepare for the arrival. When Ariel's party entered the palace grounds, Anna was waiting for her at the top of the steps of the main entrance to the palace. Ariel saw her and rode straight for the main entrance. As soon as she arrived, she jumped off her horse and ran up the stairs. She ran to Anna and hugged her. Ariel could not help herself she began to cry. She was balling and through her tears she said, "He is dead. Boris is dead." She just kept repeating herself over and over.

Anna acted quickly and put her arm around Ariel and began leading her into the palace. Anna led Ariel back to her quarters. Ariel's reaction was unexpected, but it played right into their plans. As soon as Anna and Ariel were out of sight, the sergeant and the soldiers quickly, quietly, easily captured the guards and aides.

The takeover of the palace was complete. Now all they had to do was to wait for the army to arrive.

It was a couple of hours before dawn when the messenger arrived to tell the palace that the rebels had won the battle and they would march to Twin Falls at dawn. They should arrive at mid afternoon. When Anna heard the news, she was overwhelmed with joy. She had stayed in Ariel's quarters sleeping on the floor next to her bed. She had done this because she was afraid that Ariel would do something irrational.

When Ariel arose the next morning and saw Anna on the floor, she was touched. She woke her and asked her to have her breakfast brought to her. She asked that it be done quickly because she had lots of things to do that morning. As Anna left the queen's quarters the sergeant and several handmaids were waiting outside. She ordered the maids to quickly get Ariel her breakfast and sent the others in to clean up the quarters. Then she took the sergeant back into the Ariel's quarters and told him that he would have to tell Ariel that he was in charge of the palace until the army arrived.

The sergeant agreed that Ariel needed to see that the guards were not on her side. What better ways to show this than by having the leader of the guards take her into custody? Ariel got dressed and ate her breakfast quickly. When she came out of the bedroom, she was surprised that Anna was still there. However, when she saw the sergeant of the guards there also then she understood.

She was about to start giving them both orders when the sergeant stopped her. The sergeant said, "I am sorry, but you can no longer give orders around here."

Ariel became livid and started to yell at the sergeant.

The sergeant walked up to her and grabbed her and shook her. He said, "You can scream all you want, but it won't change anything. I have control of the entire palace and staff. You will wait for the army to arrive, and when they do, Queen Linda will decide what to do with you."

Ariel felt her world fall to pieces as she listened to the sergeant. She looked over at Anna, and Anna simply shrugged her shoulders.

For Jack and Linda, it was the longest night of their lives. For Linda because she was going home; she was returning to the place where she grew up. It had been twenty years since she had been there. Honestly she had not thought that she would ever return. Not only was she returning to her childhood home but she was returning as the new queen, the rightful heir to the throne of the Kingdom. She was very nervous and could not sleep. She tossed and turned and missed her parents. For the first time in a long time she missed her parents; she cried and finally slept.

For Jack, he was coming to the end of a journey that had started twenty years ago when as a child he made a promise to his best friend. His life had been hard, and at times, he did not think that he was ever going to make it home. He would be able to see his mother. That alone made him excited. Jenna and Vanessa had told him how she had helped get him in the wagon on the night that he had killed Kain. Of course given his condition at that time he did not remember any of that night. He thanked the gods for allowing him first the opportunity to fulfill his promise and second for allowing him to defeat Boris and win the battle. With this victory, he had fulfilled his promise. Linda was now queen of the Kingdom. He also thanked the gods for the Rumalians. He thanked them for putting the Rumalians in his life; he knew that without them, none of this would have been possible. All these factors made him restless and nervous so he could not sleep. It was well after midnight when fatigue finally took him, and he slept.

When dawn finally came, Jack and Linda were ready to go. They took all the nervous energy and put it to good use. They helped prepare the breakfast meal and then helped get the camp ready to move. For everyone in the camp seeing the king (that was the way that everyone saw Jack now) and queen with their sleeves rolled up and working like one of them made a connection that would never be broken. As a result, it did not take long after breakfast for the camp to be ready to go. Shortly after dawn the army began its march to Twin Falls.

With Jack and Linda riding up in front leading the way, followed by the other dignitaries, the army, and the camp followers, they marched at a steady pace. They stopped for about an hour and a half to have lunch. Then they began the final march to the city. The closer they got, the more nervous everyone became. They had no idea how the city and palace would receive them. They did not know if they would face any resistance from Ariel. They did not know if Ariel had a reserve of men that she had left behind. How would fighting in the city affect their supremacy in numbers? All these unanswered questions and more made them all very nervous.

When the road turned back north to head into the city, Jack and Linda looked at each other and smiled. For the first time for either of them in twenty years they could see the city. It would take less than an hour to cover the distant to the city. Word spread throughout the city and the palace of the approaching army—the army led by Linda Martin, daughter of the late King Phillip and Queen Elizabeth.

Everyone was excited to have their rightful queen, a queen who was one of their own. They were also excited to meet the young warrior who had defeated Boris, fought the man beasts, killed Kain, and according to rumors would be the new king.

Excitement filled the air. As the army approached the city, Jack and Linda were stunned at what they saw. The streets were lined on both sides with thousands of people. As they entered the city proper, the people began to cheer. The further into the city they rode, the louder the cheers became. The reaction of the people made all the dignitaries relax a little. The people began shouting and chanting, "Long live the queen. Long live the rightful queen. Long live the queen and king." Hearing the cheers brought tears to Linda's eyes. When the crowd also acknowledged Jack as king, she broke into tears. She thought that the only thing that could make this moment better was for her parents to be there.

The crowd closed in around the two leaders. Everyone wanted to see the rightful queen and her new king. People just wanted to touch them and say hello. As a result, the crowd's progress was almost stopped. They moved along at a snail's pace. After two hours, they finally were approaching the gates of the palace. Linda was surprised to see the gates unchanged. She thought that Ariel would have taken down the rose and the stallions. This made her eyes water. Jack saw her reaction and reached over and took her hand.

Together hand in hand, they rode under the gates and into the palace. It looked like the entire palace staff was waiting for them in the main courtyard. The staff also joined in the cheers for the queen and her new king. As the staff approached, Linda began to recognize some of the faces, and the welcome began. Just as they were about to dismount, Jack looked at the palace and there at the top of the main steps stood his mother.

Jack jumped off his horse and broke through the crowd and ran up the stairs taking two at a time. His mother was watching him with tears in her eyes. As Jack approached her, she opened her arms, and they embraced. For several moments, they did not say anything; they just stood there holding each other. Both of them were crying. Finally they looked at each other and said hello. By now Linda was making her way up the steps. As she approached, Anna was surprised at how much Linda looked like her mother. Then she saw Silas and recognized him. They shared a warm embrace.

It was the sergeant in charge of the palace guards that brought business into the little reunion. He said, "My queen, if you will follow me to the ballroom we have a gift for you."

Linda and Jack looked at each other, and together they said, "Ariel." All the dignitaries followed Linda, Jack, and the sergeant to the ballroom.

The entrance to the ballroom was guarded by two guards. As soon as Linda and Jack arrived, they saluted by placing their fist to their heart and falling to one knee. The sergeant opened the doors. Inside in the middle of the ballroom, Ariel was pacing back and forth. There were four guards in the room with her. Hand in hand Linda and Jack walked towards her. They stopped about four feet from her. Commander Wallace and Vanessa, Jenna, and half of the dignitaries stood next to Linda. Anna, Sergeant Miller, Emily, Silas and the rest of the dignitaries stood next to Jack.

Ariel looked at Emily and with anger and hatred in her eyes spat at her. Then she faced Linda and fell to her knees and pleaded for mercy. The fake plea enraged Jack, and he slapped her so hard she fell on her back.

To show disdain for him, Ariel stood straight up and asked him, "Who are you, and why did you strike me?"

Jack took one step forward as he chuckled and said, "Who am I? I guess you ought to know. I am the one who told the entire Kingdom of the murder you and Boris committed right here in this room twenty years ago. That is who I am."

Ariel just looked around in obvious confusion. Jack continued. "I watched you and Boris kill King Phillip, Queen Elizabeth, and the rest of the royal council. I was a young boy eight years of age. I hid behind the thrones and watched you commit murder. I was horrified that is why when you later asked everyone in the courtyard to kneel I refused. You came over and punched me in the face then had exiled me.

Ariel thought back to that day, and she remembered the defiant little boy who had so proudly told her she was not his queen. Then she remembered the rest of the custom and said, "Since you were exiled and you returned, you have forfeited your life. That is the law."

Jack just laughed and said, "If I had been guilty of a crime that would be true, but you and I and everyone in the Kingdom knows that I was an innocent child. I have spent the last twenty years praying to the gods for this day, for them to allow me to bring justice to you and Boris. On this day justice is served."

Then Ariel remembered that the little boy was the son of one of the maids in the palace, but she could not remember which one. Then she saw movement off to her left and turned to see Anna moving toward her. As she realized that it was Anna's son standing there in front of her, she felt the pain of the knife in her stomach. As she fell to her knees, she looked up at Anna and tried to say something, but no sounds came out of her mouth.

Anna was standing next to Jack, and as he hit Ariel and took a step forward, she noticed the large hunting knife at his waist. She knew someone was talking, but she could not make out what they were saying. All she could think about was the knife and the opportunity she had to finally get her revenge on Ariel. Then without realizing what she was doing, she swiftly moved forward took the knife from Jack and stabbed Ariel with all the strength and force she had. As Ariel fell to the ground, she felt a satisfaction and relief that had escaped her for twenty years.

Jack took the knife from his mother, and Linda said, "Someone had to do that. You, Anna, had as much right as anyone else."

As Linda finished speaking, Ariel fell to the floor and died.

EPILOGUE

Linda and Jack spent the next two days organizing the government. Commander Wallace was promoted to marshal and put in charge of all the armies of the Kingdom. Sergeant Miller was promoted to commander and put in charge of the garrison at North Pointe. Jenna was made captain of the royal guards. Their duty was the personal protection of the queen and king. Jenna was given one hundred men to perform this duty.

Vanessa was named as the royal treasurer. Silas had recommended her for that position. As of now the royal council consisted of the queen, king, Marshal Wallace, Duchess Emily, Duchess Sheila, and Vanessa. That left no representation from the southern cities of Bartlesville and Southport. Linda and Jack knew they had to get representation from those cities. The only way to do that was to go there. So they planned a trip with the army to both cities.

On the morning of the third day after taking over, Linda, Jack, Marshall Wallace, Jenna and the army (12,500-strong) set out to Bartlesville. It took them four days to make the march to Bartlesville. When they arrived, the full garrison of five hundred men and the city council was waiting for them at the gate. At first the army thought they intended to fight. When the army was a mile from the city, the mayor, the council, and the garrison commander rode out to greet them.

The mayor took one look at Linda and said, "My queen, I knew your parents, and by looking at you, I see your mother. We are here to welcome our rightful queen."

Jack answered, "The uniform the commander of the garrison is wearing is not Kingdom issued."

The commander answered immediately, "My king, my troops and I are wearing these uniforms because they are the only ones we have. I realize that you do not know me, but I give you my personal assurance that I and my men are ready to give our lives for the rightful queen of the Kingdom."

Jack was surprised by such a strong pledge. Jack said, "Those are strong words for someone who is not from the Kingdom. So tell me why you are so quickly willing to speak such a pledge.

The commander replied, "First of all I am only one of a few, about fifty, men that are from Independent City. The rest of the garrison is men from the town. All my men, including myself, have married women from the city and made it our home. We no longer consider ourselves citizens of Independent City but of the Kingdom. Second, we are not blind we can see what Ariel's policies were doing to the Kingdom. Her greed has ruined the economy of the southern cities. We have had to be very creative to survive."

At this point, the mayor recognized Jenna. He was shocked to see her in full royal guard uniform. He said, "Your majesty why is this criminal with you and wearing the uniform of the royal guard?"

Linda said, "Why don't we ride into the city and continue this discussion inside?"

Everyone agreed, and the army began to move again.

As they rode to the city, Jack noticed some strange indentions in the ground. To him they looked like scars of a war. He asked about them and was told the story of George Long and the history of rebellion the city of Bartlesville had had against Ariel and Boris. The mayor made it a point to let them know that it was only until he became mayor that relations with the throne had improved. Jack expressed his disappointment in him. He told that he would have been more impressed if the city had continued it rebellious attitude.

When they reached city hall and everyone was seated with refreshments, Linda spoke. "Now let me answer your question about Jenna. Jenna was acquitted of any wrongdoing by Boris and Ariel. Therefore, she is not a criminal. In fact she is a heroine. After her acquittal, she rode north because she had heard rumors of a rebellion. She made the right contacts and joined our cause. She fought side by side with the men in the army. She killed as many if not more enemy soldiers than most of the regular soldiers. Here bravery and courage has won her the position of captain of the Royal Guard. You and the entire city of Bartlesville should be very proud to have one of your own in such a position."

They stayed that night and half the next day in Bartlesville. At noon the next day, the queen and the army left for Southport. The city council was very pleased with the visit of the queen and the placing of the mayor on the royal council.

They were even happier of the new and better less costly tax system that had been implemented. The entire city was in celebration of Jenna's position as captain of the royal guard. Jenna had spent many hours with her mother. She told her everything that had happened. Her mother was very proud.

On noon of the fifth day after leaving Bartlesville, the army was standing one mile from Southport as two riders rode out to meet them. They carried a white flag. It was the mayor and commander of the garrison. Like Bartlesville there was no love for Ariel and Boris in Southport. Of all the Kingdom, Southport had suffered the worst economically under Ariel.

When the queen and king and the army entered the city, the streets were lined with people. They were cheering them. This made Linda and Jack very happy. The soldiers in the garrison that were from Independent City had married local women, and those that were already married had moved their families to Southport. As a result, they considered this to be their home and not Independent City.

The city council had already heard about the changes the queen had made in Bartlesville and were anxious to ask if she would make similar changes for them. They were all very pleased to hear that indeed the queen would make the same changes in Southport. When she also announced that the mayor would be the joining the royal council, they were very pleased.

One month after having left for the southern cities, the royal party returned to Twin Falls. Once again the citizens of Twin Falls were lined in the streets and cheered the arrival of the royal couple. With the Kingdom now under complete control, it was time to turn to some more personal matters. In just one month, the double wedding was planned and held.

Linda and Jack were joined by Marshal Wallace and Vanessa in exchanging wedding vows. It was the first time in over twenty years that the entire city got involved with anything that was happening in the palace. In fact the couples would be going to various places around the city as part of the ceremony. The celebrations lasted for several days. For the first time in twenty years, the Kingdom was at peace and truly prospering again.

CHARACTERS

The Gods

Ator	–	Father of the Gods
Athena	–	Queen of the Gods
Atlas	–	Oldest child of Ator and Athena
		God of Wisdom and Honor
Pearl	–	Youngest child of Ator and Athena
		Goddess of Love and Life
Zephra	–	Middle child of Ator and
		Athena The Warrior Goddess
Zultar	–	God of Darkness & Evil
		(Brother of Ator)

The Royal Family

King Phillip Martin	–	Current ruler of the royal family line
Queen Elizabeth Martin	–	wife of King Phillip
Linda Martin	–	Daughter of Phillip and Elizabeth
		(Goes by Linnie)

The Council

Marshall Petrel	–	General of the Army
Vernon Silas	–	Royal treasurer
		(Called Silas the Counter)
Morten	–	Royal Wizard
John Winston	–	Duke of North Pointe
Adam Wells	–	Duke of Northport

Freedom Fighters

Ariel	–	Self-made leader of Independent City
Boris	–	Wizard and Sorcerer
		(Ariel's love interest)
Willard	–	Son of Ariel and Boris
		(Heir to Ariel's throne)
Kain	–	Assassin (called The Butcher)
Arianna	–	Mother of Ariel (called Queen Mother)
Bran	–	Governor of Independent City in
		absence of Ariel
Lott	–	General of Garrison at Independent City

| Buryl | – | Palace doctor |
| Master Tam | – | Teacher of sorcery and Wizardry |

Supporting Characters

Anna	–	Handmaid for Queen Elizabeth
Jack	–	Son of Anna
Betty	–	Palace servant and best friend to Anna
Emily Winston	–	Sister of Duke Winston
Vanessa Winston	–	Illegitimate daughter of Duke Winston
Sara	–	Head mistress of the First Winston Estate
Lord William Emory	–	Banker and hotel owner
Commander Wallace	–	Commander of the Garrison at North Pointe
Sheila Wells	–	Daughter of Duke Wells of Northport
George Long	–	Head of ruling council in Bartersville
Randy Long	–	Son of George Long (squired to palace at Twin Falls)
Jenna	–	Illegitimate daughter of George Long
Mark	–	Army recruit that was saved, from the man beasts, by Jack
Stg. Miller	–	Military leader of garrison at Northport

Rumalians

The Tribes:

- Arians
- Claws
- Coho
- Rumans
- Bore
- Wolf
- Crete

The Claws

Tanner	–	Chief of the Claws
Merna	–	Wife of Tanner
Jerris	–	Healer of Claws tribe
Myra	–	Wife of Jerris
Anjolina	–	Daughter of Tanner and Merna
Rail	–	Son of Tanner and Merna
Aaron	–	Head of the metal workers
Sam	–	Metalworker
Dar	–	Warrior (Jack's fighting mentor)
Claudia	–	Wife of Dar
Darius	–	Son of Dar and Claudia

The Crete

Jarod	–	Chief of the Crete
Trisha	–	Wife of Jarod
Jessica	–	Daughter of Jarod and Trisha
Tor	–	Tribal Healer

The Arians

Jerum	–	Chief of the Arians
Jade	–	Wife of Jerum
Jacob	–	Son of Jerum and Jade
Jon	–	Tribal Healer
Jerome	–	Young warrior & betrothed to Jessica

The Coho

Chet	–	Chief of the Coho
Brenda	–	Wife of Chet
Alicia	–	Daughter of Chet and Brenda (died of illness)
May	–	Tribal Healer

The Rumans

Ral	–	Chief of the Rumans
Becca	–	Wife of Ral
Raif	–	Son of the Ral and Becca
Rollie	–	Tribal Healer

The Bore

Lar	–	Chief of the Bore
Letisha	–	Wife of Lar
Rita	–	Daughter of Lar and Letisha
Cole	–	Tribal Healer

The Wolf

Kail	–	Chief of the Wolf
Sarah	–	Wife of Kail
Kolton	–	Son of Kail and Sarah
Star	–	Tribal Healer

The Horde

Sam	–	Leader of the Rumalian Mountain People
Lana	–	Wife of Sam
Faithe	–	Daughter of Sam and Lana
Gar	–	Military Leader of the Mountain People
Karn	–	Warrior and betrothed to Faithe
Garish	–	Elder
Mack	–	Elder
Wanda	–	Elder
Martha	–	Elder
Dora	–	Elder
Matt	–	Elder
Andrew	–	Elder
Nicolas	–	Elder
Shaun	–	Led attack on Crete tribe
Bran	–	Led attack on Rumans tribe
Elan	–	Led attack on Bore Tribe
Lor	–	Led attack on Coho tribe

THE END